D1072261

Writing Their Nations

Writing Their Nations

The Tradition of Nineteenth-Century American Jewish Women Writers

DIANE LICHTENSTEIN

INDIANA UNIVERSITY PRESS
Bloomington and Indianapolis

The paper used in this publication meets the minimum requirements of
American National Standard for Information Sciences—Permanence of Paper for
Printed Library Materials, ANSI Z39.48-1984.

Manufactured in the United States of America

Library of Congress Cataloging-in-Publication Data

Lichtenstein, Diane Marilyn.
  Writing their nations : the tradition of nineteenth-century
American Jewish women writers / Diane Lichtenstein.
    p.   cm.
  Includes bibliographical references and index.
  ISBN 0-253-33346-6 (cl)
  1. American literature—Jewish authors—History and criticism.
  2. Women and literature—United States—History—19th century.
  3. American literature—Women authors—History and criticism.
  4. American literature—19th century—History and criticism.
  5. Women, Jewish—United States—Intellectual life.   6. Women,
Jewish, in literature.   7. Jews in literature.   I. Title.
PS153.J4L5   1992
810.9'9287'089924—dc20   91-47015

1 2 3 4 5   96 95 94 93 92

To the memory of my mother,
Pauline Lichtenstein (1925–1990)

She died as she had lived:
strong in spirit and unswerving in conviction.

Contents

Acknowledgments

I first began to think about this project in 1983, as I was reading and rereading criticism about nineteenth-century American women. As I read, I realized that I was witnessing a process of metonymy—that is, white, middle-class Christians were "standing for" all women. In the eight years since I first noted this "part-for-the-whole" phenomenon, many scholars have helped sketch the rest of the body of literature by nineteenth-century American women. I am grateful not only to these scholars, but to the many readers and writers who have taught me to think from a feminist perspective. Without the courageous work of those who began the enterprise of feminist inquiry, I, as a "second-generation" feminist critic, would never have been able to formulate the questions that inspired this book.

Even without the feminist scholars who have influenced my reading and thinking, the list of people who contributed to the process of writing this book is long. They include students who have asked me to defend my definition of a literary tradition, colleagues who have asked me questions about the Jewish women's lives and texts, and friends who have offered intellectual and emotional support. I thank them all for their individual and collective contributions.

Some friends and colleagues deserve special thanks. Nina Auerbach and Janice Radway supported, advised, and mentored me when I first began this project. Peter Conn, Betsy Erkkila, Geoffrey Harpham, Wendy Steiner, and Larzer Ziff also helped in their own ways when I began to formulate my thoughts about American women writers. Molly Rothenberg, my friend and colleague, courageously read and commented on the entire manuscript. Georgia Duerst-Lahti, Rebecca Kugel, Tom McBride, Virginia Powell, Robin Roberts, Karen Strier, and Tom Yingling read part of the manuscript. Morris Schappes read an earlier version of what has evolved into chapter 3. Dianne Ashton and Jonathan Sarna conversed with me (in person, on the phone, and through the mail) about nineteenth-century American Jewish women. The Faculty Development Committee of Beloit College awarded me a grant for the preparation of the index, and the staff at Cradle Care provided not only loving care but peace of mind.

I am grateful to the reference and interlibrary loan staffs at the Van Pelt Library at the University of Pennsylvania, the University of St. Thomas library, and the Beloit College library (particularly Chris Nelson). I also want to thank the librarians at the American Jewish Archives, Dropsey

University, the American Jewish Historical Society, the Jewish Division of the New York Public Library, the Jewish Theological Seminary, Hebrew Union College (Cincinnati), the Philadelphia Jewish Archives, the Library Company of Philadelphia, the Free Library of Philadelphia, and the Wisconsin Historical Society.

A version of chapter 3 appeared in *Tulsa Studies in Women's Literature,* volume 6, number 2, Fall 1989, The University of Tulsa (reprinted by permission of the publisher). And some of the material in chapters 2, 4, 5, and 6 appeared in *Studies in American Jewish Literature,* volume 7, number 1, June 1988, Kent State University.

As is the convention, I have saved my thanks to family for last. But I also save these thanks until the end because they are at once both the most and least necessary. Hyman Lichtenstein, who has always been my most enthusiastic fan, has provided me with a secure anchor. Carolyn Lichtenstein, in addition to answering my computer questions, has supported me with her unshakable loyalty and love. Steven Diamond, despite his not being a "professional reader," and despite his "fear" of my ever reading his college English papers, has become one of my ablest critics; he has also been one of my truest supporters. Rachel Franni Lichtenstein Diamond, who arrived in the middle of my revising process, has infused everything I do and think with wonderment. And Pauline Lichtenstein, who died four days after I mailed this manuscript to Bloomington, taught me the meaning of strength; although she will never read this book, or this expression of gratitude, I know (and I do believe she knows) that our mutual love is inscribed on every page.

Writing Their
Nations

I.

Introducing the Tradition

Late in her life and career, Emma Lazarus wrote "The Choice," a poem which dramatizes the dilemma she faced as an assimilated Jewish woman living in nineteenth-century America. In the dramatic situation of the poem, a dream-induced spirit comes to the speaker to show her/him two paths; one, "in velvet flower,/Slopes easily to every earthly prize," while the other "narrow track skirts the abysmal verge." The spirit, who in the last line is revealed to be "Disgraced, despised, immortal Israel," makes clear that the "choice" between the two paths is more difficult than it appears, for the first path requires that the "soul" of the speaker "Follow the multitude and bind [her/his] eyes," while the second path will be lit by the spirit's "lamp." In a sense, the spirit offers no choice to the Jew who must suffer disgrace and hatred for the sake of immortal Israel's eternal light. On another level, however, the poem does clarify the decision nineteenth-century American Jews had to make, between the seemingly safe path of secularism and the more dangerous path of publicly acknowledged Judaism. For Lazarus herself and others the solution did not lie in irrevocably choosing one road or the other but rather in clearing a middle way which would permit them to live as American Jews, celebrating both of their national identities.

Although both men and women sought such a middle path, the American Jewish woman who wanted to write needed to navigate not only through the demands of demonstrating loyalty to two nations, but also around the historical obstacles which made writing so difficult both for women in Jewish life and for women in nineteenth-century America. Ironically, it was the writing itself which many Jewish women used to demonstrate the respectability of their American, Jewish, and female identities.

The primary purpose of this study is to establish nineteenth-century American Jewish women writers as *subjects* who individually and collectively deserve our attention because they form part of the canvas which was nineteenth-century American literature, and because they provide us with vivid examples of how women, Jews, and other outsiders have had to struggle to be seen on that literary canvas. In arguing for the *subject*-ness of these writers, I am describing a tradition that includes many American Jewish women writers, and does not exclude on the basis of "merit." Unlike a canon, which assumes a meritocracy of texts, with the "best," most sacred works achieving canonization, a tradition includes many of the writers and works of a specific group. This inclusive vision, I believe, provides an understanding of the group's members as whole and legitimate *subjects* rather than as inconsequential or strange objects.[1]

A tradition, as I use the term, does not depend on an "intraliterary dimension"—the "way writings receive and exploit the presence of earlier writings," as Richard Brodhead explains (13).[2] I am suggesting, instead, that a group of texts which share particular concerns—concerns born of authors' common cultural values, myths, and status—coalesce into a tradition. This tradition develops as a result of cultural changes affecting individual authors, rather than simply because earlier authors influence later authors. My definition raises the thorny question: who, then, labels which groups "traditions"? Tentatively, I would respond that because traditions develop over time, no single person can create a new tradition at a particular moment. What one can do, however, is describe a tradition which already exists.

Several feminist scholars have done this as they examined the dimensions of women's literary traditions. In *The Madwoman in the Attic* Sandra Gilbert and Susan Gubar, for example, seek to prove the existence of a "great tradition of literature by women . . . a tradition especially encompassing the works of nineteenth-century women writers who found viable ways" to write out of their unique female identities and experiences (72). Although they never explicitly categorize specific "themes" which concerned nineteenth-century women, they do imply that certain kinds of "swervings" around the male tradition mark the female tradition's most compelling characteristic—an anxiety of authorship; in particular, palimpsestic writing and representations of the "mad woman" draw writers such as George Eliot and Emily Dickinson together into a woman's literary tradition.

This tradition, which Gilbert and Gubar analyze in *Madwoman* and collect in *The Norton Anthology of Literature by Women: The Tradition in English*, suggests that "one important agenda in establishing a historical canon is to establish commonality in female experience throughout history, not difference" (Ezell 581–82). However, the preface to the *Norton Anthology* includes a corrective: texts by Kamala Das of India and Ama Ata Aidoo of Ghana, to name just two writers, "allow us to trace a number of traditions within [women's literary] history—the black, the regional, the lesbian, the working-class, and the native-American traditions" (xxx). It is not only women's literature that rests on a plurality of traditions; American literature also "has a wealth of . . . interpenetrating [*sic*] traditions," and "no one of these is more American than the others" (Brodhead viii).

Like Gilbert and Gubar, Ellen Moers has described "a literary movement apart from but hardly subordinate to the mainstream: an undercurrent, rapid and powerful" (*Literary Women* 63). This "movement" relied on "association often remote and indirect" (63). In describing a "literature of their own," Elaine Showalter also suggests that the "female literary tradition in the English novel" is strongly marked by "influences, borrowings, and affinities." She notes, however, that "we cannot show a pattern of deliberate progress and accumulation" and that this tradition is "full of holes and hiatuses," which means that "each generation of women writers has found itself, in a sense, without a history, forced to rediscover the past anew, forging again and again the consciousness of their sex" (*Literature* 11–12). Although both Moers and Showalter, and even Gilbert and Gubar, want to argue for an "intraliterary" component of women's traditions, they also recognize how problematic it would be to prove unequivocally that Emily Dickinson read Harriet Beecher Stowe, or that George Eliot read Katherine Philips.

By attempting to establish intraliterariness among women's texts, Moers and Showalter wish to identify a mechanism for distinguishing among texts which do or do not belong in a particular tradition (and to avoid using the canon's distinctions of quality and value). Such a mechanism would be useful in sharpening the sometimes blurry boundaries between traditions. Two of the critics who have been defining the boundaries of Afro-American literature have offered tentative blueprints for this mechanism. Barbara Smith, for one, who assumes that "Black women writers constitute an identifiable literary tradition" argues that "thematically, stylistically, aesthetically, and conceptually Black women writers manifest common approaches to the act of creating literature as a direct result of the specific political, social, and economic experience they have been obliged to share" (163–64). Once we identify "common approaches" as well as significant shared experiences, we should be able to describe not only the black women writers' or the Jewish women writers' traditions, but any group's literary tradition.

For Henry Louis Gates, Jr., the African-American tradition is defined "by the repetition and revision of shared themes, topics, and tropes" ("Rhetoric" 10–11). He adds, "It is no more . . . essentialist to make this claim than it is to claim the existence of French, English, German, Russian, or American literature—as long as we proceed inductively, from the texts to the theory, rather than deductively" (11). The process of defining a literary tradition, then, must include both sensitive scrutiny of texts and close attention to contexts.

Despite the distinction I am proposing between tradition and canon, the terms' very definitions raise similar questions. For example, as I begin to define the parameters of the American Jewish women writers' tradition, and "discover" writers whose names have been forgotten, I must ask why these writers have been forgotten. Is it because they were Jews, or because they were women? Or is it because they were not judged as "good" by their contemporaries? Can these two questions be separated so neatly? Clearly, the same questions could be asked not only about the boundaries of a tradition but about the hierarchical scale inherent in a canon's list of authors or texts.

In *Sensational Designs: The Cultural Work of American Fiction 1790–1860*, Jane Tompkins focuses on the canon of American literature when she asks, who judged literature, what standards did these evaluators use, and why did one author, such as Nathaniel Hawthorne, achieve canonical status when another, such as Susan Warner, did not? In response to these questions, Tompkins explains, "literary texts are man-made, historically produced objects, whose value has been created and recreated by men and women out of their particular needs." By studying the contexts of texts, she suggests, we can better understand the historical forces which produced particular writings as well as critical standards. However, we need not stop there. Indeed, we must go on, reading Warner, as well as Hawthorne, to open "the way for a retrieval of the values and interests embodied in other, non-canonical texts" (37). The "non-canonical texts" of nineteenth-century authors, including Penina Moise and Rebekah Hyneman, reveal "values" and "needs" which are just as "American" as those of Melville and Emerson; in addition, without these non-canonical texts, our vision of American literature and culture remains monochromatic and even inaccurate.

In establishing a tradition of a particular ethnic women's group we must also refocus our highly trained critical eye to see beyond conventional evaluations. While I agree with Barbara Herrnstein Smith, that the distinctions between "description and evaluation, or knowledge and judgment" (6) are not clearly drawn, nevertheless I believe that we need to recognize the critical values inherent in all ostensibly objective observations. We must try to read the words of any previously undervalued writers, such as nineteenth-century American Jewish women, as unexplored territories whose mountains and valleys need charting but not judging; our goal should not be to prove that these writers wrote like their celebrated male, Christian contemporaries (an enterprise that would most likely be built on the assumption that those men were the "best" writers of their era). Even if we cannot be unequivocally objective, because of our own cultural assumptions and values, we can become more conscious of those values and thereby attempt to read texts cognizant of our own evaluative response. Ideally, the result of such reading is a more accurate understanding of the "values and interests embodied" in all texts (Tompkins 37).[3]

I trust that the preceding discussion makes clear that my goal in presenting texts by nineteenth-century American Jewish women is not to create a rigid, narrowly defined canon but is, rather, to establish a tradition which until now has been subsumed under other headings.[4] Emma Lazarus, for example, has been studied as a Jewish author, an American poet, and a woman writer. Rarely, if ever, has she been seen as an American Jewish woman writer, connected to other American Jewish women writers struggling to reconcile the conflicting demands of their multiple loyalties. While all of the writers discussed here could fit into already established canons, of American literature, Jewish literature, Jewish American literature, women's literature, etc., we do them a disservice if we do not first see them within their own tradition. Although the potential danger of "erroneous generalization, and complicity in the institutional structures and methods of thought that have helped achieve the marginalization of women" lies within the "ghetto" some may accuse me of creating here, I agree with Elizabeth Ammons that "*not* to talk about excluded groups of writers separately . . . seems . . . equally if not more dangerous" (13). Before we can achieve a truly heterogeneous and inclusive "American literature," we must continue to identify and read unique literary traditions, to endow particular groups of writers with their own creative space—"a sentence of their own" (Rodenas 34).[5]

This metaphoric observation raises two questions: how did the Jewish women create their own space, and how do we interpret their achievements? The semiotic notion of codes can help provide answers to these questions; specifically, we can note the writers' use of Jewish, American, and female codes, and we can analyze the ways in which they created new linguistic and behavioral codes (new spaces, new identities), codes which could more fully contain their differentness. In my vocabulary, semiotic codes are closely connected to myths—the combined beliefs and values which individuals use to define themselves within and outside their culture and which others may use to distinguish one culture from another. Myths are ideals that people believe in, and they establish patterns of right behavior.

Because they call on "sacred texts, ancient wisdom, and 'things we all know—instinctively' " (Janeway 296), they seem to turn cultural institutions and practices into "natural," and therefore inviolable, conditions. Roland Barthes details this process: "Myth does not deny things, on the contrary, its function is to talk about them; simply, it purifies them, it makes them innocent, it gives them a natural and eternal justification, it gives them a clarity which is not that of an explanation but that of a statement of fact" (143). Nineteenth-century American Jewish women used a number of mythic ideals to define themselves, including the Mother in Israel and the True Woman. In addition, they believed in myths about the Jewish family functioning to preserve Judaism, and myths of the specialness of Jews. These and other myths provided the women with a way to think and feel about themselves, as well as a way for non-Jews to identify them.

Barthes also suggests that myth is related to ideology as well as to semiology (112). As I see it, myth and ideology both derive their power from people's deep beliefs in them, and both influence (at the same time they are influenced by) cultural modes of thought and behavior. What distinguishes myth from ideology, however, is that quality of sacred and unquestionable verity which myths embody. Ideology seems more avail-able to scrutiny and analysis because it does not depend to the same degree on that seeming "natural" origin of myth. A semiotic code, like ideology, depends less on the sacred aura of myth for its power and more on the details of a cultural present moment. As I will be using the terms, Jewish women used the codes available to them and created new ones, in order to find a place for themselves within the myths of their cultures.[6]

Myths can function as "cultural glue" (Schneidau 8), binding people into a community through their prescriptions for individual as well as group behavior, through their elucidation of a belief system which the culture can share, through their assurance that all is as it should be, and through their presentation of a shared history. By posing certain practices and beliefs as universals, and by proclaiming these publicly, myth helps build a group into a community/cohesive culture. For Jews, whose na-tionhood has not been defined by the inhabiting of a particular land, myth has functioned as indispensable "cultural glue."

How do myths gain and retain their potency? According to Nina Auer-bach, a "cultural myth thrives in large part because it lives below the formulated surface of its age; rarely does it crystallize into explicit gospel or precept which the conscious mind can analyze and reject" (10). It conveys its "right" patterns and beliefs through visual and verbal modes of communication, indirectly and covertly. That is what contributes to its "instinctual" and seemingly sacred quality; if it has no discernable origin, then it seems to be a simple truth.

Literacy does not preclude the need for and production of myths. In literate cultures, texts often function as primary vehicles for articulating the myths as well as for changing them. However, the relationship be-tween myth and literature is more complex than this suggests. Authors who live in a particular culture (or cultures) will be influenced by that culture's myths. Even if these authors do not consciously incorporate specific myths into their texts, the myths will influence the way they create their texts. Two different novelists can appropriate the same myth for their fiction and project it outward with unique literary plots and phrasing. For example, two of the best known nineteenth-century American women writers, Louisa May Alcott and Harriet Beecher Stowe, believed in the selflessness of women, a component of the True Woman myth, and created charcters who embody this quality. Beth March, in the former's *Little Women*, dies while in her teens; unable to dream of an adult "castle in the air," she dies, but she "softens" headstrong sister Jo in the process and thereby performs a very womanly act of spiritual guidance. Mara Lincoln, in Stowe's *The Pearl of Orr's Island*, also sacrifices her life in order to serve another—this time, her lover, a man who, in the context of Stowe's world, needs religious guidance. Although both characters grow out of the same cultural myth, each is a unique character in a unique plot.

Like Stowe and Alcott, many of the American Jewish women I studied transformed American and Jewish cultural myths about womanhood into usable forms. Sometimes, these women superimposed the myths of one culture onto those of the other; at other times, they lived with both sets, side by side. Whatever the method, the American Jewish women used the myths to strengthen their sometimes precarious positions.

To some, the Jewish women writers might seem marginal, on the outside of the "real" American literature. In effect, they are doubly marginal, as Jews and as women. Yet this peripheral position may not be a liability, as Mary Dearborn suggests in her book, *Pocahontas's Daughters: Gender and Ethnicity in American Culture:* "literature by and about those who seem to be on the edges of American culture can perhaps best represent what happens within that culture" (4). "Marginal writers" not only represent the larger culture in vivid forms, but they develop a special vision of the dominant culture from their distinctive vantage point on the periphery looking over and in. Emma Lazarus, for one, offers us such a view; she longed to be part of the American literary world, as she perceived it, but she learned, experiencing disappointment and anger in the process, that as a woman and as a Jew she would not achieve the status of a Longfellow or Bryant. The essays and poems written toward the end of her life reveal not only an awareness of her position but also the dynamics of the American literary scene as it was becoming self-conscious about itself in the mid to late nineteenth century.

Marginality and ethnicity were intricately connected for the American Jewish woman writer. Indeed, her consciousness of a necessary dual citizenship constitutes the most easily identifiable "theme" or "topic" which defines the American Jewish woman's tradition. This awareness of duality, or doubleness, is common to ethnic writers generally, as Werner Sollors explains: "whether they write in other languages or in English, ethnic writers have an acute sense of doubleness" (*Beyond Ethnicity* 249); for the Jewish women this meant double loyalties, and even, in some cases, double holidays and double sets of friends. As the following chap-

ters will reveal, these Jewish women repeatedly expressed their desire to
protect both their American and Jewish identities. Many used their writing to explore, justify, and demonstrate the premise that dual national
loyalties were possible.

I have focused my attention on Sephardic and German Jewish women,
rather than the more popularized and recognizable Eastern European
Jewish women, for two reasons.[7] The first, which seems obvious but is
nevertheless significant, is that until the 1880s, the Jewish population in
America consisted primarily of Sephardic and German Jews. Even more
specifically, Eastern European Jewish women did not begin writing in
significant numbers until the turn of the century. The second reason I am
interested in the Sephardic and German Jewish women writers is because
they have received so little attention as writers. Anzia Yezierska and
Mary Antin, both Eastern European immigrants, have recently caught the
interest of critics, and I take great pleasure in this. However, I want to
establish a historical literary context, a literary tradition, within which
we can read these early twentieth-century authors. Although German
and Russian Jewish cultures are quite different from each other, a writer
like Yezierska, choosing to write as a Jewish woman in America, shared
with Emma Lazarus and Emma Wolf certain experiences and pressures
because they were all Jewish American women writers. It is these common experiences and pressures which manifest themselves in the shared
"themes, topics, and tropes," the building blocks of a literary tradition.

Throughout the following pages, I present the Sephardic and German
Jewish women as culturally equivalent. I do this not because I think that
the two groups' differences are nonexistent or insignificant but because in
the context of class, ideals of womanhood, and conflicts between America and Judaism, the Sephardic and German Jewish women represented
themselves in ways which were nonspecific to their particular heritage.

For the purposes of this study, I am interested in analyzing the writings
of women who wrote in English, either as their first language, or as a
second language acquired early and well enough for fluency. This language competency suggests that the women who were born here considered themselves Americans or, if they were immigrants, learned English
as part of their assimilation to America. Because I am interested in
establishing a tradition of *American* Jewish women writers, the ability to
write "American" is significant. And because I wish to describe the
American *Jewish* tradition, I chose to study women who had some affilia-
tion with Judaism. In other words, the tradition I am outlining here is
composed of those women who were American Jews, not just because of
who their parents were or where they were born, but because on a
conscious level they chose to live as Jews in the United States of America.[8]

Chronologically, my study begins in 1815, the year in which Rachel

Mordecai Lazarus, a Jewish woman living in North Carolina, began corresponding with Maria Edgeworth, the British author. Although other American Jewish women, including Grace Nathan and Rebecca Franks, had written some letters and miscellaneous poems earlier in the eighteenth century, Lazarus's letters to Edgeworth appear to be the first extended corpus of work by an American Jewish woman. The study ends with the nineteenth century, although the concluding chapter includes a discussion of Edna Ferber, a successful twentienth-century writer descended from German Jews who inherited the legacy of the nineteenth century. In spanning almost an entire century, and looking ahead into another, I aim to provide a broad view of a tradition, and to provide a literary-historical context for the many American Jewish women writers who follow.

In providing this broad view, I will discuss, or at least mention, many writers. While I cannot claim to have ferreted out every letter, diary, or even poem or short story written by an American Jewish woman in English in the nineteenth century, my research has been extensive.[9] What I can claim with more confidence is that I have probably read most of the published volumes of poetry or fiction. Implicitly, this suggests that the corpus of work by nineteenth-century American Jewish women is relatively small. However, when genre distinctions and hierarchies become less important than building a tradition and including all types of writing in that tradition, then quantity in the narrowest sense should be less meaningful.

Although I will be pointing out the variety of literary types within one tradition, I feel that the conventional genre divisions limit more than expand our understanding of the nineteenth-century American Jewish women's words. As Dearborn exhorts, "In studying ethnic women's fiction, we need at times . . . to relax our standards and expectations of genre itself" (15). For the purposes of this study, we must relax our standards for all genres, not just fiction.[10] Indeed, if we do not, we may overlook "private" journals which tell stories about honoring the traditions of two cultures, and we may not accurately read a "public" published short story's encoded tale which reveals an author's fear of unwomanly fame. While we may not be able to ask exactly the same stylistic questions about a personal letter and a published poem, we can learn a great deal by asking what these writings have in common, particularly in regard to their shared "themes, topics, and tropes." In setting out to establish a tradition, we must concern ourselves less with debates over the definitions of genres and more with the interrelationships among types of writing, as well as with the problems the authors encountered in writing for public versus private audiences, or in writing at all.

Audience, like genre, becomes a complicated issue in the process of establishing a literary tradition, particularly when that tradition includes ethnic writers. According to Sollors, heightened sensitivity to audience characterizes the "ethnic" writer; she/he must

> confront an actual or imagined double audience, composed of "insiders" and of readers, listeners, or spectators who are not familiar with the writer's ethnic group. . . . Yet [her/his] audience may well be ethnic *and* American. Imperceptibly and sometimes involuntarily, writers begin to function as translators of ethnicity to ignorant, and sometimes hostile, outsiders and, at the same time, as mediators between "America" and greenhorns. (*Beyond Ethnicity* 249–50)

Although Sollors does not distinguish between the male and female "ethnic" writer, I would argue that the "ethnic" Jewish women writers carried the burden of "translation" more heavily than did the men. In their roles as educators, the American Jewish women often self-consciously directed their public writing toward an audience, either to confirm that being a Jew was noble and vital, or to improve the status of Jews among non-Jews. As a matter of fact, the "mediating text of the American ethnic woman is written very much with a sense of an audience; that audience . . . is the ethnic text's professed reason for being," Dearborn explains (40).

Contemporary Jewish audiences enthusiastically praised Penina Moise, Rebekah Hyneman, and Emma Lazarus, among others, for their commitment to Judaism as expressed in their womanly method of cajoling unobservant Jews to return to tradition and explaining Jews and Jewish values to non-Jewish audiences. Although these women were entering a public realm through their writing, they were doing so primarily for the sake of Judaism. The woman writer used this rationalization herself for her writing. Whether she wrote for a Jewish newspaper, and could therefore feel "safe" within her Jewish world, or for a secular magazine, knowing that she was making herself vulnerable, she often used her belief in Judaism and her roles within Jewish custom to justify the writing.

A Brief History of Jews in America

From the beginning, America received Jews with an ambivalent welcome. In 1654, a group of twenty-three Jews fleeing from Brazil and its Portuguese control, arrived in New Amsterdam. Arnold Wiznitzer hypothesizes that "the newly arrived Jews consisted of four adult men, six adult women and thirteen young people and children" (92). Although many historians believe that these early immigrants were Sephardic Jews, Wiznitzer suggests that at least some of them were "Ashkenazic Jews from Germany and Italy" (93). To their disappointment, Peter Stuyvesant initially forbade these weary Jews from staying in his small colony, arguing that

> The Jews who have arrived would nearly all like to remain here, but
> . . . fearing that owing to their present indigence they might become a
> charge in the coming winter, we have, for the benefit of this weak and
> newly developing place . . . deemed it useful to require them in a
> friendly way to depart; praying also most seriously in this connection,
> for ourselves as also for the general community . . . that the deceitful
> race,—such hateful enemies and blasphemers of the name of Christ,—
> be not allowed further to infect and trouble this new colony. . . .
> (Schappes, *Documentary History* 1–2)

Seven months later, in April 1655, the Dutch West India Company granted these first "American" Jews permission to stay, provided that "the poor among them shall not become a burden to the company or to the community" (Schappes 5). Despite restrictions on their activities, including prohibitions against holding public religious services, the Jews quickly became productive members of colonial society.

Bringing traditions and rituals with them from Spain and Portugal, via Brazil, Curacao, Surinam, Barbados, and Jamaica, the Sephardic Jews set the American Jewish cultural tone through the eighteenth and into the nineteenth century. "Despite the fact that prerevolutionary American Jewry was overwhelmingly Ashkenazic (German-Polish) in ethnic origin, the Sephardic style [of liturgy] had become the traditional American rite" (Marcus, "American Colonial Jew" 80). This Sephardic style was Orthodox in its orientation and practice.

During the eighteenth century, Ashkenazic Jews from Germany, Poland, and other European countries joined the Sephardic Jews in the American colonies. During the Colonial period, "the immigrant Jews were young and unmarried generally," according to Doris Groshen Daniels. These young men

> arrived alone, without families, from Holland and England, although
> some did travel directly from small towns in Germany and Poland.
> Unlike Christian settlers of the same period, they were not interested
> in land; they were merchants, not farmers. Most Jews had been mem-
> bers of the middle or lower middle class in small towns in Europe and
> . . . brought a small amount of money for investment. . . . The typical
> Colonial American Jew, therefore, was generally a middle class
> urbanite, in some form of trade, and anxious to move up socially and
> economically. (378)

By 1776, Jewish communities were thriving in Rhode Island, New York, Pennsylvania, North Carolina, and Georgia, although Jews lived in all thirteen colonies; the total Jewish population was between 1,000 and 2,500 (.04–.1 percent of total population). By 1820, the number had grown to between 2,700 and 3,000 (.03 percent of total population); by 1840, 15,000 (.09 percent); and by 1850, 50,000 (.22 percent). The numbers become even more dramatic as the century progresses: 230,000–280,000 by 1880 (.46–.56 percent); 400,000–450,000 by 1890 (.64–.71 percent); and 938,000–1,058,000 (1.23–1.39 percent) by 1900 (Sarna, "Appendix" 296).

Despite their growing numbers, or perhaps because of them, Jews continued to experience an ambivalent reception from America. Even after they served faithfully in the Revolutionary War, and even with the protection of the Bill of Rights, Jewish men were prohibited in some states from voting or holding public office. It was not until 1826, for example, that Maryland amended its constitutional requirement that public officials declare their belief in Christ and Christianity. This southern state's policy was not exceptional. In 1861, the Congress of the United States stipulated that a chaplain in the Union army had to be a Christian. Although Congress amended this requirement in the following year, the original policy demonstrated that Union and Christianity were inseparable. "Jews realized that they could win equality in popular eyes only by demonstrating that being Jewish in no way conflicted with being American. They had to prove that non-Christians could still be loyal and devoted citizens" (Sarna, "Impact" 24). But, "no single action and no single speech could break down centuries of popular prejudice. Jews had *continually* to prove their patriotism. The battle against anti-Jewish stereotypes was a never-ending one" (25).

Although Jews constantly proclaimed fidelity to America, anti-Semitic incidents increased during the second half of the nineteenth century. One of the most publicized of these involved Joseph Seligman, a prominent New York banker, who in 1877 was denied accommodations at the Grand Union Hotel in Saratoga Springs. From then until well into the twentieth century, resorts commonly "restricted" their clientele to non-Jews. The Seligman case demonstrated that although many Jews had achieved respectable economic positions by the last quarter of the nineteenth century, they could never feel completely secure if neither their government nor social peers chose to accept them as equals. Hard work, devotion of time and money to philanthropy, and responsible citizenship did not automatically insure a Jew's access to echelons of power and leisure.

The ambivalence America expressed toward Jews became even more dramatic when thousands of Eastern European Jews began arriving in the last two decades of the nineteenth century. To the Sephardic and German Jews who were already established and assimilated these oppressed, poor, desperate immigrants seemed to threaten not only their own relative security but their American national identities as well.

Many of the German Jews achieved financial security through the efforts of hard-working men who began life in America as peddlers in the south and midwest, selling cloth and ribbon, trinkets and tools, to isolated farmers and residents of small towns. When the peddler acquired enough capital, he invested in a store, often a dry goods store, usually in the south or midwest, where he had peddled. The success of Benjamin Bloomingdale and Levi Strauss are well known, but even less spectacularly successful German Jewish men became prosperous business proprietors in towns and cities all over the United States.

Columbus, Ohio, provides a vivid example of German Jewish men's success. According to Marc Lee Raphael, by 1872 "every retail clothing store in Columbus was owned by a German Jew" (438), and all of these store owners were economically secure. In other, larger cities, too, German Jewish men were involved in clothing sales or manufacturing. "An account published in 1888 claimed that 234 of the 241 clothing manufacturers in [New York] were Jews, doing an annual business $55 million" (N. Cohen 29). One year later, in 1889, the

> Bureau of the Census studied 18,000 Jews, of whom four-fifths were German immigrants or their descendants. . . . Among other things, the survey disclosed that about 50% of the men were wholesale or retail merchants; 20% were accountants, bookkeepers, and clerks; 2% were bankers, brokers, and company officials; 5% were professionals; and less than 1% were peddlers. . . . Of the 10,000 families, 40% had one servant, 20% had two, and 10% had at least three. (N. Cohen 30)

The statistical picture presents German Jewish men as heavily involved in one industry—clothing manufacturing and sales—and as economically secure.

German Jewish women shared with the men a desire to find a safe, comfortable place to live, as Jews. As the following chapters will clarify, however, for women, who were denied access to the business and political worlds, writing functioned as one of the primary means for finding that safe place. With their words, the Jewish women affirmed their Jewish and American identities and achieved a degree of success.

What originally motivated the German Jews to emigrate? According to Rudolf Glanz, during the 1820s, "Germany was engulfed by a tempestuous flood of chauvinism, when an anti-Semitic movement spread throughout the country," prompting an increase in emigration. Even more Jews left Germany and came to America after 1848, "after the failure of the revolution and the blighting of all hopes of the German Jews for a full emancipation, particularly in Bavaria, where the Jews obtained no rights whatsoever" (*Studies* 89).

Despite the anti-Semitic attitudes and policies which might have forced them to leave Germany, many of the German Jewish immigrants retained strong ties to German culture. It was not uncommon to send children to German-speaking schools and to subscribe to German language newspapers, for example.

These German Jewish immigrants brought with them the ideas and rituals of the developing Reform movement. Reform Judaism, which had its roots in the German Enlightenment, "was a conscious effort to adjust Judaism to the nineteenth century temperament." Reform Judaism convinced Jews "that they were not compelled to make a choice between Judaism and modern European culture, that there was no inherent contradiction between Judaism and the environment" (Korn, "German-Jewish" 108). In practice, Reform Judaism allowed men and women to sit together in synagogue, organ music and choirs to provide music during services, and girls to be confirmed along with boys.[11] In other words, it molded Judaism so that it would resemble American Christianity. Because a "vibrant Judaism in America required both continuity with its historical Jewish heritage and sufficient Americanization to render that tradition intelligible and respectable to Jews and non-Jews alike[, t]he Reform movement in America, the best example of conscious and purposeful Americanization of Judaism," was successful (N. Cohen 161).

This need to Americanize Judaism has been deeply felt by American Jews who have wanted to continue to practice Judaism as Americans. Indeed, "American Jewish history . . . is . . . unified by a common vision, the quest to be fully a Jew and fully an American, both at the same time" (Sarna, "Introduction" xiii). The tradition of American Jewish literature by women expresses this same quest to demonstrate, over and over again, that loyalty to one nation does not mean a denial of loyalty to another.

Three of the five chapters that follow are arranged around particular themes which I use to construct the parameters of the American Jewish women's tradition: American and Jewish womanhood (chapter 4); American and Jewish nationality (chapter 5); and American Jewish womanhood (chapter 6). The two exceptions to the thematic arrangement are "Mythic Ideals of American and Jewish Womanhood" (chapter 2) and "The Words and Worlds of Emma Lazarus" (chapter 3). Chapter 2 functions as context for the texts and authors in the tradition, while chapter 3 focuses on the writer whose work most vividly represents the qualities that define the tradition of nineteenth-century American Jewish women writers.[12] I hope that by examining "the repetition and revision of shared themes," and by proceeding formalistically or "inductively, from the texts to the theory" (Gates, "Rhetoric" 10–11) (all the while recognizing the dangers and limits of assuming that these texts do exist in ways more concrete than simply my subjective reading of them), I will be accurately charting the writings that constitute the tradition. These writings suggest that nineteenth-century American Jewish women valued the privilege of free expression and learned to use it in their personal struggles to be female citizens of both the American democracy and the ancient Jewish nation. For these women, writing was not a harmless hobby or a lucrative occupation but was, more often, a means for reconciling the demands of womanhood and their two nations. What and how they wrote will constitute the "subject" of this book.

II.

Mythic Ideals of American and Jewish Womanhood

In "Politics and Culture in Women's History: A Symposium," Temma Kaplan observed that it is "impossible to speak of 'women's culture' without understanding its variation by class and ethnic group" (DuBois et al. 44). Although Kaplan was speaking in general terms, her admonition has particular relevance to this study, because without an appreciation for the variety of women's cultures, we would probably overlook the experiences and traditions of American Jewish women. At the same time, however, we must recognize that there was a dominant American women's culture in the mid-nineteenth century, that that culture was white, middle-class, and Christian, and that a Jewish woman who wanted to be accepted as American had to conform to at least some of the dominant culture's myths.

For women in mid-nineteenth-century America, the white, middle-class, Christian model of propriety emerged as the True Woman. I begin this chapter with a summary of True Womanhood in order to establish the traits, behavior, and sometimes even values which Jewish women emulated in order to seem American. In the second part of the chapter, I discuss another powerful cultural myth: the Mother in Israel. Although I will be detailing some strikingly important similarities between these two mythic ideals, I do not intend to provide a neat point by point comparison, a comparison which might be schematically pleasing but which also might oversimplify, and therefore distort, complex cultural processes.

The American True Woman

True Womanhood: Origins and Development

Emerging in the early nineteenth century, the Cult of True Womanhood

16

had become firmly entrenched in white, middle-class America by the mid-nineteenth century. Geographically, the notion of a woman's sphere originated in New England and then spread to the rest of America, as Nancy Cott postulates in *The Bonds of Womanhood*.[1] The "canon of domesticity" was "rooted in the experience of Yankee middle-class mothers" but was "applied to the female sex as a whole," Cott explains (17). She also argues that this mythic ideal was a middle-class phenomenon, "a cultural preference for domestic retirement and conjugal-family intimacy over both the 'vain' and fashionable sociability of the rich and the promiscuous sociability of the poor" (92). As a middle-class ideal, the True Woman functioned to categorize people in a nation that wanted to see itself as classless. Instead of organizing society around income level or social connections, America would classify its citizens according to "natural," and therefore indisputable, differences: race and sex. Ironically, of course, such a system did not abolish inequalities; it merely displaced them.

Nor did the system achieve its goal of completely abolishing class divisions: some women (usually white and middle- or upper-class) could hire out a number of domestic jobs, while other women (immigrants, slaves and free blacks, working class) had to work in a factory or another woman's home. Thus, as Gerda Lerner points out, the True Woman was really not a classless ideal but was rather an upper-class, white image which women emulated in order to resemble those of a higher status ("The Lady" 190). Although the Cult of True Womanhood did make women equal through its stipulation that their identities should be inseparable from family and home, it also glorified the Truest Woman as one who could devote all her time to domestic duties. Therefore, the perfect True Woman necessarily had to be middle- or upper-class.

Like all cultural myths, True Womanhood did not remain static. As American culture changed, so did the ideal of womanhood. In the final decades of the nineteenth century, demographic as well as financial shifts, such as the ever-increasing number of immigrants and the growth of industrial capitalism, contributed to tremendous changes in where and how Americans lived. Both cause and effect of these changes was the disintegration of a clear definition of America. According to Alan Trachtenberg, "political battles and ideological campaigns in the Gilded Age took the appearance of struggles over the meaning of the word 'America,' over the political and cultural authority to define the term and thus to say what reality was and ought to be" (73). More specifically, the consensus on what a proper American woman was and ought to be was also changing. As women began to join the professions and seek experiences beyond the home, the True Woman began to see herself as a new woman, capable of earning her own living and leading an independent life. In increasing numbers, these new women chose to explore their educational and professional options, either before or instead of taking on the roles of wife and mother. This is not to suggest that suddenly all American middle-class white women rejected their domestic roles in favor of public professions. On the contrary, well into the twentieth century, many women, and men, held firm in their beliefs that a woman's duty was to serve others selflessly.[2]

True Womanhood: Definitions

According to Carroll Smith-Rosenberg, the True Woman was expected to be "gentle and refined, sensitive and loving. She was the guardian of religion and spokeswoman for morality. . . . Her sphere was the hearth and nursery" ("Hysterical Woman" 655–56). The True Woman was responsible for "guiding the more worldly and more frequently tempted male past the maelstroms of atheism and uncontrolled sexuality" as well as for bestowing "care and love, peace and joy" upon husband and children. She had learned that "aggression, independence, self-assertion, and curiosity were male traits, inappropriate for the weaker sex and her limited sphere." Deprived of the opportunity to "achieve in any area considered important by men and thus highly valued by society[, s]he was . . . to remain a child-woman, never developing the strengths and skills of adult autonomy" (655–56). And under no circumstances was she to question the authority that defined her sphere.

In her definition of True Womanhood, Barbara Welter delineates four "cardinal virtues" by which a "woman judged herself and was judged by her husband, her neighbors and society." These included "piety, purity, submissiveness and domesticity. Put them all together and they spelled mother, daughter, sister, wife—woman. Without them, no matter whether there was fame, achievement or wealth, all was ashes. With them she was promised happiness and power" (21).

The four qualities that defined a woman were both cause and effect of the division between the private and public spheres. Because women believed in their roles as protectors of the hearth, moral guides of brothers and husbands, and educators of children, they contributed to the polarized structure upon which American middle-class culture was built. At the same time, that construct told women that they were suited for such a domestic existence because they were ill equipped to enter the competitive world and because their special female natures made them ideal for family and home duties.

The idealized home, which both defined and confined the True Woman, was "supposed to be a cheerful place, so that brothers, husbands and sons would not go elsewhere in search of a good time" (Welter 31). The men in the family should *want* to stay at home, finding the peace and love of the fireside more alluring than the ephemeral excitement of the billiard table and dance hall. And always sacred home life "had to express the highest moral and Christian values. The woman had to guard against any outside influence that might breed corruption or scandal" (B. Harris 34).

Despite all the rhetoric that glorified her domestic responsibilities, the True Woman's influence was indirect, and, ironically, even this power of influence was carefully circumscribed: "the wife, as the mistress of the home, was perceived by society and herself as the moral superior of the husband, though his legal and social inferior" (Degler 8). Being "inferior" meant that "in those areas of interaction between home and society . . . the husband held sway" (Chambers-Schiller 75). Although women were told that they were superior within the domestic sphere, that sphere actually had limited impact on the public world. Marxist historians have been helpful in analyzing this power differential in the male and female spheres; in her important article "Separate Spheres, Female Worlds, Woman's Place: The Rhetoric of Women's History," Linda Kerber summarizes the Marxist critique, noting that it "offered an explanation of the way in which [the] separation [of spheres] served the interests of the dominant classes." In addition, according to Marxists, "Separate spheres were due neither to cultural accident nor to biological determinism. They were social constructions, camouflaging social and economic service, a service whose benefits were unequally shared" (14).[3]

How did individual women live with the reality of these separate and unequal spheres? Not surprisingly, the psychological and emotional process of attempting to turn inferiority into superiority required tremendous effort on the part of women, and it produced only partially successful results. Kathryn Kish Sklar's biography of Catharine Beecher emphasizes the conflict between the ideal of centrality and the reality of marginality. As Sklar describes her, Beecher had difficulty finding a comfortable place within her culture; at the same time that she was advocating myths of domesticity, she was leading an active, public life. Intelligent and opinionated, she advocated education for women so that they could be teachers of others, yet she often grew impatient with her own schools and projects. Although Beecher was extreme in the discrepancy between her public avowal of domesticity and her private violation of some of its major tenets, she did seem to understand that in order to be respected as a loyal American, the nineteenth-century white, middle-class, Christian woman had to support domesticity either in her actions or her words.

If she did not, she was not fulfilling her duty as an American. Indeed, it was through her domestic duties that the True Woman demonstrated her civic responsibility, particularly in the first half of the century. In her capacity as mother, for example, she was expected "to raise up a whole generation of Christian statesmen who could say 'all that I am I owe to my angel mother'" (Welter 38–39). It was understood that in order to survive as a healthy, virtuous democracy, the nation needed its mothers to keep corruptible men uncorrupted and to rear the succeeding generations of "moral, trustworthy statesmanlike citizens" (Cott 94). In other words, women, although they could neither vote nor hold public office, were expected to contribute to the American nation; presumably, their influence was no less vital for being indirect.

Such indirectness reveals an inherent contradiction at the heart of the True Womanhood myth: appear inactive but act tirelessly. Thus the ideal True Woman who contentedly supervised her hearth and family, in reality ran clubs, organized church activities, and performed deeds of charity, both before and after the Civil War. Superimposed on the image of the demure and submissive wife was the strong and efficient manager who kept home and family functioning.

The True Woman as Christian Ideal

The perfect True Woman also had to uphold Christian values, not only for herself and her family, but for the whole nation. According to Mary Kelley, nineteenth-century Protestants had replaced the "omnipotent God of Calvin, who stood in judgment over sinful human beings, determined their fate, and elected few among many," with a "loving if still demanding God" (*Private Woman* 289–90); as a result, individuals became more responsible for their own lives and afterlives, as well as for "demonstrat[ing] commitment toward others" (290). It seemed natural, then, that women, who were deemed more morally virtuous and who took *others'* concerns so seriously, should become the spirit-keepers of America.

Amanda Porterfield, in *Feminine Spirituality in America*, argues that women took on this role because the "home, and thereby women, lost economic status during the late eighteenth and early nineteenth century, but gained in religious authority, a development reflecting the secularization of American public life and the isolation of religion as a personal, family affair." Porterfield further explains that "As religion became a matter of family persuasion, women became arbiters of religious life, persuasive religious authorities as well as exemplars of religious devotion" (58). Ann Douglas has argued that women were able to gain such prominence in spiritual affairs because institutions that defined and maintained religious practices lost prestige and authority.[4] I would complicate the cause/effect dynamic and add that those institutions lost power because the family, and women, became so central in American Christianity.

"The Cult of Single Blessedness"

In church or at home, the True Woman was expected to be wife and mother, as well as daughter and sister. How, then, did a single woman fulfill the domestic obligations of womanhood? The answer to the question is the subject of Lee Chambers-Schiller's *Liberty, A Better Husband.* Chambers-Schiller describes another mythic ideal, the Cult of Single Blessedness, which developed alongside the Cult of True Womanhood. This Cult of Single Blessedness

> upheld the single life as both a socially and personally valuable state. It offered a positive vision of singlehood rooted in Protestant religion and the concepts of woman's particular nature and special sphere. It promoted singlehood as at least as holy, and perhaps more pure, a state than marriage. As developed from 1810 to 1860, the central tenet of single blessedness noted the transitory nature of "domestic bliss" and encouraged the search for eternal happiness through the adoption of a "higher calling" than marriage. Whether moral or intellectual in nature, such a vocation was considered "thrice blessed": blessed to the individual because it guarded the integrity of her soul; blessed of God because through it she committed her life to His work; and blessed to those for whom her efforts ensured a better life. (18)

Despite the exalted rhetoric and the promise such rhetoric held out, being an " 'old maid' was hardly an honorable status" (Degler 152). In reality, "unwed [women] experienced considerable stress and conflict in their single lives. The Cult of Single Blessedness held up an ideal that could not be realized both because of the contradictions inherent within it and because of cultural attitudes and social structures that inhibited its full expression" (Chambers-Schiller 173). In a culture that assigned well-defined roles to its inhabitants, deviance from those roles would require tremendous will and sacrifice on the part of the "rebels." Ironically, many of those who did "rebel" by not marrying or bearing children still had little time for pursuing their individual interests either because they found themselves responsible for parents, siblings, nieces, or nephews, or because they had to earn a living, generally as governesses or teachers, occupations which required long, difficult hours and offered small salaries and low social status.

Chambers-Schiller argues that single women enabled "middle-class Americans to cope with the social upheavals of economic development and population redistribution." During the antebellum "transition period," she continues, "the services of single women eased the costs of social and economic change and made viable the family structure which characterized the new industrial order" (40). So, the Cult of Single Blessedness developed to fill economic and social needs, not only of single women, but of American middle-class culture; such a reading of history suggests that the idea of greater autonomy and independence for spinsters was a fiction used to maintain a ready supply of cheap and willing labor.

Women Writers

One occupation *did* offer a woman more prestige and money: writing. Although it presented its own challenges and dangers, writing provided a woman, single or married, with a way to earn a living and establish her individuality but avoid taking a long stride outside the home. Even when a woman wrote, however, she had to remember her duties as wife, mother, sister, and daughter. "Women of genius . . . were urged to make it clear in their lives and in their work that they understood [that their] domestic duties came before their work" (Welter 76). Often the nineteenth-century woman writer's work reveals the frustrating dilemma of fusing two seemingly contradictory identities—public writer and private woman. In her analysis of this problematic identity, *Private Woman, Public Stage,* Mary Kelley emphasizes the ambivalence the "literary domestics" (those who wrote best-selling novels about women and the home) experienced as they perceived themselves to be encroaching on the male sphere and male activities, such as earning money in the public arena, while desperately trying to maintain their personal sense of private, domestic propriety. Most of the women Kelley studied accepted the rules made by their patriarchal culture, and they tried to play their "proper" roles even as they earned money and immense popularity.

Susan Coultrap-McQuin also describes a paradox experienced by women writers: "they had a place in the literary world, yet that world often rendered them invisible" (7). Thus writers such as Rose Terry Cooke, Harriet Prescott Spofford, Rebecca Harding Davis, Louisa May Alcott, Louise Chandler Moulton, Sara Payson Parton (Fanny Fern), Sara Jane Lippincott (Grace Greenwood), and Maria Cummins achieved great popular success at the same time that their white "gentlemen" publishers sometimes failed to invite them to literary parties, and reviewers evaluated their work using criteria that had more to do with standards of genteel femininity than literary qualities. And even when they did conform to a critic's view of femininity, these "authoresses" found themselves caught in a "catch-22. Women, who were expected to write of domestic scenes, were criticized for doing so" (17).

Despite such mixed messages, the five writers Coultrap-McQuin examines in detail (E.D.E.N. Southworth, Harriet Beecher Stowe, Mary Abigail Dodge, Helen Hunt Jackson, and Elizabeth Stuart Phelps [Ward]) "did not seem to accept the idea that a literary career was inappropriate for women; they were not particularly anxious about being a woman who was pursuing literary work" (20). Their comfort, Coultrap-McQuin argues, was the result of the "overlapping nature of expectations about Victorianism, womanhood, and authorship" (20); because "American Victorianism encouraged moral, didactic, and patriarchal approaches to life"

(7), and because writing was viewed as "an embellishment, a luxury, a pursuit for the leisured or for those with a lucrative career and time to spare" (13), an "authoress" could maintain her identity as a woman and a writer simultaneously.

No matter how comfortable she was, however, a nineteenth-century woman had to have experienced ambivalence about her writing, if for no other reason than because she was a woman. In their now famous rereading of Harold Bloom's "anxiety of influence," Sandra Gilbert and Susan Gubar argue that most nineteenth-century women writers (British and American) experienced an " 'anxiety of authorship'—a radical fear that [they could not] create, that because [they could] never become a 'precursor' the act of writing [would] isolate or destroy" them (*Madwoman* 49). For Jewish women, as will become apparent in the following chapters, this "anxiety of authorship" was exacerbated by a centuries-old tradition which excluded them from serious study of holy texts, as well as by a feeling of uncertainty in their new home, America.

The myth of True Womanhood was firmly rooted in America's dominant white, middle-class, Christian culture and as such it mandated that all women in America had to conform to the myth on some level if they wanted to be counted as American women. Such a task could prove difficult if one's family was not Concord Christian but Hamburg Jewish; in the latter case, one would need to study True Womanhood carefully by reading widely circulating popular magazines such as *Godey's Ladies' Book* as well as popular novels and stories, and by noting non-Jewish Amerians' details of dress, manners, and attitudes toward husbands, children, and America itself. Ironically, the Jewish woman also learned that even as they taught her how to be included, the myths of True Womanhood excluded her from the culture she defined as American.

The Jewish Mother in Israel

The Mother in Israel: Origins and Definitions

The nineteenth-century American Jewish woman, as she revealed herself in her own words, understood that two nations asked for her loyalty and that her loyalty would be measured by how well she adhered to mythic ideals of womanhood. As the previous section has detailed, the American middle-class ideal manifested itself in the True Woman. The Jewish ideal projected itself through the Mother in Israel who, like Deborah in the Old Testament (Judges 5:7), the original mother in Israel, was dedicated to defending her children, the Jews.

According to Rachel Adler, "the term 'mother in Israel' . . . is an expression used to describe a power which is institutional" (247) and "which depicts the mother role as a power-role involving leadership, daring and protectiveness on a societal rather than simply a familiar level" (249).[5] As it came to be used in nineteenth-century America, the appellation Mother in Israel described the model "Jewess," the wife, mother, daughter who dedicated herself to the well-being of her family and, through the family, the Jewish nation. She was the Old Testament matriarch transposed into the modern world; religiously committed and capable, she could conquer any task if it benefited the "familiar" parents, children, husband or the "societal" temple and Jewish community.

The myth of the Jewish family communicated the essential syllogism: survival of the Jews depends on strong Jewish families, and strong families rely on devout, able women, so Jewish survival depends on woman's commitment and strength. Specifically, the Jewish woman was "responsible for the moral development of the family, being endowed with an exceptional capacity for moral persuasion" (Hyman, "Other Half" 109). As the center of the family, the nineteenth-century American Jewish woman believed that she had a special, even religious duty, to instill in her children the knowledge and feelings which would insure the survival of the group; the Mother in Israel taught her children fear of prejudice and potential violence directed against Jews, as well as pride in surviving without a homeland and in spite of countless attempts at decimation.[6]

The Jewish woman's belief that her life was centered in the home was reinforced by nineteenth-century American attitudes; indeed, "in mid-nineteenth century America . . . Jewish women were scarcely distinguishable from their non-Jewish middle-class counterparts" (Baum et al. 32). By the end of the century, Jewish women had even "internalized the view that theirs was the duty to reign as the spiritual element within the home" (Baum et al. 33). Despite the overlap between responsibilities of the True Woman and of the Mother in Israel, some important differences emerge when we start examining the cultural rationale for home duties.

The True Woman ostensibly created a warm and inviting space in order to protect her husband, brother, and sons from the saloon, gambling hall, and even brothel. The Mother in Israel, on the other hand, did not try to shield her men from temptation but, rather, provided a refuge where they could study the laws of Judaism; she established a safe home which could function as a sanctuary from a world that distrusted Jews. "To the Jew, more than to the man of any other race is home a sanctuary, an asylum, the one place on earth where, if anywhere, happiness is for him attainable," wrote Alice Rhine, a Jewish woman, in 1887 ("Race Prejudice" 530). Accordingly, the Jewish man was not choosing between home life and society as was the Christian; he valued the home as one of the few places where he could proudly and unapologetically *be* a Jew. And the

Jewish woman feared not the particular consequences of a husband's worldly ways but the annihilation of an entire people.

For most of the nineteenth century, the idealized Mother in Israel carried out her duties within a family, in relation to children and to men. Because she did not enjoy many rights under Jewish law, a woman without a father or a husband was almost invisible. Legally, religiously, economically, and socially, she needed a man for and through whom she could perform her duties, just as the American True Woman did. It is not surprising, then, that "marriage remained the clear purpose in life for female Jewish youth" (Glanz, *Jewish Woman* 2, 17) during most of the nineteenth century in America.

The Jewish woman who never married and never bore children of her own faced the same dilemma the single Christian woman did: how could she demonstrate her womanliness? By functioning as a surrogate mother to nieces and nephews, or to a whole school full of children. Or she could forge a new identity, outside the domestic circle, as did Emma Lazarus, who is the subject of the next chapter. Like the Christian woman, however, the Jewish woman who remained single or unattached to someone's children, and therefore implicitly rejected the myths of the Jewish family, had to work doubly hard to earn the respect of her co-religionists, often by devoting herself to the welfare of the Jewish community.[7]

It should be noted that within Jewish culture marriage was as important for men since every individual had an obligation to uphold the precious Jewish family. "In Jewish tradition marriage and family life is not viewed as a compromise between the holy and the profane, between the spirit and flesh," Marshall Sklare explains. He continues: "to marry is a *mitzvah*, a religious commandment. . . . In Jewish culture the obligation of marriage and family life is prescribed for everyone" (*America's Jews* 74). Indeed, "only he who had founded a house in Israel was worthy to be considered a full-fledged member of the community; only she who had become a Mother in Israel had realized her destiny," according to Bernard Cohen (107).

In nineteenth-century America, the idealized Jewish marriage received support from non-Jews who also glorified the function of marriage in Jewish culture. The rapid economic rise of German Jewish immigrants, for example, was perceived to be dependent on the stability of Jewish married life—on the husband who worked diligently to provide for his wife and children, and on the wife who dutifully and lovingly tended to the needs of her home, her husband, and her children (Glanz, *Jewish Woman* 2, 89).

As the example of marriage makes clear, Jewish tradition and law have become intricately intertwined through the centuries since the ancient Hebrews received commandments regarding their daily lives. The interdependence of tradition and law has had a particular impact on Jewish women. Although "Jewish law does not . . . define with any precision whatsoever a 'proper' or 'necessary' role for Jewish women," according to Saul Berman, "it is nevertheless clear that since for most of [Jewish] history, . . . continuation as a people depended upon the voluntary selection by women of the role of wife-mother-homemaker, the law would and did encourage the exercise of that choice" (121). Whether or not actual laws stipulated that a woman's first obligation was to her family, Jews believed in this "truth" as if it were law.

Blu Greenberg also suggests that "what was a sociological truth about women . . . was codified in many minute ways into Halakhah ["the body of Jewish religious law" (4)] as religioethical concepts, binding upon future generations" (4–5). Like Berman, Greenberg proposes that the spirit, if not the letter, of the law maintained specific roles for women. Paula Hyman goes one step further than Berman and Greenberg, pointing out that although the Jewish woman has been honored for her roles within the family, she has been legally denied many religious and civic privileges. Halakhah, she argues, "exempts women from all positive time-bound mitzvot ["commandments, usually referring to good deeds" (Beck 283) such as communal prayer and study] because of the nature of their family obligations" ("Other Half" 106). She adds,

> within the framework of traditional Judaism, women are not indepen-
> dent legal entities. Like the minor, the deaf-mute, and the idiot, they
> cannot serve as witnesses in a Jewish court, except for a few specified
> cases. They do not inherit equally with male heirs; they play only a
> passive role in the Jewish marriage ceremony; and they cannot initi-
> ate divorce proceedings. ("Other Half" 106)

Because nineteenth-century American Jews accepted these traditions and laws as integral to Judaism, they relegated the ideal Jewish woman to the home, and they emphasized that her primary role was to contribute to the preservation of the Jews. It should not surprise us, then, that as a whole, the nineteenth-century American Jewish women writers were conservative—they acted as conservators of their culture(s). Most of them followed traditional middle-class paths into marriage and motherhood, or into teaching/caring for others. And in their verbal rhetoric, they tended to follow prescribed conventions (of genre, subject matter, and structure) because they believed in the mythic ideals which shaped their cultural and creative contexts, and because they felt that by following what they perceived to be appropriate forms, they themselves and their writing would be accepted. However, even as these women subscribed to and activated the public codes of American and Jewish middle-class cultures, they attempted to create for themselves new identities, identities that would allow for greater personal and creative flexibility.[8]

The Jewish woman in nineteenth-century America learned her prescribed Jewish roles through formal advice, conversations with mothers and grandmothers, and through newspaper articles, rabbis' sermons, and speeches, almost all of which were written by men. Given Judaism's patriarchal structure, it is not surprising that men were advising women how to act, think, and feel, as they had been doing for centuries. But the tenor of the advice was different in America, because America was different. A country founded on the principles of freedom and choice (at least for its white, male citizens), as well as on the separation of "church" and state, promised Jews greater opportunities than any other country. But it also presented threats—of secularism, dilution of customs, intermarriage, etc. So Jewish leaders, almost all of whom were men, advised and asked women to continue to play their roles of Mothers in Israel, dedicated to preserving the Jewish nation in America.

However, even as they asked the women to remain faithful "Jewesses," these men shaped their request to fit American standards. In 1835, for example, Isaac Leeser, an important conservative religious leader who published *The Occident and American Jewish Advocate*, an influential newspaper, from 1843 to 1869, delivered a sermon on the education of Jewish women. "It is not to be denied," Leeser declared, "that it is almost entirely useless for the female to become learned in the strictest sense of the word; it would unsex her, if she were to study the legal profession; if she were to step abroad as a physician." Not the public sphere, "But her home should be the place of her actions; there her influence should be felt, to soothe, to calm, to sanctify, to render happy the rugged career of a father, a brother, a husband, or a child" (129–30). Leeser molded the Jewish ideal of woman and family into a Christian American shape, stressing the influence a woman should have on the men in her family. And in proclaiming, "far better will it be that our daughters grow up religious women and excellent housewives than that they be elegant musicians, skillful painters, graceful dancers, or pretenders to sciences which to the great majority of females must be quite useless" (132), he could have been addressing upper-class Christian Americans; there is nothing specifically Jewish in his statement.

Less than a decade later, in 1842, Nathaniel Levin of Charleston, South Carolina, also advised Jewish women of their roles in America. In delivering an address to the Society for Instruction of Jewish Youth, Levin stated that woman's influence, which emanated from her delicacy, mild disposition, warm affection, and loveliness, was one of the most "powerful and efficient causes of [society's] progress in refinement and civilization" (152). Levin voiced the American belief that woman's influence at home paralleled her influence in society: "Her domestic virtues confer on home all its comforts and allurements; her presence in society humanizes law and imparts a more lofty honour and a more refined state of morals to the civil relations" (153). *Influencing* those around her to be more civilized, the woman's "refining tenderness . . . cheering confidence, and . . . consoling faith . . . awaken [the] noble emotions of [man's] soul and excite him to the generous and lofty pursuits of patriotism and philanthropy" (153).

The Jewish woman's domestic responsibility, like the Christian woman's, included educating Jewish children at home and in organizations such as the Society for Instruction of Jewish Youth. Levin told his audience that women had a "hallowed task" in "upholding the *temple* of the *Jewish mind*, and giving perpetuity to that faith which threw the majesty of Heaven from the harp of David, and which wrapped Isaiah's hallowed soul in fire" (155); by instilling in children positive feelings about and knowledge of Judaism, Jewish women contributed to the continuation of their nation. They were well suited to this task because they possessed "patience under difficulties . . . devotion under opposition . . . [and] unwavering constancy of purpose under all circumstances" (156).

Both Leeser's and Levin's words echo Christian Americans' discussions of women's nature and roles. Influenced as these Jewish men were by American middle-class culture, they, and many other Jews, believed in the ideals of American womanhood. The transition from beliefs about Jewish womanhood to American womanhood was not difficult to make in mid-nineteenth-century America; the Jewish myths which for centuries had told women to keep the family and, thus, Judaism intact, easily molded themselves to American myths which stipulated that women, because of their special traits, were to oversee the domestic realm for the good of all.

Leeser and Levin were by no means the only men who reminded women of their sacred roles. With the power of their public offices, many rabbis, as well as editors of Jewish newspapers, could and did influence the direction of American Judaism. These editors functioned as "national leaders . . . who, until the establishment of the twentieth-century defense agencies (American Jewish Committee, Anti-Defamation League), were the self-appointed guardians of Jewish rights in the U.S. and abroad." In addition, the editors were "responsible for establishing a network of ongoing communication among the Jews of different cities as well as between American and foreign Jewries" (N. Cohen 46). The energy and personality of the editors, as well as their political and religious beliefs, defined each individual American Jewish paper.

In their roles as "guardians," many of these editors articulated strong convictions about Jewish women and their responsibility to safeguard the sacred Jewish family. One of these "guardians," Abram S. Isaacs, the editor of *The Jewish Messenger*, one of the "leading nineteenth-century Anglo Jewish newspapers," which was "traditionalist in its outlook" (Singerman 424), reiterated the ideals expressed by Leeser and Levin but with a particular emphasis on the Jewishness of the Mother in Israel.[9] Isaacs wrote in an 1875 editorial, "A Lesson to Mothers," that from the mother "the child learns to lisp the first words, and by her it should be taught to whisper its first prayers to the Father of Mercy" (4). The following year, in "Our Daughters," he wrote, "The women of Israel have at all times been the conservators of our hallowed creed. When the sterner sex have been faithless, they have remained faithful to their religion, and have instilled by their example the balm of hope into the hearts of their daughters" (4). Concerned as he was with the diffidence assimilated American Jews displayed toward Judaism, Isaacs felt compelled to remind women of their responsibility to preserve Judaism by keeping the family observant and, even more specifically, by teaching their daughters to keep the faith even when the men were becoming lax in their observances.

Four years later, in 1879, Philip Cowan placed his editorial, "Home Influence," on the first page of the premiere issue of his *American Hebrew*, a weekly newspaper whose " 'editorial staff comprise[d] men of diverse shades of opinion on ritualistic matters in Judaism, but men who [were] determined to combine their energies for the common cause of Judaism' " (Madison 18–19). The prominent position of the editorial suggests that Cowan felt he had a mission to remind American Jews of their traditions and duties, particularly in regard to the "Hebrew's attachment to his [sic] faith," an attachment which stemmed from "home influence":

> This is a power which can never be overrated. It binds many a son of our race to his religion, and especially in lands far distant from the home itself is its magic manifested. The memory of early surroundings clings to us through life, and . . . when we think of the calm happiness they [home customs] infused in the hearts of all, there are few of us who would not gladly again enjoy it. Such happiness, peaceful and holy, obtained in the old Jewish homes. (Cowan, "Home Influence" 1)

Cowan went on to lament that such influence had waned in recent years; Jewish homes resembled Christian homes, and children did not learn patriotic sentiment:

> The great danger to Judaism is not so much the spread of unbelief, as the decay of proper home influence. This is the only antidote for the

poison which infects our children, and when home influence is again
. . . an influence for purity, affection and happiness, nourished in the
atmosphere of religion, then shall the ancient love for our faith be
again restored. (1)

Cowan implicitly warned parents, and more specifically mothers and
wives, to make their homes Jewish homes, with the observance of Jewish
rituals and the teaching of Jewish values, in order to keep children in the
fold and thus ensure the future of the Jews. The simple equation was,
again: woman preserves the home, and home preserves Judaism.

Obituaries in Jewish periodicals, like the explicit statements of editors,
also emphasized the ideals of Jewish womanhood, repeatedly praising a
woman for her gentleness, piety, devotion to children and husband, and
service to Judaism. One such obituary, which appeared in the April 1852
issue of *The Occident and American Jewish Advocate*, Isaac Leeser's
"traditional" newspaper, eulogized Mrs. Bella Hart:

> With a degree of energy and perseverance, not often equalled in her
> sex, but which, together with piety, charity, and kindliness, formed
> the leading traits in her character, she thenceforth devoted herself to
> the bringing up and prosperity of her children. A strict observance of
> God's holy law, and orthodox from conviction, she made it her first
> care to imprint on their minds, that strong religious feeling, that firm
> adherence to principle, that pure sentiment of integrity and honour
> which she herself had imbibed from her own pious parents. . . . Nor
> was her activity limited to the well-being of her own family. But with
> a heart ever ready to feel, and a hand ever open to relieve the
> distressed, her ample means, and truly beneficent disposition, enabled
> and prompted her to do much good, whilst her singleness of purpose
> and genuine modesty prevented her charity from every degenerating
> into ostentation. (64)

This portrait of Bella Hart describes not a real woman, but, rather, a
mythic Mother in Israel, a quiet champion of Judaism. The exalted, but
static rhetoric freezes Bella Hart in an untouchable frame, ironically
isolating her from the family and community she presumably served so
valiantly.

Another obituary in *The Occident* (January 1867), also froze a woman,
Sophia David, in a portrait of the perfect Jewish woman. This Mother in
Israel

> well exemplified the beautiful life of a true, devoted, and faithful
> daughter of Israel, and in her, therefore, were united all those higher
> virtues that impart value to woman in all relations of life. Her devo-
> tion to her husband and children was heightened by a still stronger
> devotion to the principles and teachings of her faith. (480)

Just as the word "therefore" establishes a neat dependence between womanly virtues and Jewish responsibilities, so does the whole eulogy strictly define the parameters of a Jewish woman's activities and values. Seemingly immutable, the mythic ideal militated against individuality, in life and even in death.

Although both Bella Hart's and Sophia David's obituaries appeared in the *Occident*, the image they projected of the Mother in Israel was one which all American Jews recognized and respected for most of the nineteenth century as indispensable for the welfare of the Jewish nation. These obituaries, in addition to essays, speeches, and editorials such as the ones above, had to have had a tremendous impact on American Jewish culture. At the same time that they reflected the myths about Jewish families and Jewish women, they also contributed to the articulation and strengthening of those myths. In a continual reciprocal relationship, myth and text affirmed but also modified the other's designs.

As the following chapters will delineate, Jewish women believed in and articulated the prescriptions for their own ideal behavior, particularly in the first three quarters of the nineteenth century. Yet it was the Jewish men who spoke loudest and most forcefully about these ideals, believing, as they did, with all their cultural conditioning, that Judaism had survived and would continue to survive because of the strength of the Jewish family, which in turn survived because of the Jewish woman. Facing the potential disintegration of Judaism in permissive America, the men clung perhaps even more tenaciously to the old ideals which had served Judaism so well in the past. By rearticulating the familiar myths, the men were doing their part for the good of the Jews.

On another level, they were safeguarding their privileged, powerful positions in the patriarchy of Judaism. As "others" in their adopted nations, Jewish men could exert control only within Judaism, over those with even fewer rights: Jewish women. Jewish men were not unique in their desire and need to maintain power over women. Simone de Beauvoir tells us that men "cannot be blamed for not cheerfully relinquishing all the benefits they derive from the myth [of Woman, the Other], for they realize what they would lose in relinquishing woman as they fancy her to be" (xxv). Conveniently, nineteenth-century American Jewish men retained their patriarchal "benefits" through religious and cultural sanctions, and, as the sermons and editorials reveal, they continually reminded themselves and women of their seemingly inalienable Jewish rights.

The Late Nineteenth-Century Mother in Israel

Changes in Christian American women's lives in the last decades of the nineteenth century affected Sephardic and German Jewish women, who by this time were assimilated, established, and self-conscious about their American identities. For the American Jewish woman, these changes were exciting, but also frightening, because as it became more difficult to determine the correct "feminine" behavior, it became more difficult to prove one's American identity through acting the part of the proper American woman. At the same time, proving one's loyalty to Judaism still required a primary commitment to the home and family; myths of American Judaism continued to equate a strong and loving family and home with the preservation of Judaism. The Jewish American woman of the late nineteenth century was not oblivious to the changes occurring around her, and she became increasingly aware that being female in both American and Jewish cultures was problematic, as well as that being a Jewish American woman was a unique identity with unique challenges.

Not surprisingly, a number of Jewish men clung to traditional ideals, even while they were advocating the "advancement" of women. Some other men simply seemed to ignore the ways in which American women's lives were changing. One man who fits into this second category was Reverend M. Spitz. In his "The Model Wife," which first appeared in the *St. Louis Republican* and was reprinted in the *American Israelite* in 1882, "the 'accomplished Jewish woman' . . . is the pride of our race . . . best supporter of our faith, and the pillar of strength of our domestic felicity." The "accomplished Jewish woman," who was a "high priestess," fanned the light of faith "into her husband's soul when he had to go out into the cruel world" and "diligently planted" the light "into the hearts of her children by which she made them strong for the coming struggle." She lit up and warmed every corner of her home, the "sanctum sanctorum of Jewish life," and barricaded it so that "the fiercest storm from outside would not reach and extinguish the light" (1).

Spitz transformed the term "accomplished Jewish woman" from an accolade of achievement into a restatement of the Mother in Israel's traditional function. The Jewish woman's accomplishments were not in the fields of medicine, art, science, or even social work, but in the home; it was there that she had "accomplished" the task of keeping Judaism alive through many dark ages, and for this she was to be cherished. Spitz reminded women that they had to be particularly vigilant now, not against anti-Semitism, but against the attitude of assimilated Jews who were ignoring the Sabbath and not attending synagogue. Progress would mean nothing if it spelled out the disintegration of Judaism.

Even Kaufmann Kohler, an outspoken advocate of Reform Judaism, maintained traditional views of women late into the century. In an 1888 lecture he delivered at Temple Beth-El in New York, Rabbi Kohler stated that "Woman stands for soul-power. Her strength lies in persuasion" (3). She must use this persuasion to "unfold those qualities which [man], in the hard struggle of life, failed to cultivate within himself" (3). In Kohler's estimation, "Self-sacrificing Esther [of the Old Testament] is the true type of womanhood" (7) because she saved the Jews through a "sympathetic nature" that "lent her that irresistible charm which won her the king's heart, and overawed her people's foe" (4). On a realistic note, Kohler recognized that not all Jewish women were Esthers; through proper education, however, even "the daughters of the poorer classes" could learn to serve others (7). Once properly educated, a woman would influence her children and husband for good, and she would exert her influence in "the first and the only normal sphere of womanly devotion and self-sacrifice"—the home (5). Not only does Kohler reveal his class bias but his American and Jewish perspective; that is, Esther, one of the female heroes of the Bible, becomes, in this rabbi's eyes, a model Mother in Israel as well as a mid-nineteenth-century True Woman. Although he concedes that something is wrong with women's education, his analysis of the problem, and his proposed solution, argue for traditional, rather than progressive, values and behavior.

Some obituaries, like Spitz's essay and Kohler's speech, also emphasized the ideals of Jewish womanhood without taking into account the transformations in women's lives. A March 18, 1887 eulogy for Bertha Cohn, which appeared in the *American Hebrew*, could have been written half a century earlier.

> . . . faithful and devoted to her family, never losing faith in God under the most trying circumstances, the deceased was one of those mothers in Israel who are insensibly a power for good in the world's work. The consciousness of a pure life extended beyond the psalmist's limit should furnish consolation to those who miss her genial presence. (85)

Bertha Cohn was remembered for being a faithful Jew, a mother, and a devoted family nurturer, a "Jewess" who accomplished good in the world through influencing her family and possibly through civic work. The ideal Jewish woman was still the Mother in Israel who, even in an age of change, could save Judaism by fulfilling her centuries-old duties. By reiterating these myths, Jewish men convinced themselves that certain "truths," such as woman equals protector of home and Judaism, immutably guaranteed the future of Judaism.

Even those men who were more progressive in their outlook did not completely abandon the traditional view of women's roles. Rabbi Henry Berkowitz, D.D., for example, who wrote "Dowries for Our Daughters" for *The Menorah* (B'nai B'rith's official publication) in 1891, proposed that every daughter, as well as every son, be capable of earning her own living. "Let the hundreds of dollars spent on hollow accomplishments be spent on making a girl self-helpful" (71), Berkowitz proclaimed. Giving each daughter an "avocation in life," however, was to insure her material well-being in the event that she did not marry; wedlock continued to be the primary "life pursuit" of a woman.

In responding to a debate over whether conventional dowries for daughters should be reinstituted, Berkowitz argued that new dowries for Jewish daughters should contain: preparation to assume a free and independent place in the world (71); "an even stronger development of their womanly traits" so that they might "make the men with whom they are brought into contact more manly, more refined, more considerate, more noble" (75); and "a sincere religious training" (75). This last item was particularly important because woman's nature is the "intenser nature, the tenderer susceptibility" which gives her "a moral and spiritual superiority over man." "Mother's love is divine," and through its "sublime power," woman "becomes the true educator of the race" (75).

Where Berkowitz seemed to be struggling to reconcile tradition with "progress," Reverend Dr. Joseph Silverman seemed to be making a valiant attempt to hold on to tradition. In his "Place of Woman in Modern Civilization," which also appeared in *The Menorah* (December 1896), Silverman articulated his belief in the "inherent force of a mother's love and devotion" and her ability to influence men (401). To clarify his point, he listed three fields in which woman could be effective: home, church, and world (403). In all three, she should use her powers of influence to guide others, particularly in religious matters: "Woman needs no other field of work than that of religion and philanthropy. In these two she can conquer. Here none will dispute with her. In all other fields she is only an intruder. Here she is in her element. . . . Her place is where the spirit of love alone holds sway" (404).

In concluding, Silverman discussed the newly formed National Council of Jewish Women. He viewed the organization as a force which would "stem the tide of overwhelming irreligion"—the "insidious poison of indifference, of atheism, of agnosticism, ignorance, materialism and love of worldly pleasure" (405). He submitted to the council the problem of a "revival of religion in the Jewish home . . . religious training of the young . . . congregational life and of making the synagogue the centre of Israel's thought and action . . . [and] the sanctity of the Sabbath" (405–6). By accepting the council as a force, Silverman validated a Jewish woman's organization and recognized its power. But by assuming that its role would be the individual Jewish woman's role writ large, he relegated that power to carefully circumscribed and unobtrusive spheres. The National Council of Jewish Women, as Silverman defined it, could have been called The National Council of Mothers in Israel.

Even as the twentieth century drew closer, American Jewish men continued to articulate the seemingly timeless dicta that Jewish women had the responsibility to make a Jewish home for their families and thereby help keep Judaism alive, and that Jewish women's special qualities of morality and refinement enabled them to influence their husbands, children, and the Jewish community for the better. By reminding women of their responsibilities to family and Judaism, these men sought to battle against the indifference to and ignorance of Jewish laws and customs which had become widespread in the late nineteenth century. They also attempted to retain the power with which centuries of law and tradition had endowed them, as men. But because they also recognized that Jewish women were looking beyond their homes and families, they tried to modify their traditional views at the same time that they struggled with the dilemma of protecting Judaism in a rapidly changing modern America.

While Jewish men were prescribing correct behavior for their mothers, daughters, and sisters, a number of these American Jewish women were exploring the how, what, and why of representing their identities and their roles, as the following chapters will outline. In conforming to the myth of American womanhood while also valuing and preserving their Jewish religion and culture, Jewish women forged not only original selves but a unique literary tradition as well.

III.

The Words and Worlds of Emma Lazarus

The New Colossus

Not like the brazen giant of Greek fame,
With conquering limbs astride from land to land;
Here at our sea-washed, sunset gates shall stand
A mighty woman with a torch, whose flame
Is the imprisoned lightning, and her name
Mother of Exiles. From her beacon-hand
Glows world-wide welcome; her mild eyes command
The air-bridged harbor that twin cities frame.
"Keep, ancient lands, your storied pomp!" cries she
With silent lips. "Give me your tired, your poor,
Your huddled masses yearning to breathe free,
The wretched refuse of your teeming shore.
Send these, the homeless, tempest-tost to me,
I lift my lamp beside the golden door!"

Through Emma Lazarus's imagination, the famous Statue of Liberty has come to articulate symbolically the ideals which America collectively believes about itself. Although Lazarus did not invent the image of a young nation free from the prejudices and restrictions of "ancient lands," her poem has helped solidify the belief that America has meant opportunity and freedom for Jews, as well as other "huddled masses." The metamorphosis of this "wretched refuse" into American citizens has been the result of an ironic celebration of the outsider, the "homeless" newcomer, as an insider who brings new vitality to her/his adopted nation.[1]

Also ironic is the new colossus's gender, an irony Lazarus sharply focuses in her literary lens. With the poem's help, the statue stands as a symbol of womanhood which defies traditional stereotypes of passivity and demureness. This "mother" is a "mighty woman" who promises not the easy comforts of gold-paved streets but the challenges of economic, political, and social freedoms. Not the sentimentally glorified True Woman whose mothering took the form of gentle guidance and warm consolation, she is, rather, the Woman whose majestic strength supplied a nation with courage. She also personifies Deborah, the original Mother in Israel who valiantly defended her Jews, as well as the nineteenth-century Jewish woman who created for her family a refuge from a potentially hostile world. The Mother of Exiles is a regnant figure from whom both Americans and Jews could draw strength.

I begin the discussion of American Jewish women writers and their literary tradition with Emma Lazarus not merely because this author is the most easily identifiable of the group, but because she so dramatically "speaks for" the whole tradition in three significant ways: she addressed many of the themes of the tradition in her work, including a concern about ideals of womanhood, of Jewishness, of Americanness, and the fusion of identities; she wrote fiction, essays, and poetry; and she wrote from the mid-1860s through the 1880s, a crucial period for the American Jewish woman writer. "The New Colossus" itself, written in 1883, embodies the themes and concerns of the American Jewish woman's tradition in its projection of strong yet "womanly" traits, both Jewish and non-Jewish, as well as in its projection of the potential value of outsiders, such as Jews, to the growing American nation.

Although I have suggested that Lazarus typifies the other writers in the tradition, I must qualify my statement. Unlike many of the others, Lazarus enjoyed economic and social privileges; she never had to work or to marry to find security, nor did she have to take on familial responsibilities for frail parents, siblings, or nieces/nephews. Lazarus was born into an old, wealthy American Jewish family on July 22, 1849. Her father, Moses, was descended from a Sephardic Jewish family, and her mother, Esther Nathan, was the daughter of respectable German Jews.[2] Emma, like her three older sisters, two younger sisters, and one young brother, probably studied mythology, music, American poetry, European literature, as well as German, French, and Italian with private tutors.

It is not only Lazarus's education and freedom from familial duties that mark her as privileged. It is also the financial and emotional support she received from her father. Moses Lazarus, a successful sugar merchant, provided his family with material comforts in the fashionable sections of New York and Newport, Rhode Island. Even more importantly, this atypical father fostered his daughter's writing; in 1866, when Emma was only seventeen, he had *Poems and Translations Written between the Ages of Fourteen and Sixteen* printed "for private circulation." Of course, Emma dedicated the volume "To My Father."

As sheltered and special as her childhood was, Lazarus could not remain isolated from cultural pressures to conform to the ideals of the True

Woman and the Mother in Israel. However, she did not define herself
through conventional female roles but, instead, through her literary identity. With her proud belief that as an American she was privileged to enjoy
many freedoms and that as a Jew she had a rich ancient heritage, she
verbally constructed a unique American Jewish self. Even more to the
point, she built an identity that seemed to follow established gender
codes even as it functioned outside those codes.

Although she was not the only Jewish woman who wrote, Lazarus was
one of the few who was not a writer and a wife, mother, educator, or
caretaker. She was also unusual because she self-consciously sought to
establish literary credentials in the world of American letters. Even with
these aspirations she could not and did not openly relinquish her assigned
female roles—instead, she subtly molded them into unique forms. Like
Deborah, she would fight against those who sought to annihilate the
Jews, but unlike the more conventional Mother in Israel, she would fight
with words, aiming her attack at Christians who did not understand or
accept Jews, and at Jews themselves who had become complacent and
therefore vulnerable to anti-Semitism. While Lazarus's literary accomplishments and sensibility mark her as unusual within the tradition of
American Jewish women writers, many of her concerns and methods
place her centrally within that tradition.

Exploring and Expanding the Myths of Womanhood

In contrast to Mary Kelley's "literary domestics" and to other Christian
and Jewish women, including Rebekah Hyneman and Octavia Harby
Moses, Lazarus exhibited very little conflict about stepping onto the
"public stage" of authorship. In fact, she knew with surprising sureness
that she wanted and deserved the role of American author. At the same
time, she understood that because she was a woman she would encounter
obstacles in pursuing a literary career, as her sonnet "Echoes" acknowledges:

> Late-born and woman-souled I dare not hope,
> The freshness of the elder lays, the might
> Of manly, modern passion shall alight
> Upon my Muse's lips, nor may I cope
> (Who veiled and screened by womanhood must grope)
> With the world's strong-armed warriors and recite
> The dangers, wounds, and triumphs of the fight;
> Twanging the full-stringed lyre through all its scope.
> But if thou ever in some lake-floored cave
> O'erbrowed by rocks, a wild voice wooed and heard,
> Answering at once from heaven and earth and wave,

Lending elf-music to thy harshest word,
Misprize thou not these echoes that belong
To one in love with solitude and song.

(Poems of EL 1, 201)

The speaker of the poem, who recognizes that she is at a disadvantage because she cannot share with men the common literary subject of wars' "dangers, wounds, and triumphs," turns her own experiences into assets, valorizing the female poet's "elf music" and "echoes." However, as is too often the case with women's art, the valorization emerges as a poor rationalization for limitations. The title, "Echoes," for example, while it suggests the potentially powerful subterranean nature of women's writing, also reminds us that an echo's sound is an after-effect, a by-product, whose tone grows fainter with each repetition. The word "veiled" in line 5 reinforces the imagery of the title, suggesting as it does the way in which nineteenth-century American, and Jewish, women were "screened" by their domestic duties; it also suggests that a female artist needs to hide her work in secret codes and even conceal her true story in a palimpsest, as Sandra Gilbert and Susan Gubar have argued (*Madwoman* 73). Through the speaker of the poem, Lazarus admitted that women artists must compromise in order to be heard at all. Yet she did not compromise in her belief that she could and would be an American author. Rather than allowing the "veil" to stifle her, Lazarus used it to "screen" and protect her compelling confidence.

In a manuscript notebook, Lazarus dated "Echoes" October 18, 1880; she was then thirty-one years old.[3] By this time, Lazarus had been writing for more than a decade and was entering her most productive and inspired period. Already established as a writer rather than a wife or mother, she would have been declared an "old maid" according to the standards of her cultures. The poem's significance seems accentuated in such a context; to a woman whose identity emanated from her pen and not her womb, any limitations imposed upon verbal creativity would have been experienced as a profound denial of self.

Lazarus again expressed frustration with limited expectations and privileges in a second sonnet entitled "Sympathy," one of her few other poems explicitly about women. Unlike "Echoes," however, "Sympathy" describes personal, rather than literary, limitations.

Therefore I dare reveal my private woe,
The secret blots of my imperfect heart,
Nor strive to shrink or swell mine own desert,
Nor beautify nor hide. For this I know,
That even as I am, thou also art.
Thou past heroic forms unmoved shalt go,

To pause and bide with me, to whisper low:
"Not I alone am weak, not I apart
Must suffer, struggle, conquer day by day.
Here is my very cross by strangers borne,
Here is my bosom-sin wherefrom I pray
Hourly deliverance—this my rose, my thorn.
This woman my soul's need can understand,
Stretching o'er silent gulfs her sister hand."

(Poems of EL 1, 217)

"Sympathy" stands out dramatically within the corpus of Lazarus's work because of its candid expression of both women's struggles and the author's identification with other suffering women, to whom she offered her "sister hand" in a gesture of solidarity. The poem is, however, typically Lazarus in the way that it employs conventional codes (acceptable poetic form—sonnet, Christian imagery—a cross, a rose, a thorn) to represent a potentially controversial issue. Unfortunately, we do not know the date or occasion of the poem. Despite this, we can use it to establish one of the concerns of the Jewish woman's literary tradition: the search for identification with other women, both to validate one's own experiences and to share "struggles" along with triumphs.

Lazarus's only two works of fiction, *Alide: An Episode of Goethe's Life* (1874) and "The Eleventh Hour" (1878), also articulate the tensions and frustrations which the author experienced as an artist and a woman. *Alide* is based on Goethe's own autobiographical writings, which chronicle a love affair between the young writer and a country woman, Fredericka Brion (Alide Duroc in the novel). The story reaches its bittersweet climax when the lovers part; both presumably understand and accept that Fredericka is not Goethe's spiritual or intellectual equal.

Lazarus developed Goethe as a "great" man whose "simplest action [is] fresh and original," who is "generous of . . . soul," and who "shed[s] a peculiar glory upon whatever claims [his] regard" (102–3). Her inclusion of Goethe's thoughts on *Hamlet* explain her feelings about her own creativity:

> "But from the moment that his capacities are disclosed to him by the revelation from another world, he is bound by the highest duty to man—that which he owes himself—to discard everything that can cramp or impede the development of his own nature, and the fulfillment of the sacred office to which he is called. The beauty and sweetness of Ophelia's character can not be exaggerated, yet she is no mate for Hamlet." (153)

Toward the end of the novel, we share Alide's pain in giving Goethe up, and yet it is Goethe, the man, with whom Lazarus sympathized and identified. Below the surface of Goethe's story, *Alide* narrates the tale of a young female artist who felt the calling to a "sacred office" but whose gender and cultural limitations impeded her. Lazarus envied Goethe's right and ability to break earthly bonds in order to find the fulfillment of his artistic capacities. It is the "great" male writer, whose calling was so powerful and privilege was so sure, whom Lazarus admired.

"The Eleventh Hour," which was published in *Scribner's* magazine, traces the alienation and bewilderment of a young Romanian artist, Sergius Azoff, who has left his European home to experience the American liberty he had dreamed of. Once again, Lazarus's sympathies lie with the male artist who, in this case, experiences alienation because of his nationality and temperament. Sergius is disappointed not only by the seeming sham of American freedom, but also by the state of art in this young nation. But as Dick Bayard, the husband of one of Sergius's art students, tries to explain, " 'America is a country where art and beauty must and will thrive, though in the present transition-period of upheaval and reconstruction, it is impossible to discern what forms they will assume' " (256). Through Dick, Lazarus urged herself and other American artists to be patient, and, more subtly but more importantly, to cultivate America's unique artistic expression.

Lazarus had little liking for the women in the story, as we see in her treatment of Ellen Bayard. The author called her an "arch-woman, simple and cunning, vain and disinterested, noble and petty, capable of entering with ardent enthusiasm into the thoughts and feelings of others, yet always retaining in the fervor of her generous emotion an undefined pleasant consciousness of her own sympathetic qualities" (244). And still she appears better than most of her wealthy New York sisters who also dabble in art. Lazarus seems to have needed to distance herself from Ellen, from the woman she might have become, who used her creativity not to paint or write seriously, but to spin fantasies of her power over potential lovers. Lazarus did not want to be the dabbler in art or the manipulator of men. She wanted to be Sergius Azoff (or Goethe), who, despite his foreignness and differentness, could find a powerful outlet for his spirit.

Unlike her fictional character, however, Lazarus was a woman, bound to the myths of the True Woman and the Mother in Israel. She could not escape gender expectations, even, or especially, in the world of letters. When Lazarus died, *The American Hebrew* brought out an "Emma Lazarus Memorial Number" (volume 33, December 9, 1887). Many literary notables wrote, expressing their admiration and sorrow. Edmund C. Stedman's eulogy dramatically reveals the attitude of the literary establishment toward Lazarus, the woman poet: "While thoroughly feminine, and a mistress of the social art and charm, she was—though without the slightest trace of pedantry—the natural companion of scholars and thinkers" (68). Although Stedman is perhaps extreme in his rhetoric, others who also wrote to *The American Hebrew* voiced similar, if subtler, gendered expectations for Lazarus and her art.

Lazarus's sister Josephine, a progressive thinker and writer herself, also contributed to the poet's "womanly" image.[4] Josephine described Emma in an 1888 biographical eulogy printed in *The Century* and then used as an introduction to *The Poems of Emma Lazarus*[5] (copyrighted by two of Emma's sisters, Mary and Annie, in 1888), as a "true woman, too distinctly feminine to wish to be exceptional, or to stand alone and apart, even by virtue of superiority" (*Poems of EL* 1, 9). Toward the end of the sketch, Josephine added, "To be born a Jewess was a distinction for Emma Lazarus, and she in turn conferred distinction upon her race. To be born a woman also lends a grace and a subtle magnetism to her influence. Nowhere is there contradiction or incongruity" (*Poems of EL* 1, 38). In ascribing culturally acceptable "feminine" attributes to her sister, Josephine misrepresented Emma's burning desire to "stand apart" as a "superior" writer, as well as her need to resolve the "contradictions" inherent in her dual citizenships. I believe that such misrepresentation not only by Josephine but by other literary critics such as Stedman has contributed to the blunting of Lazarus's artistic achievements, for in reducing Emma to a proper woman, Josephine and others ignored, and ultimately contributed to the erasure of, all that was vital and original in the author's life and work.[6]

Of course, the attitudes expressed by Stedman and Josephine Lazarus should not surprise us, given the strength of gender myths in mid-nineteenth-century middle-class America. However, what contributes to the interest of the situation is Lazarus's own manipulation of the cultural codes. As we have seen, she created a specifically female persona in "Echoes," a persona which the public accepted as truly Lazarus. Ironically, that persona permitted Lazarus entry into the American literary nation by "veiling" or protecting her. As long as the "screen" projected an image of propriety, she could write as she wanted to. Her use of male artists as role models throughout the early years of her career forms part of this screen. Later, however, when she discovered her own authority, she dispensed with these straw men and wrote in a unique, powerful voice.

The Rhetoric of Lazarus's Jewish Identity

Many scholars have debated when and why Lazarus became a public spokesperson for Jews. Some claim that she always had a Jewish consciousness, while others argue that the Russian pogroms of the early 1880s incited her to reclaim her Jewish identity.[7] Although I side with the former group, I do so within the context of a more specific issue: how

Lazarus used her poetry and essays to create a compromise among her Jewish, American, and female identities and, especially, to enfranchise herself. Although most contemporaries saw her first as a woman, and then as a writer, an American, or a Jew, Lazarus viewed her identity as an author as primary, and it was through this role that she both came to accept herself as a Jew and affirm her Americanness. While other writers within the tradition also used their writing to mediate conflicts, only Lazarus concentrated so intensely on her literary self.

An early poem that exhibits Lazarus's process of utilizing verbal codes to establish national loyalties and mediate conflicts is "In the Jewish Synagogue at Newport" (1867). Lazarus's poem echoes Henry Wadsworth Longfellow's "The Jewish Cemetery at Newport," as the opening stanzas of each illustrate:

> *Longfellow:*
> How strange it seems! These Hebrews in their graves,
>   Close by the street of their fair seaport town,
> Silent beside the never-silent waves,
>   At rest in all this moving up and down!
>
> The trees are white with dust, that o'er their sleep
>   Wave their broad curtains in the sound wind's breath
> While underneath these leafy tents they keep
>   The long, mysterious Exodus of Death.
>
> *Lazarus:*
> Here, where the noises of the busy town,
>   The ocean's plunge and roar can enter not,
> We stand and gaze around with tearful awe,
>   And muse upon the consecrated spot.
>
> No signs of life are here: the very prayers
>   Inscribed around are in a language dead;
> The light of the "perpetual lamp" is spent
>   That an undying radiance was to shed.

The poem's derivative nature suggests that the eighteen-year-old Lazarus was inspired more by a male American poet's words than by heartfelt devotion to her people and that Lazarus emulated Longfellow's poem in order to validate her own American literary voice. It also raises the possibility that she felt more comfortable approaching a Jewish topic after a venerated American poet had blessed it, and more comfortable keeping some distance from the Jewish subject by describing it through an acceptable American literary form.

Yet it is *this* Longfellow poem that attracted Lazarus's attention. And where Longfellow's speaker stands in the Jewish cemetery contemplating the demise of the Jewish nation, Lazarus's speakers stand in the Jewish synagogue, in the "sacred shrine" which is "holy yet." The Jews and their "consecrated spot" are still living, still powerful. Even at this young age, Lazarus was attempting to find her own creative space, space which consisted of both pre-existing poetic codes and new Jewish American female codes; by modifying traditional American literature, Lazarus embarked on a literary career that would eventually find its greatest strength in a symbiosis of American and Jewish forms and subjects.

A decade after Lazarus wrote "In the Jewish Synagogue at Newport," Gustav Gottheil, the Rabbi of Temple Emanu-El in New York, asked Lazarus to translate and write hymns for a new collection. Lazarus did translate "three of the Hymns" for the rabbi, but explained in a letter dated February 6, 1877, "As for writing hymns myself, 'the flesh is willing, but the spirit is weak.' I should be most happy to serve you in your difficult and patriotic undertaking, but the more I see of these religious poems, the more I feel that the fervor and enthusiasm requisite to their production are altogether lacking in me" (Schappes, *Letters* 20). A few weeks later, on February 25, she added, "I cheerfully offered to help you to the extent of my ability, and was glad to prove to you that my interest and sympathies were loyal to our race, although my religious convictions (if such they can be called) and the circumstances of my life have led me somewhat apart from our people" (Schappes, *Letters* 21). Implicitly, Lazarus was telling Gottheil that poetic forulmae were more familiar and comfortable for her than were religious feelings. Categorizing herself as a secular Jew who felt loyalty and sympathy for her "race," nevertheless she was still distant from her Jewish identity in 1877.

Five years later, Lazarus published three essays in *The Century* over a ten-month period. When read together, the essays reveal the verbal process through which Lazarus grew to accept her Jewish identity more openly. In the first of these essays, "Was the Earl of Beaconsfield a Representative Jew?" (April 1882), Lazarus discussed Herr Georg Brandes's study of Benjamin Disraeli. Brandes had decided that Disraeli was not a representative Jew because " 'the Jewish mind has revealed itself in far more affluent and nobler forms than in Disraeli's comparatively limited mental range' " (939). Lazarus contested Brandes's argument with her own definition of "representative," suggesting that it did not mean the greatest example of a Jew, but, rather, the "epitome of the race features common to both [Spinoza and Shylock]" (939). Disraeli, who was not a "first-class man," was actually narrow, arrogant, proud, vengeful, and ambitious, but also supplely intelligent, morally courageous, dazzlingly talented, and triumphantly energetic, according to Lazarus (942). Embodying both the worst and the best of Jewish traits made Disraeli "representative."

The two essays that followed were less equivocal. Instead of apologizing for Jews, Lazarus instead began defining and defending them. We can clearly see the change of approach in "Russian Christianity vs. Modern Judaism," from the May 1882 issue of *The Century*, in which Lazarus responded to an essay by Madame Z. Ragozin, a Russian woman. Ironically, Ragozin's article, "Russian Jews and Gentiles," which blamed the Jews for their own persecution in Russia, had appeared in the same issue with Lazarus's "Was the Earl of Beaconsfield a Representative Jew?".

Throughout her refutation of Ragozin's arguments, Lazarus controlled her anger: "Of these horrors [heard from Jewish immigrants to America about pogroms and life in Russia], no one in whose veins flows a drop of Jewish blood can speak with becoming composure" (54). Not only was Lazarus criticizing Ragozin's misreading of historical events, she was making a personal plea for an accurate understanding of Russian Jews and their situation, and she was publicly including herself among those who could feel the agony of her fellow Jews.

In the third *Century* essay, "The Jewish Problem" (February 1883), Lazarus was even more forthright in her conviction that she was a spokesperson for Jews. The "problem," that "This scattered band of Israelites, always in the minority, always in the attitude of *protestants* against the dominant creed, against society as it is, seem fated to excite the antagonism of their fellow-countrymen" (602) is "as old as history and assumes in each age a new form," Lazarus informed her audience (602). The solution? The founding of a state in Palestine for Jews by Jews. Because of proposals such as this, as well as similar ones in "An Epistle to the Hebrews" and in several of her poems, Lazarus is credited with being an early Zionist.[8]

Lazarus stressed in "The Jewish Problem" that she was talking about a global (particularly Russian) problem; American Jews had been accepted in their adopted nation, for the most part, and would have no need to leave for Palestine. It was actually incumbent upon privileged American Jews to help their less fortunate co-religionists find a new home. Despite the predominant tone of righteous benevolence, Lazarus's motivation for proposing that a Jewish state be established in Palestine was not purely altruistic; class tension permeates her argument. Understanding as she did the precarious status of Jews even in America, and wanting to retain her own relatively respectable middle-class position, she feared the anti-Semitism which the ever-increasing presence of poorly educated and economically deprived Eastern European Jews might spawn. Like Rebekah Kohut, Rosa Sonneschein, and others within the tradition, she wanted the conspicuous immigrants to go elsewhere or immediately shed their un-American costumes and habits.

Despite her proclamation that American Jews were relatively safe and secure, Lazarus recognized that

> Even in America, presumably the refuge of the oppressed, public
> opinion has not yet reached that point where it absolves the race from
> the sin of the individual. Every Jew, however honorable or en-
> lightened, has the humiliating knowledge that his security and repu-
> tation are, in a certain sense, bound up with those of the meanest
> rascal who belongs to his tribe, and who has it in his power to
> jeopardize the social status of his whole nation. (608)

Lazarus expected more from America than narrowmindedness and found
it difficult to accept anti-Semitism from the American citizens she respected. Yet the new vision she gained from learning about the Russian
pogroms forced her to reassess her own status in America, and she found
it vulnerable.

The complexity of Lazarus's feelings about her Jewish identity helps
explain her fascination with Heinrich Heine, a poet who also had to
reconcile a secular outlook with a Jewish birth.[9] In addition to her
translations of his works, *Poems and Ballads of Heinrich Heine* (1881),
Lazarus wrote "The Poet Heine," again for *The Century* (December 1884).
In this piece, Lazarus implicitly explained her strong affinity for Heine:

> A fatal and irreconcilable dualism formed the basis of Heine's nature,
> and was the secret cause not only of profound unhappiness, but of his
> moral and intellectual inconsistencies. He was a Jew, with the mind
> and eyes of a Greek. . . . In Heine the Jew there is a depth of human
> sympathy, a mystic warmth and glow of imagination, a pathos, an
> enthusiasm, an indomitable resistance to every species of bond-
> age. . . . On the other hand, the Greek Heine is a creature of laughter
> and sunshine, possessing an intellectual clearness of vision, a plastic
> grace, a pure and healthy love of art for art's own sake. (210)

According to Lazarus, when two such antagonistic natures were imprisoned in one body, "contradictions . . . struggles . . . tears . . . vio-
lences" ensued. What saved Heine, however, was what saved Lazarus from
the contradictory forces in her own nature: poetry, and the "artist capacity of playing the spectator to the workings of his own mind" (210–11).
Lazarus recognized in Heine the ability to understand the "internal incongruity" (211) of one's mind and shared with him the need to synthesize conflicts into creatively inspired visions.

Lazarus also recognized in Heine a feeling for Jews which was similar to
her own; it "was a sympathy of race, not of creed" (216), of cultural
outlook if not of religious faith. Despite Heine's having been baptized and
educated in Catholic orders, Lazarus sensed that he had retained a Jewish
spirit: "What the world thought distinctively characteristic of the man
was often simply a mode of expression peculiar to his people at their best"
(215–16). In repeatedly describing him as a fundamentally Jewish poet,

Lazarus established Heine as a model of the Jew whose poetry was inescapably Jewish even when most secular. In painting her picture of Heine's life and work, she was also creating a self-portrait of the Jewish artist who could retain a worldly sensibility.

Always self-conscious of her role as author, Lazarus came to accept her Jewish identity through writing about Jews. In reaction to Brandes's and Ragozin's words, she became a more outspoken Jew. And with her own words, she would continue to fight in behalf of Jews and claim her rightful place in the Jewish nation. Ironically, her strategy for declaring citizenship in the Jewish nation should have made her more of an alien. It was through acting as a Mother in Israel that she should have been granted citizenship. But Lazarus stretched the parameters of this role, playing the part of Deborah, with her pen as a weapon. In using a writing implement as an instrument of education and mediation, she resembled writers like Rachel Mordecai Lazarus and Nina Morais (Cohen), who articulated careful, logical arguments to explain and ameliorate the negative stereotypes of Jews when they wrote for non-Jewish readers.

In their roles of educators, Lazarus, Leah (Lee) Cohen Harby, Mary Cohen, and Emma Wolf also felt compelled to address other American Jews to enlighten them about both their privileged status in America as well as their vulnerability. Lazarus herself spoke to American Jews in "An Epistle to the Hebrews," a series of fifteen "letters" that appeared in *The American Hebrew* between November 1882 and February 1883, the same period during which the *Century* essays were published. In alluding to the New Testament's Letter to the Hebrews, Lazarus urged American Jews not to permit apathy to replace a firm belief in the promise of salvation. More specifically, she appealed to American Jews to reflect upon their history and to understand their present and future conditions so that they might preserve their special identities.

The first of the letters implicitly explains Lazarus's own journey to her present Jewish consciousness:

> Firmly convinced as I am of the truth of the axiom that a study of Jewish history is all that is necessary to make a patriot of an intelligent Jew . . . I shall undertake from time to time to bring before the Jewish public such facts and critical observations gathered in the course of my studies as I think calculated to arouse a more loyal spirit and a more intelligent estimate of the duties of the hour. (8)

The repetition of "study/studies," and "intelligent" emphasizes the secular nature of Lazarus's endeavor. History, rather than religious faith, a "sympathy of race but not of creed," inspired Lazarus and many other assimilated American Jews to reclaim Judaism as a viable cultural identity.

In letter number five, Lazarus explained that Jews need to understand their history because without accurate information, they have no grounds upon which to refute Christian prejudices and therefore might believe negative stereotypes. Lazarus pointed out in this same letter that many Jews wished to conform to standards set by Christians, but that they did so at great cost: "our own people in default of sufficient acquaintance with the well-springs of our national life and literature are apt to be misled by the random assertions of our Gentile critics, and are often only too apt to acquiesce in their fallacious statements" (29).

In the preceding letter, she had explained that Jews are the "*Intensive form* of any nationality whose language and customs they adopt. . . . Whether owing to our circumstances or our character, we reflect the general color of the people who surround us, and usually succeed in giving it a shade deeper dye" (21). The author warned that such complete assimilation could be detrimental if Jews also conformed to the anti-Jewish sentiments of the adopted nation. Jews, she said, actually need to be more tribal, not, as many had suggested, less: "we have not sufficient solidarity to perceive that when the life and property of a Jew in the uttermost provinces of the Caucasus are attacked, the dignity of a Jew in free America is humiliated. . . . Until we are all free, we are none of us free" (30). The implicit message to Lazarus's Jewish readers was, conform but do not forget. This was a warning that Lazarus herself had recently begun to heed.

Despite the rhetoric of solidarity in letter four, in letter eight she proposed that Palestine, rather than America, become a haven for Eastern European Jews. As she also suggested in "The Jewish Problem," over *there* (far away from America), *they* could establish their own free country without the difficulty of having to assimilate to America and in the process relinquish valued laws and customs. Lazarus's thinking stemmed in part from an understanding that the relative stability of Sephardic and German Jews rested on a precarious base. She explains:

> Even in free America, we have not yet succeeded everywhere and at all times in persuading the non-Jewish community to accept or reject us upon our personal merits, instead of condemning us as a race for the vices or follies of individual members. This species of injustice, from which we occasionally suffer, in common with some other races, is the inevitable consequence of our representing an unpopular minority in opposition to a dominant and numerically overwhelming majority. (78)

Here, in the final letter, Lazarus openly acknowledged that despite its credo of liberty and justice for all, America was not immune to the disease of anti-Semitism or other forms of prejudice. Such an acknowledgment gains significance in light of Lazarus's usual public rhetoric about America's freedom and tolerance. It suggests that from her "study of Jewish history" she had learned that Jews must always be on their guard, particularly when seemingly hospitable circumstances lulled them into complacency.

When viewed as a whole, "An Epistle to the Hebrews" again reveals Lazarus verbally constructing her Jewish identity. By addressing an assimilated American Jewish audience, she was also speaking to herself, becoming increasingly convinced of the need for Jewish solidarity. Her more frequent use of the pronoun "we" rather than "they" to refer to Jews informs us of this need on a rhetorical level. The strategy was useful in convincing the Jewish readers of *The American Hebrew* to listen to her, one of their own. The "we" was also a signal that Lazarus was much surer of her Jewish identity and eager to claim it as her own.

The same new confidence is evident in the volume of poetry which was published by *The American Hebrew* in 1882. *Songs of a Semite* included *The Dance to Death*, a five-act poetic tragedy, as well as seven original poems, one translation and two imitations of Heinrich Heine, and translations of three Spanish Hebrew poets. The title of the volume and the publisher were public proclamations that Lazarus wanted to be identified as a Jewish poet.

The Dance to Death[10] demonstrates once again that it was in this capacity, as writer, that she would both confirm her Jewish identity and champion the Jewish cause. Although Lazarus presumably wrote the tragedy "a few years" earlier (Schappes, *Letters* 35), she informed "the Editors of the *American Hebrew*" on May 25, 1882, that she thought "it would be highly desirable" to publish *The Dance to Death* "now [after news of Russian pogroms had reached the United States], in order to arouse sympathy and to emphasize the cruelty of the injustice done to our unhappy people" (Vogel 144).

The Dance to Death is an imitative dramatization of Richard Reinhard's prose narrative, *Der Tanz zum Tode* (1877). Despite its derivative quality, it "implie[d] rare gifts of sympathy and discernment," according to a contemporary review in *Lippincott's* (volume 31, 216). The story centers around the Jews who were condemned to die in Nordhausen, Germany, in 1349, for an outbreak of the plague. What makes the drama so powerful is the courage and dedication of the Jews. When they realize that the edict for their death will stand, they ask their assassins to build a pyre, upon and around which they will dance as they burn to death. In the poem, these defiant Jews will die proclaiming their devotion to God:

> Ours is the truth,
> Ours is the power, the gift of Heaven. We hold
> His Law, His lamp, His covenant, His pledge.

> Wherever in the ages shall arise
> Jew-priest, Jew-poet, Jew-singer, or Jew-saint—
> And everywhere I see them star the gloom—
> In each of these the martyrs are avenged! (Act 5, sc. 3)

Lazarus was one of these "Jew-poets" or "Jew-singers" who took on the responsibility of avenging the unwarranted deaths of countless Jews. By representing her writing as action, Lazarus became a part of Jewish history and affirmed her citizenship in the Jewish nation.

In several poems from the collection, Lazarus translated historical Jewish figures and past glories of the Jewish people into contemporary situations in order to inspire nineteenth-century Jews to fight new battles against Russian pogroms and world-wide prejudice. For example, "The Crowing of the Red Cock" suggests a way for Jews to fight these battles—not with swords, but with the courage to forget. The Jew is not a coward

> Who singly against worlds has fought,
> For what? A name he may not breathe,
>   For liberty of prayer and thought.
> The angry sword he will not whet,
> His nobler task is—to forget. (Lines 32–36)

What the Jew must forget is the pain of the "lust of mobs, the greed of priest, / The tyranny of kings, combined / To root his seed from earth again." Lazarus herself seems to have wanted to forget this history in order to reconcile her Jewish consciousness with her secular outlook, but in order to forget she first had to remember.

In another poem published in *Songs of a Semite*, "The Banner of the Jew," Lazarus calls upon "Israel" to "Wake" and "Recall to-day / The glorious Maccabean rage." Again, we see the poet exhorting contemporary Jews to act in the spirit of their ancestors:

> Oh for Jerusalem's trumpet now
>   To blow a blast of shattering power,
> To wake the sleepers high and low,
>   And rouse them to the urgent hour!
> No hand for vengeance—but to save,
> A million naked swords should wave.
>
> Oh deem not dead that martial fire,
>   Say not the mystic flame is spent!
> With Moses' law and David's lyre,
>   Your ancient strength remains unbent.
> Let but an Ezra rise anew,
> To lift the *Banner of the Jew!* (Stanzas 4, 5)

Proud, even defiant, Lazarus is no longer one of the "sleepers." Feeling the urgency of her identity as a Jew, she had begun to use her pen as a "naked sword," prepared for battle against complacent Jews and anti-Semitic non-Jews.

As "The Crowing of the Red Cock" and "The Banner of the Jew" reveal, by the 1880s, Lazarus had reconfirmed her commitment to Judaism; this commitment had become a subject of her poetry as well as a major focus in her life. However, conflict remained. Even as she was singing loudly in a proudly defiant Jewish voice, she felt alienated from Eastern European Jews, who shared a "creed" but not a "culture" with her.

Despite, or because of, her ambivalence toward Eastern European Jews, Lazarus took some public steps to help her "co-religionists" assimilate. In addition to writing about Jews, she met immigrants at Ward's Island, and she helped establish Jewish agricultural communities as well as the Hebrew Technical Institute. Yet it was for her words in behalf of Jews that she earned the most respect.

Cyrus L. Sulzberger, a prominent Jewish philanthropist, expressed a common feeling when he wrote,

> no words of praise can be too great for one who . . . voluntarily returns to the old household, publicly proclaiming herself one of its members, and bringing to it not alone a heart filled with sympathy, but the pen of a prophet to arouse the moral sense of Jew and Gentile. It was an act of heroism on the part of Emma Lazarus, performed at a cost she alone could know—thus to put herself at the head of a cause which was so unpopular in the general world. (79)

This eulogy, which appeared in *The American Hebrew*'s "Memorial Number" (volume 33, 1887), confirms that it was by the pen that Lazarus identified herself publicly as a Jew, and by the pen that she fought most valiantly in behalf of Jews. Like many of the other American Jewish women writers, including Nina Morais (Cohen) and Adelina Cohnfeldt Lust, Lazarus wrote most vividly and passionately when she fought against anti-Semitic bigotry and Jewish complacency. Because she came to believe deeply in the righteousness and rights of Jews, she felt an intense responsibility to speak out in behalf of "her" people.

American Literary Identity

We must remember, however, that Lazarus's "interest in literature was not limited to Jewish topics even after she became 'all Israel's now.' She was a stout advocate of an American national literature" (Harap 297). A self-identified American writer on the one hand, and an increasingly outspoken Jew on the other, Lazarus could not ignore either national identity: she had to cultivate each to its fullest. She would not have been as effective in behalf of Jews if she had not believed deeply in America's freedoms or if she could not have expressed herself as a writer, and she could not have been as moving a writer if she had not discovered how important her Jewish identity was. Particularly in the 1880s, Lazarus sought to create a strong, integrative voice which would establish her as a serious American, as well as a Jewish, writer.

Such a voice required a "native ground," as Alfred Kazin has described it. He explains that American "writers' absorption in every last detail of their American world together with their deep and subtle alienation from it" has been the "greatest single factor about our modern American writing" (*On Native Grounds* ix). What Kazin and others have not noticed is that an American Jewish woman writer such as Lazarus also experienced alienation, but it was alienation that grew not from feeling estranged on her own soil, but from a sense of confusion about what being an American required. Before Lazarus and the other writers in the tradition could share the discomfort of being a stranger in their own country, they first had to prove that they were citizens of the country. A writer who could not take a "native ground" for granted because of her ethnicity and gender would never find easy access to the dominant American literary culture.

Despite the difficulties, Lazarus valiantly struggled to claim this "native ground." Especially because she did not shape her identity around the roles of wife or mother, her entry into the world of American letters became all-important. The figure from whom she requested the most help in her endeavor was Ralph Waldo Emerson.[11] The two probably met soon after the appearance of Lazarus's first volume of poetry, *Poems and Translations: Written between the Ages of Fourteen and Sixteen*, in 1866. The meeting must have been amicable, for the younger and older writer began a correspondence that lasted from 1866 until Emerson's death in 1882.

In two early letters, dated February 24 and April 14, 1868, Emerson established himself as Lazarus's mentor: in the first letter, he wrote that her poems had "important merits," and in the second, "I should like to be appointed your professor" in both reading and writing (Rusk 3, 4). Later that year, Emerson complimented Lazarus's new poem, "Admetus": "All Hail! You have written a noble poem, which I cannot enough praise" (November 19, 1868, Rusk 9). To show her gratitude, Lazarus dedicated "Admetus" "To My Friend, Ralph Waldo Emerson" in her second collection of poetry, *Admetus and Other Poems* (1871). During the next few years, Emerson advised the young poet about what to read and how to improve her poems.

For her part, Lazarus admired Emerson for his embodiment of the American spirit, and she respected the influence he had had on American literature. As she wrote in an 1882 *Century* essay, "Emerson's Personality," Emerson was "the antithesis of all that is mean and blameworthy in our politics and pursuits, for he also is the legitimate outcome of American institutions, and affords an eternal refutation of the fallacy that democracy is fatal to the production and nurture of the highest chivalry, philosophy, and virtue" (456).

Two years later, in 1884, Lazarus wrote a sonnet for the opening of the Concord School of Philosophy (untitled poem included in "Emerson and the Concord School" 55). In the poem, she named Emerson "Master and father," and called herself one of his "children." The first eight lines detail the impact Emerson has had on Lazarus and other American writers:

> As, when a father dies, his children draw
> > About the empty hearth, their loss to cheat
> > With uttered praise and love, and oft repeat
> His own familiar words with whispered awe,
> The honored habit of his daily law—
> > Not for his sake, but theirs, whose feebler feet
> > Need still his guiding lamp, whose faith, less sweet,
> Misses that tempered patience without flaw—

His disciples miss his guidance and patience, but because his "presence [is] in the sacred air," they do not weep that he is gone. A daughter of this American spiritual father, Lazarus imbibed the sage's instruction on life, nature, and art. Like a dutiful daughter, she would continue to exalt the father's work and influence. To Lazarus, Emerson was the American spirit, and she revered him for this Americanness.

I believe that Lazarus sought Emerson's approval to validate her identity as an American writer as well as to reassure herself that she was a worthy interpreter of American experiences. After all, if *the* American literary father thought highly of her work, then it must be "American" and valuable. Because Lazarus's trust in Emerson was intimately connected to her identity as an American author, his decision not to include any of her poems in his anthology *Parnassus* (1874) shook her confidence, as well as her attitudes about America. However, the reportedly shy, always respectful young woman discovered the strength of her own voice when she responded to her mentor regarding his omission:

> I cannot resist the impulse of expressing to you my extreme disappointment at finding you have so far modified the enthusiastic estimate you held of my literary labors as to refuse me a place in the large and miscellaneous collection of poems you have just published. I can only consider this omission a public retraction of all the flattering

opinions and letters you have sent me, and I cannot in any degree
reconcile it with your numerous expressions of extravagant admiration. . . . Your favorable opinion having been confirmed by some of
the best critics of England and America, I felt as if I had won for myself
by my own efforts a place in any collection of American poets, and I
find myself treated with absolute contempt in the very quarter where
I had been encouraged to build my fondest hopes. . . . May I not now
ask which alternative I am to adopt—whether I must believe that the
few years which have elapsed since you wrote me those letters [of
praise] have sufficed to make you reverse your opinion of my poems,
or whether that opinion was even then ill-considered and expressed in
stronger language than your critical judgement warranted! (December
27, 1874, Schappes, *Letters* 11–13)

Lazarus had been insulted, and by the very man whom she had trusted as
her judge and teacher. She had begun to believe in herself as a writer of
real ability, having been praised by Ivan Turgenev (Rusk 17) and William
Cullen Bryant (Vogel 27), as well as by Emerson. For this twenty-five-year-
old woman whose identity depended on her words rather than on her
maternal roles, Emerson's omission must have been more than just a bad
review; it must have felt like a betrayal and a public announcement that
her poetry did not belong with Longfellow's and William Cullen Bryant's.
Emerson's inclusion of poets such as Mrs. C. F. Alexander and Tom Taylor
could only have fueled Lazarus's fury.

Although we will probably never know the reasons for Emerson's edi-
torial decision, or how he responded to Lazarus's letter, we do know that
Lazarus "forgave" Emerson because in 1876 she visited the Emersons in
Concord for a week during which time she established a friendship with
Emerson's daughter, Ellen, and made the acquaintance of Bronson Alcott
and William Ellery Channing (*Poems of EL*, 1, 12).

Despite the apparent reconciliation, Lazarus's feelings for her old mentor changed permanently; never again would she idolize him as an infallible god. This is made clear in "Emerson's Personality," in which she
wrote,

Let me not be understood as implying that his literary judgment was
infallible . . . in defiance of all canons, very inferior as well as obscure
writers might be exalted by him to a dizzying eminence, almost lifted
into immortality, by one of his golden sentences, simply because such
a writer had struck or tried to strike that note of moral aspiration with
which every chord of Emerson's great heart throbbed in unison. . . .
His friends and correspondents had to make liberal allowance for this
splendor of enthusiasm which led him to magnify the merits of
others. (454–55)

Obviously referring to herself as one of the "obscure writers" as well as
one of the "correspondents," this passage reveals tremendous insight and

confidence on Lazarus's part. Finally immune from Emerson's "poetic hyperbole," she could candidly evaluate her relationship with the great sage and assess her own abilities. Even more importantly, she learned that she should never again completely trust America's rhetoric of equality for all. In an indirect but powerful way, Emerson's rejection compelled Lazarus to recognize her precarious status in the world of American letters, because she was both a woman and a Jew.

She never completely relinquished her belief in America's ideals or literature, however. In her 1881 essay, "American Literature," for example, which appeared in *The Critic*, Lazarus set out to defend American literature against George Edward Woodberry's claim (in the May issue of the *Forthrightly Review*) that America had no tradition, and that America's poets had left no mark. Lazarus, who felt strongly that there were, indeed, an American tradition and respectable American authors, wrote that Emerson had given rise to an American "school of thought and habit of life" (164). Writers who had been trained in this school included Hawthorne, Whitman, Lowell, Holmes, and Stowe. Lazarus contrasts with that of the claim that "the literary history of the past fifty years compares favorably with the past fifty years in England—the only period with which it can, with any show of justice, be compared" (164). Lazarus took a defensive stance in the essay, feeling compelled to prove the viability and worth of American literary figures, as well as of American values and experiences. In justifying American literature, she was justifying her own identity as an American author.

Throughout her career, Lazarus sought justification in order to claim a patch of "native ground" upon which she could establish her literary identity. We see this private search veiled by a public exhortation in an early poem, "How Long!" *(Admetus)*:

How long, and yet how long,
Our leaders will we hail from over seas,
Masters and kings from feudal monarchies,
    And mock their ancient song
With echoes weak of foreign melodies?

That distant isle mist-wreathed,
Mantled in unimaginable green,
Too long hath been our mistress and our queen.
    Our fathers have bequeathed
Too deep a love for her our hearts within.
· · · · · · · · · · · · · · · ·
The distant siren-song
Of the green island in the eastern sea,
Is not the lay for this new chivalry.
    It is not free and strong
To chant on prairies 'neath this brilliant sky.

> The echo faints and falls;
> It suiteth not, upon this western plain,
> Our voice or spirit; we should stir again
> The wilderness, and make the plain
> Resound unto a yet unheard-of-strain.
>
> (Stanzas 1, 2, 7, 8)

We hear Lazarus expressing frustration with America's insecurity about its literature. It is time, she writes, to protect ourselves against that British song which cannot accurately or honestly express America's uniqueness. But it is not only America's uniqueness she is defending; it is also her own. In calling for an authentic American "strain," she sought to stake out a national as well as a personal "native ground."

Her search brought success. She published in mainstream magazines such as *Lippincott's* and *The Century,* journals which also praised her poetry. The opening lines of an 1871 review of *Admetus* from *Lippincott's* typify this praise:

> There is very much to commend and very little to condemn in the longer poems in the volume, and the same remark will apply to some, at least, of the shorter pieces. They exhibit careful study, intelligent and conscientious labor, vigor of thought and diction, and a superiority to all the artifices by which popularity is sought and sometimes gained.

Although the review goes on to qualify its first statements, pointing out that the author will gain even more poetic power when she "look[s] at life with the same clear eyes with which she has studied the legends of the ancient world" and when "emotions and sympathies deeper and stronger than the contemplation of heroic ideals can awaken shall give ardor and inspiration to her verse" (527), nevertheless such praise must have reassured the young woman of twenty-two.

During the following sixteen years, Lazarus's citizenship in the American literary world became even more solidly established. She advised E. Clarence Stedman on the manuscript for his essay, "Poetry in America," which appeared in the August 1881 issue of *Scribner's* (Schappes, *Letters* 67), and corresponded with Thomas Wentworth Higginson to thank him for his appreciation of "American Literature" (Schappes, *Letters* 29). She also exchanged letters with John Hay, to discuss her translations of Heinrich Heine,[12] and with William James (Schappes, *Letters* 48–49). Although Lazarus has not passed "the test of time" for a variety of economic, political, gender, and ethnic/religious reasons, it is important to note that in the 1870s and 1880s, she was known to other American writers and to the American reading public.

American Jewish Identity

Lazarus found her own American Jewish creative space in the last decade of her life, when she wrote powerfully about Jews at the same time that she wrote about her belief in America and American literature. Her contributions to *The Century* magazine make this resolution concrete. "Emerson's Personality," the eulogy for the dean of American letters, appeared in July 1882, "Was the Earl of Beaconsfield a Representative Jew?" in April, and "Russian Christianity vs. Modern Judaism" in May. To regular readers of the magazine, Lazarus would have been known as an essayist concerned with Jewish issues as well as American literature. She had become an insider, contributing not only "Jewish" pieces to a mainstream periodical, but the commemorative piece on one of America's most venerated literary figures.

Ironically, Lazarus became this literary insider by valorizing the outsider. "The New Colossus," her best-known contribution to mainstream American literature and culture, is the culminating symbol of this process. In the poem, Lazarus valorizes the alien who finds in America a home—a native ground composed of many alien grounds. Through the celebration of otherness, Lazarus conveyed her deepest loyalty to the best of both America and Judaism and, ironically, strengthened her "outsider" status so that it would become valuable.

Another poem, written in 1883, also projects the Jewish pride and gratitude to America Lazarus felt during this fruitful period of American and Jewish literary production. As the title suggests, "1492," focuses on the "two-faced year" when Spain expelled its Jews and Columbus landed in America. As Lazarus imagines the historical irony of 1492, the Jews, the "children of the prophets of the Lord," will find haven in a "virgin world where doors of sunset part." This new world proclaims,

> "Ho, all who weary, enter here!
> There falls each ancient barrier that the art
> Of race or creed or rank devised, to rear
> Grim bulwarked hatred between heart and heart!"

Echoing "The New Colossus" in sonnet form and exuberant rhetoric, "1492" more explicitly focuses on Jews—rather than the generalized "huddled masses"—and their unique historical experiences. The poem also implicitly reminds American Jews not to take freedom for granted; despite the optimistic conclusion of the poem, the juxtaposition of the two history-altering events of 1492 functions as a warning that a nation's hospitality can quickly become hostility.

Pieces for *The Century* and poems such as "1492" demonstrate Lazarus's own vision of an American Jewish persona. But how did others view her? Sulzberger's eulogy typifies the admiration and respect American Jews felt for her. Many non-Jews also recognized her literary "talent" but could not separate her achievements from her Jewish identity. As Kazin writes, "being a Jew had certainly distinguished her in the literary world of Victorian America. She was that still exotic figure, that object of Christian curiosity, 'the Jew'—and to descendants of the New England Puritans, straight out of their bible" ("The Jew as Modern Writer" 37).

The sympathetic and admiring letters received by *The American Hebrew* (and printed in the "Memorial Number") when Lazarus died of cancer in 1887 illustrate Kazin's observation. John J. Whittier, for example, wrote, "With no lack of rhythmic sweetness, she has often the rugged strength and verbal audacity of Browning. Since Miriam sang of deliverance and triumph by the Red Sea, the Semitic race has had no braver singer" (67). And John Hay noted that Lazarus's death would be felt by Jews and American literary figures. He explained that Lazarus's death "is not only a deep affliction to those of her own race and kindred; it is an irreparable loss to American literature . . . her place is already secure among our best writers" (70). While these comments seem somehow negative, serving as reminders that Jews can never be "just" Americans and writers, they also dramatize the possibility that Lazarus's being a Jew might have distinguished her positively. Perhaps it was *because* she was Jewish that she caught the attention of other American literary figures, and perhaps they valued the unique contributions Lazarus made as a Jew to American literature.

Unlike many of the tradition's other writers, who found a path to publication in Jewish volumes, Lazarus wrote for non-Jewish journals as much as she did for Jewish publications. Her more heterogeneous audience provided her with the opportunity to write about less parochial subjects. But she also sought out these journals because her interests were not exclusively Jewish. She later used her wider readership as a force in behalf of Jews. Since she had already established a reputation among non-Jews, she could be an influential voice in the fight against anti-Semitism. It was vital to her that her Americans understand her Jews, and that her Jews understand the uniqueness of America's relative acceptance of Jews. She needed each to understand the other so that she would not have to choose between the two.

In its December, 1879 issue, *Scribner's* magazine compiled twenty "Poems by American Women" (volume 19, 196), including a sonnet by Lazarus, "The Taming of the Falcon." In the poem, the falcon, tamed by its master, is docile on earth, "but in the awful sky,/Reigns absolute, unreached by deed or word,/Above creation, through eternity" (lines 10–12). The other nineteen poets, including Elizabeth Stuart Phelps and Rose Terry Cooke, who expressed conventional sentiments on God, flowers, and love, safely followed the linguistic codes which established specific requirements for propriety in female poetry and which mirrored similar standards in behavior and sensibility. Lazarus, in contrast, might appear to obey these rules, but in her sky, her poetry, her spirit would soar freely.

Lazarus provides us with an unusual but also representative model of the American Jewish woman who constructed a complex self with verbal building blocks. Like the other writers in the tradition, Lazarus was sensitive to the gender myths of both her cultures; this sensitivity led her to focus her attention on the limitations imposed by traditional female roles as well as on the privileges of being a Jew, an American, and an American Jewish woman. Despite her alien status in American and Jewish ideology which defined male as normative, she successfully established her own ground on her own terms. On that ground, she could assertively express her tensions, her frustrations, and her joys. When she sang in her "woman-souled," "wild voice," she dared to hope that her lyre would twang "full-stringed through all its scope." When she exalted the glory of the Jews, she wrote herself into the dispersed nation. And when she praised America for its freedoms, she reassured herself that such freedoms truly existed.

IV.

American and
Jewish Womanhood

Until the 1890s, American Jewish women published only one novel, several volumes of poetry, and a small number of short stories, poems, and essays scattered in periodicals. Then, in the comparatively bountiful final decade of the century, they published at least seven novels and multiple essays, as well as a magazine—*The American Jewess*—ostensibly devoted to their particular concerns. This increase in published works, modest as it is, reveals more than the simple demographic fact that more Jews were living in the United States. It also suggests that American Jewish women were taking advantage of the expanded opportunities being offered to all white American women as well as feeling more comfortable in public roles because they were more assimilated and therefore more "legitimate" Americans. In other words, they were discovering their own space, a space in which they could celebrate unique blends of their American and Jewish identities. Through the process of creating this space, and then within the space once they had found it, American Jewish women gained power. It is important to note that each woman created and used this space in her own way, that she employed a personalized code to navigate through the American and Jewish myths.

According to Susan Coultrap-McQuin, "by the middle of the nineteenth century, many women writers could be comfortable with their own literary aspirations, though undoubtedly there were others whose attitude toward themselves reflected their society's ambivalent or negative views" (20). Although she is referring in general terms to American and British women, Coultrap-McQuin's statement reminds us that Jewish women were writing within and against a white, middle-class, Christian women's tradition that was itself ambivalent about the status of women writers, and that no matter how mainstream she and her writing appeared, the Jewish woman would always be an "other" who had to contend with ambivalent or negative views about her and her writing. It should not surprise us, then, that so few Jewish women embraced literature as a public activity.

This chapter is arranged around the theme of womanhood. Like many of their Christian counterparts, a number of Jewish women were self-conscious about their roles as women, particularly in the last decades of the century when "the woman question" was receiving so much attention. To provide a context for the theme, I begin with some examples of the ways in which Jewish men viewed Jewish women's writing. Next I discuss Jewish women's relationship to the myths of American womanhood, and then I move to the Jewish women's handling of the myths of Jewish womanhood. Through both sections runs a more persistent theme, that of American Jewish womanhood. By this I mean that in the majority of cases, the writers within the tradition attempted to synthesize the American and Jewish myths of ideal womanhood. In each of the two main sections of the chapter, I present the writers and their texts in a roughly chronological order; the writings move from the early half to the later half of the century and thereby take into account the changes affecting women. So, while the chapter has the theme of womanhood as its focus, it also utilizes a chronological construct at times to help sharpen the material.

Throughout the nineteenth century, editors of Jewish periodicals expressed concern over the limited literary production of American Jews, although they recognized that the small number of Jews in America was a primary factor in this dearth of writing. An editor of the *Asmonean*, an Orthodox publication (1849–1858), suggested several additional reasons for this limited production: "the heterogeneity of the immigrant Jews and their retention of 'foreign' culture—German immigrants continued to use German in their publications—and the preoccupation of the Jews with business concerns" (Harap 270).

Of course, it was primarily men who were "preoccupied" with "business concerns," while women presumably had more leisure time to write. In a *Jewish Messenger* editorial, the author (who was most likely the editor Abram Isaacs) implored "The Daughters of Israel" in 1876 to use this "free" time to write and to write in behalf of Jews: "Desiring that our females should co-operate with those who wish to elevate Israel to the rank they are destined to occupy, we call upon them to exert their refined mind for the benefit of our common cause." He continued, explaining

> Our sole motive is to ask [women] to devote some of their spare time, which is now employed in matters which do not profit, for the benefit of that cause of which the matrons of old were the most faithful and zealous professors. We require them to dip their pens in ink and letters of gold will flow from their writing. (4)

Although "This may appear an undertaking beyond their power" because "their native modesty will shrink from attempting an act which they feel will be a failure," they should not be deterred. "The good they will be able to accomplish should spur them on, and success will be sure to crown their efforts if but rightly directed" (4).

By invoking "matrons of old," Isaacs implicitly exhorted nineteenth-century Jewish women to play the role of Mother in Israel—educator as well as champion. Despite the respect such an identity carried with it, Isaacs, the male editor, paternal guardian of Judaism, could not grant his female readers full autonomy. He sent his female readers mixed messages: contribute to the Jewish cause with your words, but do not assume too much independence. It is no wonder women hesitated about writing publicly, for such "action" might be interpreted as a violation of ancient commandments *not* to turn to public work away from the home and family.

In 1892, Isaacs wrote another piece on Jewish women writers, "The Jewess in Authorship," which appeared in *The Ladies' Home Journal.* Stressing that the "work of the Jewess in authorship will hardly vary in quality and tone from that of her non-Jewish sister" once the former has "a little more time for development," Isaacs nevertheless believed that the Jewish woman would make unique contributions to American and British literature because of her gender and her religion: "womanhood and womanliness will guide her right, and as the religious instincts of the Jewess are innate, and her domestic qualities strong, one may expect her to champion all that is pure, and sweet, and wholesome" (17). In these lines, as well as in the final paragraph of the essay, Isaacs again implied that the "Jewess in Authorship" had an obligation to uphold the tenets of the Mother in Israel. Even in the progressive 1890s, "With every barrier razed that once checked her progress, with the universities, the arts, the sciences all open to her," the Jewish woman will celebrate her gender and her heritage:

> Whatever record may be hers in the future, whatever achievements she may claim as her own, she will write no unworthy line, utter no false note, if she be true to the ideals of Judaism and womanhood. She has everything to spur her on—in the broad republic of letters there are no distinctions of sex or creed, class or condition, race or nationality. (17)

Ironically, Isaacs was simultaneously celebrating the unique identities of Jewish women and defending their rightful place in the American "republic of letters." Even more, he was arguing for the Americanness of Jewish women, using their similarity to the predominantly white, middle-class, Christian readers of the *Ladies' Home Journal* as his proof.

Another influential editor, Isaac Leeser *(The Occident and American Jewish Advocate)*, also solicited literature by women. However, he only published literature that promoted his image of the American Jewish woman, a figure who embodied traits of the idealized Mother in Israel. In many of *The Occident's* short stories, female characters are intelligent, graceful, and devoted to family members and loved ones, especially ailing fathers. On the rare occasions when a young Jewish woman forgets her faith, she meets with ruin and even death. By articulating myths of ideal Jewish womanhood, such stories impressed upon the female readers of *The Occident* what was expected of them, and they reinforced male readers' beliefs about Jewish women. Leeser's restrictive editorial policy, as unintentional as it might have been, could hardly have inspired many women to explore their literary potential.

Despite the urging of editors such as Isaacs and Leeser, few Jewish women wrote. Perhaps this was the "result of a defect in the education of Jewish girls" (Glanz, *Jewish Woman* 161), although this hardly seems like a convincing explanation in light of the large number of Christian American women who also received limited educations but who wrote. Nor is it convincing to point only to Jewish myths that demanded undistracted attention to home and family; again, many Christian women wrote in spite of the demands of similar myths. What does seem more plausible is that the gender roles within Judaism which prescribed that it was the man's responsibility to study, to know God's words, and the woman's responsibility to provide comfortable conditions in which the man could read and write, restricted women. Gilbert and Gubar's analysis of the "anxiety of authorship" helps explain the restriction; the woman writer's battle, they hypothesize, is "against [men's] reading of *her*. In order to define herself as an author she must redefine the terms of her socialization" (*Madwoman* 49). "Socialized" to feel incapable of writing, as well as to feel unfeminine and even un-Jewish if they stepped outside prescribed roles, Jewish women only occasionally, and with great caution, ventured to express themselves in poetry, fiction, and essays during most of the nineteenth century.

However, as the century drew to its close, more Jewish women felt compelled to articulate their concerns and conflicts, addressing either secular audiences about stereotypes of Jews and anti-Semitism or Jewish audiences about Jews' status in America. Their movement away from safe explorations to outspoken proclamations of their identities indicates both a step away from traditional Judaism's dictates and a step into the American public arena. Jewish women realized, as Emma Lazarus had, that they could be forces for change in spheres other than the domestic. In exploring and developing new creative spaces, they wrote about Judaism and anti-Semitism, formed the National Council of Jewish Women, joined the work force as volunteers and paid employees, and took philanthropic work seriously. But in so doing, they did not ignore the domestic sphere or the responsibilities associated with it. In an attempt to reconcile the old and new "contested" myths of womanhood, many of the women pointed out that they were fulfilling their domestic duties through public activities; care of impoverished immigrants was an extension of caring for the family, for example, and even writing about anti-Semitism was another form of preserving Judaism.

Jewish Women and American Womanhood

Although they resembled Christian women in their familial obligations, Jewish women did not need to fight the image of the helpless, fainting "child-woman." Because so many of them felt they played a vital role in preserving the Jewish nation through the Jewish home, Jewish women had a strong sense of purpose and identity. They believed in their duties as women particularly because they perceived them as special and necessary for the survival of the Jews. They accepted the responsibility for being teachers of morality, for example, not to guide children and husband past "maelstroms of atheism and uncontrolled sexuality" as was the Christian woman's duty (Smith-Rosenberg, "Hysterical Woman" 666) but, rather, to save them from spiritual annihilation (through a loss of Judaism) and literal annihilation (through overt anti-Semitism). Despite these significant differences between Christian and Jewish myths, the women within the literary tradition I am describing were American women and as such conformed on some levels to the myths of American womanhood, as the following group of writings demonstrates.

Rebecca Gratz (1781–1869) epitomizes the early nineteenth-century Jewish woman whose belief in domestically related responsibilities for women stemmed from a synthesis of Jewish and American values. One of ten surviving children of Michael Gratz and Miriam Simon, she spent her life in the protective environment of her well-established and highly respected German Jewish family. Although Gratz remained single all her life, she dedicated herself to her family by mothering her sister's orphaned children as well as by writing letters to and visiting relatives. She also demonstrated commitment to her communities through the establishment of the Hebrew Sunday School Society in 1838 and the Philadelphia Orphan Society in 1815.

In the many letters which she wrote to friends and family, Gratz articulated a strong belief in the standards of feminine decorum. A wife, she explained in 1846, should be a "help meet, and a guide and a guard and a companion . . . [and] should make [her husband's] home a little Paradise" (Philipson 329). As for a mother, she added a year later, "there can be no love more pure more perfect or more enduring than a mothers [sic]— what a blissful refuge to the stricken spirit. . . . Alas! who can estimate the loss of a mother to a young family—the training eye of maternal watchfulness not only forms and regulates the character of her offspring but clears their path from unseen and unsuspected dangers" (Philipson 339).

Women, according to Gratz, occupied a designated sphere; one of the horrors of the Civil War ("this unholy strife") was that it forced women to "step out of the sphere God designed them to fill in such times of trouble" (Philipson 430). Women, even those who remained unmarried, had the responsibility of using this special sphere for the proper influence of men. Gratz explained to her sister-in-law in 1834 that unmarried men in particular had need of womanly influence:

> Whatever the lords of creation may imagine they are infinitely the most helpless beings in the decline of life unconnected by the ties of family—the sedentary habits of women keep them only dependent for a few comforts on their friends—but the man who has no one to influence and console him, when vehement passions, painful diseases and disappointed pride cross his vexed spirits—is a sad spectacle of suffering and helplessness.

Woman's duty was to "rescue" single men "from the worst effects of bachelorship—a care-for-nobody independence" (Philipson 206–7).[1] Clearly echoing True Womanhood rhetoric, Gratz's words reveal the similarities between Christian and Jewish women's gender roles. However, we must not be misled by these similarities. As we will see in chapter 5, Gratz never abandoned her Jewish values or identity, remaining particularly adamant in her views on intermarriage.

Although the passages just quoted sound like oversimplifications, other letters reveal Gratz's awareness of the relative powerlessness of women in her cultures. For example, in an 1824 letter to her sister-in-law Maria Gist Gratz, who had just given birth to her third son, Gratz wrote, "tho' I dare say you would have welcomed a girl with equal joy, I am sure for the poor child's sake you should be more happy as in the arrangements of this working-day world the men have honors and glory—while the weaker vessels are more heavily laden'd by care" (Philipson 68). In an even more revealing passage, from the same 1834 letter which outlined the duty of women toward unmarried men, Gratz explained that as an unmarried woman she felt she had to "repay" her brothers' "goodness" by "keeping up a domestic home with those charities alive, which may rescue them" (Philipson 207). "Repayment" was particularly important because "we who have neither fortune to support, nor other right to an establishment must endeavor to set up a claim to usefulness in some subordinate way to reconcile us to the idea of not being a burden to our relations" (207). The "rights" of a "burdensome" single woman were severely limited, as Gratz herself recognized.

Like Gratz, Rebekah Gumpert Hyneman (1812–1875) wrote from the perspective of a traditional outlook. The daughter of a Jewish father and a Christian mother, Hyneman chose very deliberately to live her life as a Jew, marrying a Jewish man and living according to Orthodox standards. She also seems to have followed the codes for both a True Woman and a Mother in Israel; as a mother, she devoted herself to her sons, and as a wife, to the memory of her husband after he disappeared on a business journey.

Given the life she led, it should not surprise us that Hyneman wrote often about women, and that much of what she wrote reflects a convergence of American and Jewish gender roles. In her story "The Lost Diamond," published in *The Occident* in 1868, she conveyed her belief that women had the right and power to bring wandering men back to the haven of religion, in this case Judaism. A young physician, Lascelle, who had been "passing" for a non-Jew, tells Anna Malchoir, the Jewish woman he loves,

> you have brought my heart back to its original faith. . . . I could not, looking upon your fortitude, your affection, and cheerfulness even under trials and tribulations, remain insensible to the cause which enabled you to be what you were. And thinking thus, my mind flew back to my boyhood's days, and all the beauties of our sacred religion which, in my sinfulness of heart, I had laid aside came back to me, and led me, I humbly trust, to make my peace with God. (170)

Anna re-educates Lascelle about the strength of Judaism and offers him the means by which he can reconcile himself with God. Hyneman's belief in woman's special duties as preserver of the family through her role as moral educator represents one of the ways in which an American Jewish woman could follow the myths of both Jewish and American female propriety.

Hyneman also projected images of conventional Mothers in Israel who resembled True Women in many of her poems collected in *The Leper and Other Poems* (1853). "Female Scriptural Characters," which also appeared in *The Occident* between 1846 and 1850, for example, transform heroic biblical figures into nineteenth-century American women. Even as she sang the praises of Sarah, Rebekah, Leah, Rachel, Miriam, Ruth, Naomi, Esther, Jochebed, Deborah, Huldah, Judith, and Hannah, the mother of the seven martyrs, Hyneman reduced these women's valorous deeds to acts of feminine propriety. She addresses Deborah, the original Mother in Israel, as follows:

> And thou, gentle woman, so meek in thy might,
> God-fearing and loving, thou aidest the fight,

And thy song, as we trace it, recalls thee as when
Thy presence gave hope to the fortunes of men.

In Hyneman's literary projection, the brave Deborah becomes an acceptable True Woman, not a valiant warrior. Powerless even in her powerfulness ("meek" in her "might"), she inspires rather than leads men.

The description of Judith, another valiant hero, also juxtaposes strength and demureness:

> She leaves that scene of blood behind,
>   And speeds through many a lonely dell;
>
> . . . .
>
> How fearfully her woman's soul
> Had mocked at Nature's soft control—
>   How well her mission sped!
> Oh! not by woman's gentle hand
>   Should blood be shed or victory won;
> Yet, for her God, her love, her land,
>   What hath not woman done?

Hyneman extols Judith's courage but assures us that her actions grow out of love of country and God. She is not hardened to battle or murder but, rather, masters her feelings of repugnance in order to serve. Hyneman uses the contrast between the woman's "gentle hand" and the blood of the battle to heighten the incongruity of the scene. Neither the True Woman, nor even the Mother in Israel, has a regular place on the battlefield; the proper woman's war is against immorality, nonobservance of religious laws, and family members' illnesses.

The poem "Woman's Rights" *(Leper)* makes this last point explicit. Despite the provocative title, the poem tells us not that a woman has the right to vote or work, but rather she has the "right" "to soothe the couch of pain" as well as to make man's home an earthly paradise and "to teach the infant mind." Woman, Hyneman tells her audience,

> . . . is a flower that blossoms best, unseen,
>   Sheltered within the precincts of her home;
> There, should no dark'ning storm-cloud intervene,
>   There, the loud-strife of worldings never come.
> Let her not scorn to act a *woman's* part,
>   Nor strive to cope with manhood in its might,
> But lay this maxim closely to her heart—
>   That that which God ordains is surely right.

This poem reinforces the impact of "Deborah" and "Judith"; the biblical heroes acted not as surrogate men, but as True Women who acted to save their nation and the extended family of the Jewish people. They exercised their "right" to serve others.

Like Gratz, Hyneman identified "women's rights" and women's natures as divinely created and therefore equally as fixed as an individual's sex. In her beliefs and in her rhetoric, Hyneman mirrored as well as strengthened the myths of her cultures. She utilized conventional characters and actions to transpose her beliefs into literary forms, but she also contributed to the process whereby such literary conventions became mythic in their impact. In Hyneman's work, the American True Woman and the Mother in Israel were indistinguishable; this author actually avoided choosing sides in the "contest" between the myths of her cultures by ignoring the existence of the contest. By conforming to general standards of genteel femininity and emphasizing the similarities rather than the differences between American and Jewish women, she found her own creative space and validated her own identity as an American Jewish woman.

She also legitimized her identity as an author by writing conventional poetry, by staying within safe, acceptable "feminine" bounds. In the preface to *Leper*, she wrote,

> "It is a good lesson," says Hawthorne, "though it may be a hard one, for a person who has dreamed of literary fame, and of making himself a rank among the world's dignitaries by such means, to step out of the narrow circle in which his claims are recognised, and to find how utterly devoid of significance beyond that circle, is all that he achieves and all that he aims at." I am now stepping out of that charmed circle, and tremble lest the above truth may be too rudely enforced. In presenting my unassuming little volume to the public, I feel more than the usual share of timidity attendant upon such ventures, for I come before them unknown and unnamed.

She proceeded to explain that she expected her co-religionists to overlook faults in the poems, but "to those whose path is not as mine, and who may not be disposed to judge with equal leniency, I have no excuse to offer, but screen myself behind the shield of insignificanc[e]" (iii). Obviously self-conscious about her "proper" roles, Hyneman chose to frame her poems in a typical apology, itself a female convention.

Also typical are poems such as "On an Infant" and "The Dying Sister," which express unoriginal sentiments in familiar rhetoric. The final stanza of "On an Infant," for example, reads,

> Here earth's sweetest treasures around thee shall bloom,
>   And affection its holiest vigils will keep;
> Bright flowers shall scatter their sweetest perfume,
>   And angels watch over thy visionless sleep.

And the first two stanzas of "The Dying Sister":

> I am dying, dearest sister,
>   The death-damp is on my brow,
> Which thy dear hand is pressing;
>   Yes, I am dying now.
>
> I feel it in the quivering
>   Of each faint and feeble breath,
> And my fast receding senses
>   Assure me this is death.

Despite Hyneman's timidity in "stepping out of that charmed circle," she really had little to fear. Nothing in these poems suggests that the poet wanted to challenge the roles that had been prescribed for her, as a woman or a woman author.

Octavia Harby Moses (1823–1904) is another poet who accepted her roles as an American and Jewish woman.[2] Even less self-identified as a writer than Hyneman, her volume of poetry was not published until eleven years after her death, by her children and grandchildren, although many of the poems were written in the middle of the nineteenth century. The very title of the collection, *A Mother's Poems: A Collection of Verses*, explains how Moses's family remembered the woman and the author. The title also accurately reveals that Moses perceived her art as something additional to the birth of her seventeen children (fourteen of them survived). Most of the poetry was inspired by family members and everyday occurrences; the only public event that sparked Moses's creativity was the Civil War.

The Harbys were an old, established South Carolina family; Isaac Harby (Octavia's father) was one of the founders of the Society of Reformed Israelites in 1824, the first Reform congregation in America. After Octavia married Andrew Jackson Moses at the age of sixteen, she lived in Sumter, South Carolina. Her loyalty to the South, her "native . . . beautiful land" ("To the South," line 18), and the Confederate cause never wavered.

A Mother's Poems clarifies that Moses saw her role of nurturer and supporter as primary. In "God Help the Poor (Written during the Confederate War)," she described this female identity:

> Oh! Woman, ray divine from Heaven,
>   Give from thy lesser store,
> To thee is every good work given,
> Strive as thou never yet hast striven
>   And help the starving poor! (Stanza 7)

Moses also conveyed her beliefs about men's roles:

> Oh! Man with more than plenty blest,
>   Give from thy liberal store!
> So shalt thou know a mind at rest,
> Sweet the wife's kiss, the child's caress,
>   For thou hast helped the poor. (Stanza 6)

According to Moses, both men and women had the responsibility to help others, but they were to perform their duties in uniquely "masculine" or "feminine" ways within clearly marked spheres of influence.

Moses obviously accepted her responsibilities as a mother of the Confederacy, and she believed that she could remain loyal to the South even as a Jew. "To the South" (1863) strongly expresses that Southern loyalty:

> Oh! shame to thee, land of the South!
>   Shame on the inglorious day,
> When thy sons and thy daughters, thy mothers and sires,
>   Shall yield to the Northerner's sway.
>
> Oh, where is the pride of thy youth?
>   Where the glory encircling thy brow?
> Has the laurel wreath faded which proudly you wore?
>   Then recall its bright freshness e'en now!
>
> Let us end the long contest of years,
>   Let Liberty warm every heart,
> Let Liberty's war cry resound through the land,
>   'Till its echo doth fill every part.
>
> Ye have waited too long for the day,
>   Arm, arm ye! right brave Southern men!
> Ye must conquer them now, or forever be slaves,
>   On your necks they will trample again.
>
> Only yield up thy rights with thy life,
>   My native, my beautiful land,
> Let the battle go hard, better die than to wear
>   One moment the coward's black brand!
>
> The North preaches freedom to those,
>   Who know not the bliss it bestows,
> Shall we, who were born amid freedom's bright homes,
>   Surrender our rights to our foes?
>
> Never! Never! my brothers, my friends,
>   Awake! rouse ye up for the strife!

'Tis your honor you fight for, your wives and your homes;
    Struggle hard—'tis for Freedom and Life!

Despite the references to slavery and freedom which we can see as ironic, both because of the American situation and because of Jewish history, the poem articulates Moses's convictions not only about the Confederacy but also about women's roles. She believed that a woman could and should battle through her men—by inciting them to protect and serve.

Moses's only poem self-consciously on her art, "To Poetry" (1857), describes the author's disappointment when poetry has fled from her, and her yearning for it to return:

Oh Spirit Immortal! why, why dost thou wander,
    In paths that allure thee afar
From this earth, once illumed by thy beaming splendor,
    Till it shone like some light-giving Star.

Hast thou floated to scenes that are fairer than ours?
    Art thou hid in thy sky's deepest blue?
Or art thou embalmed in the heart of the flowers,
    To heighten their perfume and hue?

I miss thee—I miss thee—I sigh for those fancies
    That filled every hour with beauty,
That lightened life's cares with the sweetest romances,
    And to pleasure transmitted each duty. (Stanzas 1–3)

Poetry was a pleasant recreation, or, at most, a balm for life's hardships. It helped the poet express her feelings and cope with tragedy; it was a pastime to be squeezed in among daily chores, not a vocation demanding concentration and dedication. Whether in "To Poetry" and "To the South," or "To My Daughter Rebecca" and "Anita (A day of unspeakable anguish—July 14, 1882. Anniversary of Anita's death.)," Moses reinforced myths about women and women writers by simply echoing traditional views, rather than challenging them with fresh imagery or controversial questions. Like Gratz and Hyneman she ignored the "contested space" between her cultures.

Another mid-century writer who accepted and glorified the roles of the American woman and of the Americanized Mother in Israel without apparent conflict was Penina Moise (1797–1880). Best known for *Fancy's Sketchbook* (1833), presumably the first volume of poetry published by a Jew in America, Moise also lived her life as a Southern Jewish woman. Like Gratz, she never married, but devoted herself to her parents, her sickly mother in particular, her students in the school which she, her sister, and her niece ran, and her community (in 1854 she nursed many through a yellow fever epidemic). Also like Gratz, she promoted the education of Jewish children by serving as the superintendent of Jewish Sunday schools in Charleston, South Carolina. Moise's poetry appeared in such secular periodicals as *The Charleston Courier* and *Godey's Ladies' Book*, and in the Jewish periodical *The Occident and American Jewish Advocate*. She also wrote hymns for Beth Elohim in Charleston, one of the oldest Reform congregations in America.

Those hymns were published by Beth Elohim in 1857/8 (the Jewish year 5618). These religious songs cover obedience to God's will, duties toward others, duties toward ourselves, etc. Most are directed at general audiences. One Sabbath hymn, however, number 154,[3] stands out because it is addressed to women:

> Daughters of Israel, arise!
>   The Sabbath-morn to greet,
> Send songs and praises to the skies,
>   Then frank incense [*sic*] more sweet.
>
> Take heed, lest ye the drift mistake,
>   Of heaven's hallowed hours,
> And from those dreams too late awake,
>   That show you but life's flowers.
>
> Leave not the spirit unarrayed,
>   To deck the mortal frame;
> With gems of grace let women aid,
>   Charms that from nature came.
>
> With jewels of a gentle mind,
>   More precious far than gold,
> Brightened by love, by faith refined,
>   And set in chastest mould.
>
>   Wife! mother! sister! on ye all
>   A tender task devolves;
> Child, husband, brother, on ye all,
>   To nerve their best resolves.
>
> Your hands must gird the buckler on,
>   The mortal weapons cleanse,
> By which that battle may be won,
>   That in self-conquest ends. (*Secular* 136)

The last two stanzas in particular remind the female congregants of their moral responsibility for husbands and children. This responsibility is a "tender task" which the woman will gladly assume because it will keep her loved ones safe. Given the context of the exhortation, Moise implies that religious instruction should compose a significant portion of the woman's battle plan. But it could be any religion's lessons that should be taught. Hymn number 154 could have been written by a Christian True Woman for other Christian True Women. The emphasis on the woman's duty to protect her family through indirect influence reinforces key similarities between myths of Christian and Jewish American woman- hood. Also significant about the poem is the way in which Moise used it to include herself in the female congregation although she never cared for a literal husband or child. She fulfilled her general role as moral protector through poems such as this, as well as through her teaching and social service. As Lazarus and Gratz demonstrated, a woman could fulfill her destiny even as a metaphoric mother.

Hymn 154 is by no means the only poem Moise wrote which supported conventional attitudes about women's identities. For example, "On the Death of Mrs. R. Cohen, who, with her two children, perished in the Edwina, on Monday, June 25th" functions like the obituaries that trans- formed real women into unapproachable saints:

> For though no marble orator proclaims
> Her devotional and lofty aims,
> The hearts inscription ne'er can be effaced
> On which her moral image has been traced
> The gentle guardian of domestic bliss,
> 'T was hers to press the ruffled plume of peace
> Enchanting by her mien and manners bland.
> In duty's sphere she waved a magic wand,
> Subdued ambition sought no loud acclaim,
> Her partner's plaudit was her highest fame,
> Alas! for him whose bosom feels the shaft
> Deeper, as mem'ry doth her worth ingraft
> The wild disorder of his wandering glance
> Seeks her, incredulous of Fate's romance;
> Three broken chords life's harmony destroy.
>
> . . . .
>
> Oh! balmy pity thou a barrier rear
> Nor let deep sorrow darken to despair,
> Thy power shall lift his thoughts to purer spheres
> And fervid faith exhale the mourner's tears.

(Secular 209; lines 19–33, 39–42)

Moise places R. Cohen firmly within the domestic sphere, identityless without her husband's name (we know her only as Mrs. R. Cohen) and her husband's praise. Remembered as a type, rather than for her individual traits or worldly accomplishments, this woman became, in death, a symbol of the ideal woman.

Writing primarily in the middle of the nineteenth century, this first

group of writers (Gratz, Hyneman, Moses, and Moise) did more to maintain than to challenge myths of womanhood. By the last few decades of
the century, however, most Jewish women became conscious of the
changing myths of American womanhood at the same time that they
valued traditional myths. Jenny Kleeberg Herz, for example, wrote an
essay, "Daughters of Columbia," which simultaneously glorified "new"
women's and True Women's achievements.

Herz's essay, which was printed in the October 1892 edition of *The
Menorah*, begins with the proclamation, "Every nation brings forth its
own distinct type of womanhood . . . [because] woman, the more plastic
half of mankind, is the offspring of circumstances, moulded by surrounding conditions" (243). America, the essay continues, "has brought forth
various types of womanhood, so different in all main particulars, yet
sisters withal, alike daughters of glorious free Columbia" (243). What
made American women sisters were the "innate" traits of independence,
self-reliance, and energy, "transmitted from mother to daughter for many
generations" (243). Herz proceeded to chronicle this transmission, pointing out that "the revolutionary war . . . stimulated Columbia's daughters
to actions of heroism and self-denial" (244) and that women had served as
nurses during the Civil War. By the time Herz was writing her essay
women had demonstrated their "ability" and "capability to succeed" as
writers, physicians, actresses, educators, and philanthropists, as well as
"inventors, journalists, reporters, printers, dentists, publishers, librarians, agriculturists, florists, undertakers, druggists, shoemakers,
storekeepers, etc." (249).

Although Herz praised women for their achievements, she retreated
into conventional rhetoric when she described mothers:

> That woman's influence has greatly added to the rapid progress of our
> country, can not be doubted, for the intellectual and moral growth of a
> country is stimulated by its mothers. When mothers excelled in deeds
> of heroism, sons could not be cowards; when mothers demanded
> equal rights for all, sons would not endure servility; when mothers
> demanded co-education, sons would not remain illiterate. Hence the
> prosperity of America. (250)

Despite Herz's earlier claim that mothers "transmitted" independence,
self-reliance, and energy to their daughters, here she emphasized the
mother's service to her sons. Daughters, she implied, will use their
strength and "self-denial" for men, not for themselves.

In most of her essay, Herz projected a vision of American women united
by gender rather than divided by race or religion. On the last page,
however, she noted that "charity is not limited to race or creed" and that
women's service societies which barred "conscientious Jewesses" were

"uncharitable" (250). Obviously cognizant of her identity as a Jewish woman, as well as of anti-Semitism, Herz sought an America—a protected space—which recognized and accepted her. Her celebration of the achievements of the "daughters of Columbia," including the non-Jewish and Jewish American writers "Anne Bradstreet, Margaret Fuller Ossoli, Harriet Beecher Stowe, Alice and Phebe Carey, Grace Greenwood, Fannie Fern, Jennie June, Gail Hamilton, Mary Dodge, Sarah E. Jacobs, Emma Lazarus, Rebekah Hyneman, etc." (248), was a technique for calling off the contest between her American and Jewish selves. Such a list must have reassured the Jewish readers of *The Menorah* that despite some anti-Semitic attitudes, America would still count Jewish women among the "daughters of Columbia."

Nina Morais (Cohen) (1855–1918) was also interested in analyzing gender tensions in a secular context, as her essay "Limitations of Sex" makes clear. Morais was the daughter of an eminent Philadelphia rabbi, Sabato Morais. According to the *Universal Jewish Encyclopedia*, she attended both private and public schools in Philadelphia, taught school, lectured, and wrote (volume 3, 254). In 1886 she married Emanuel Cohen, a lawyer, with whom she settled in Minneapolis. She maintained her interest in literature and "social service," founding the Minneapolis section of the National Council of Jewish Women.

Morais's "Limitations of Sex" was a critique of a Miss Hardaker's "Ethics of Sex"; both Hardaker's essay and Morais's response appeared in *The North American Review* (in July 1880 and January 1881, respectively). Morais's "object" was "to show that Miss Hardaker's physiological and psychological statements are inaccurate and incomplete in themselves, and valueless in their application to a permanent ethical code." Specifically, Morais argued that

> physical size cannot be shown as a factor in [women's] mental development; that the ratio between normal quantity of brain and of brain power has not been scientifically determined; that no essential variation between the constitutions of male and female brains is known to exist; and that existing mental traits cannot be found indicative of the real female nature, because no scope has been afforded to womanly endeavor. (94)

As the last point in the preceding list specifies, Morais took an "anti-essentialist" stance, believing the *cultural* prohibitions limited women's public achievements. She explained that the "masculine nature, from its long-continued contact with wider interests and more numerous ideas, has acquired more accurate habits of thought." It was this that had given men "the real advantage," but, Morais hypothesized, "time, whose every division shall record greater mental effort for accuracy on the part of woman, can remedy the discrepancy." She continued optimistically:

The results of freedom are already felt. The pressure of unmoved prejudice bearing upon each woman who seeks a new channel of activity, and the invariable law of competition calling for the survival of the fittest, make her stimulus to exact habits of thought greater than that which urges her male competitor. With such impulses a habit ought to be acquired in a few generations. (91)

Morais concluded her essay by explaining that this new "habit" will offer to a woman many options other than marriage. No longer needing the "self-protection" of wedlock, she will marry "only if it appear to better her condition . . . [and] she will sanctify marriage by removing the fictitious sexual distinctions which the power of the male has imposed upon the dependence of the female." The final sentence of the argument, "Equality, intellectual and moral, is the key to the sexual problem" (95), implies that men, as well as women, must change their "habits" or attitudes.

Annie Nathan Meyer (1867–1951) also explored the need for men to change in her novel *Helen Brent, M.D.: A Social Study* (1892). Meyer, a Daughter of the American Revolution, a descendant of two of the oldest and wealthiest Jewish American families, cousin of Emma and Josephine Lazarus, wife of a prominent New York physician, and a mother, helped establish Barnard College while still in her early twenties.[4] In addition to *Helen Brent*, she also wrote sketches, plays, a history of Barnard College, *Barnard Beginnings*, as well as an autobiography, *It's Been Fun*.

Early in her writing career Meyer edited a collection of eighteen essays, all by American women, entitled *Woman's Work in America* (1891). Including articles entitled "Woman in the Ministry" by Rev. Ada C. Bowles and "Woman in Philanthropy—Care of the Indian" by Amelia Stone Quinton, this volume, Meyer explained in the preface, was to function as both a "record" and an "inspiration." More specifically, it was:

1. To set certain plain facts, shorn of all sentiment, before the world in accessible form;
2. To preserve the record of a great, brave, and essentially American struggle;
3. To serve as a stimulus to many women who are working along a very weary road;
4. To hold up before the entire sex in every sphere of life only the highest standard of excellence. (vi)

Julia Ward Howe, in her introduction, expanded upon Meyer's goals by explaining that because a "respect for labor lies at the very foundation of a true democracy . . . the great uprising of industries among women, are then not important to women alone, but of momentous import to society at large" (1). Meyer's volume, according to Howe, would "furnish evidence to confute calumny, to convince the doubtful" regarding the attainments of women (2).

When asked by a "well-known editor and poet (a man)" why she did not include a chapter on "Women in Marriage," Meyer responded that, as far as she knew, "women had never been denied that privilege." Sounding very progressive, she included those work arenas where "women, if entrance were not absolutely denied them, were at least not welcomed, nor valued" (iii–iv). Yet seven of the eighteen chapters were devoted to various kinds of philanthropy, one of the few public domains in which middle-class women could work. Meyer, who went so far as to recognize the need for a book on woman's work in America and to solicit essays by women committed to the subject, ultimately kept the volume uncontroversial, securely ensconced in middle-class propriety.

Helen Brent also remains in the secular middle class. However, it ultimately moves beyond neatly charted territory when the main character resolves the irreconcilable conflict between marriage and career by deliberately forsaking wedlock for professional fulfillment. Helen Brent, a physician, dedicated to the success of a new women's hospital, loves and is loved by Harold Skidmore, a lawyer. Despite his admiration of her dedication to medicine, Harold expects Helen to substitute marriage for career: "how else could a home be made; a family reared?" (37). To his arguments, Helen responds forthrightly, " 'to give this [her work at the hospital] all up for you, is to make myself fall utterly in my eyes, and I could never be happy without the respect of my own self' " (40).

Nor can she be happy knowing that other women lack this self-respect, so she strives through her work " 'to make all women find themselves' " (104) and recognize " 'the true dignity of the individual' " (105). This is a difficult task because " 'women have lived so long in such a narrow sphere that their judgement is warped. They have become conservative through seeing only one kind of existence going on' " (102). Meyer suggests that most women would marry Harold, influenced by cultural expectations to find love and socially sanctioned security more alluring than work.

Although Helen's statements imply that women must alter their habits of thought and behavior if they want to "find themselves," Meyer explicitly declares, like Morais, that gender inequalities can only be corrected when men are " 'educated to allow greater liberty of thought and action in their wives, to seek in them companionship in marriage, to seek sympathetic cooperation, not merely physical gratification, nor the mere oiling of the household machinery' " (54). Harold, who is intelligent and more progressive than many other men, learns this only after the beautiful but vapid woman he marries leaves him for another man and then dies as the result of her dissipated life.

The central dilemma of the novel—career or marriage—reflects a key

issue of "new womanhood," which Meyer defines early in the novel:
" 'The new womanhood is a development, an enriching of the old womanhood—not, in any sense, a narrowing down, nor a dwarfing of our noblest
conceptions. It means growth in every direction' " (21). New womanhood
represents potential of the individual and of society. For Helen, it expresses itself in "a fierce longing that her whole nature could rise and
expand, grow as it was intended it should grow—full, proportioned, equa-
ble, beautifully rich in all the blessings of life; not warped, thwarted,
stunted" (53). Sadly, such glowing passages do not tell the whole story.
The fact is, Helen pays for her career with loneliness. While the character's pain might suggest that the novel is covertly subverting its own
intentions, I believe that it remains consistent in its strong message that
the decision not to marry Harold was the correct one. The ennui and
frustration that Helen would have experienced as a result of abandoning
her work would have been worse than the loneliness she feels at the end
of her day at the hospital. Although *Helen Brent, M.D.* oversimplifies
some complex conflicts, it illuminates the tensions American women
felt in an era when myths of traditional female propriety were explicitly
being challenged.

Emma Wolf (1865–1932) also fictionalized the issues surrounding late
nineteenth-century female independence, although she never constructed the conflict between career and marriage as neatly as did Meyer.
Wolf, like Meyer, was a member of a respectable Jewish family.[5] She was
educated in San Francisco schools (*Who's Who in American Jewry*, 1926)
and wrote five novels between 1892 and 1916.[6] According to Rebekah
Kohut, Wolf was "one of eight daughters" and was "handicapped from
birth by a useless arm, but there was no defect in her mentality. Her
memory was the most remarkable" Kohut had ever seen (*My Portion* 61).
It seems that she never married.

In two of the four novels she published in the final decade of the
nineteenth century, Wolf examined the meaning of womanhood in secular American contexts. In *Joy of Life* (1896), she explored new womanhood.[7] The central female character in the novel, Barbara Gerrish, has
gone to college because she "wanted to develop" (71). Very proud of the
A.B. she earned at twenty-three, she values her independence (72). Nevertheless, after several years of genteel tutoring, she turns down an offer "as
instructor of physiology and hygiene in a girls' school" because, "for all
her independence, she was hungering for somebody to love" (73). Nearly
twenty-six, she makes her brother Robert, a newspaper reporter in River-
ton, California, the recipient of her love.

Robert calls Barbara a "New Woman," " 'a cross between a something
and a nothing; a woman who wants to climb the fence, catches her skirts
in a nail, and commences to shriek for some one to come and help her
over' " (119). Barbara defensively responds by saying,

"when you mean, by the term [new women], the women who believe in and ask for the right to advance in education, the arts, and professions with their fellow-men, you are speaking of a phase in civilization which has come gradually and naturally, and is here to stay. There is nothing new or abnormal in such a woman. But when you confound her with the extremists who wantonly disown the obligations and offices with which nature has honored them, you do the earnest, progressive women great wrong." (121)

Despite this proud proclamation, Barbara calls herself a " 'traditional woman' " (121) whose *"maternal* instinct" (151) compels her to say, " 'I believe that when a woman turns out a noble son or husband she is doing glorious patriotic work; and a true woman asks for nothing better' " (122). The last quotation is not spoken sarcastically; rather, it springs from the character's struggle to reconcile her education and earlier goals with more traditional expectations which she also valued.

A Prodigal in Love (1894) is not so much about the transition from True Womanhood to new womanhood as it is about the tenacity of female roles. Even at the end of the nineteenth century, Wolf could write a novel in which the central character (Constance Herriott) sacrifices her youth to care for her orphaned sisters and forces her next youngest sister (Eleanor) to marry Hall Kenyon when she thinks, mistakenly, that they have been lovers. Constance demands this marriage even though she herself is in love with Kenyon. Here, the strong, capable woman martyrs herself and her happiness for her sister's and the family's honor.

After Eleanor and Kenyon marry, the wife must perform a difficult womanly duty: to teach her husband that he cannot disappear for days at a time when he is confused or angry. Eleanor guides Kenyon to the lesson by disappearing herself. She explains her actions: " 'This recurrence had to be stopped, and I was the only one to save him—I, in my love for him. So I hurt him, willingly though painedly. To shock him almost to death was his only salvation from such a violent disorder' " (251). The traditional woman had the obligation to reform and redeem her man and thereby display her strength of character indirectly.

Eleanor compounds her indirect power when she rewrites a book manuscript of Kenyon's and makes it her text. She tells Constance that she began by "annotating" Hall's words in order to make them more human and less artistic. Then, she explains, " 'I came to strike out here, to add there; and finally—finally . . . I found the way—I wrote between the lines! I wrote my heart out. I have written there what few women would care to reveal; but it is written, not spoken' " (252). In this passage, Wolf informs us that woman's creative space might be found in unlikely, and seemingly crowded places; in this narrow space, she supplies us with her own encoded message. Not only do we see the power of a text, but we see how much more powerful that text can be when it feels the "human" influence of the woman's voice. When she wields the pen, woman can actually improve upon man's efforts, teaching him valuable lessons by exposing the subtle but indispensable ingredients in his own creation. Although potentially overlooked or underestimated, woman's indirect method of communicating serves its purpose in *A Prodigal in Love,* providing both author and character with an avenue for expression and achievement.

Meyer's and Wolf's fiction about non-Jewish women reflects the conflict between the older myths of True Womanhood which required that women be family careproviders and influencers for good, and the newer myths which projected images of women as intelligent, independent participants in the world beyond the home. They used their novels both to explore the skirmishes along the borders between the myths as well as to suggest ways to achieve peace between them. Like Herz and Morais, they believed in the progress women had made in the final decades of the century and envisioned a future in which changes would continue to improve the lives of women. The fact that this second group of women, including Morais, Meyer, and Wolf, could choose to write on secular subjects for secular audiences and that Herz could publish her essay on the accomplishments of American (including Jewish) women in a Jewish paper indicates how much freedom Jewish women had obtained by the last two decades of the century. Seeking neither to escape from Judaism nor to "pass" for non-Jews, these women were striving to find their place among American women, and by discussing their female identities within American, rather than Jewish, contexts, they emphasized their right to be counted as Americans.

Jewish Women on Jewish Womanhood

Throughout the nineteenth century, the myths of Jewish womanhood remained surprisingly consistent. Even toward the end of the century, as she gained increasing freedom to enter the public realm, whether for an education or to perform charitable deeds, the Jewish woman was still supposed to be, first and foremost, a wife and mother who preserved Judaism through her maintenance of a solid and loving family.

It is clear that Sophia Heller Goldsmith (1848–1929) had internalized these expectations and had converted the myth of the Mother in Israel into an actual way of life by carrying out her duties, as she saw them, to raise Jewish children and make for the family a Jewish home. Her "In Remembrance of My Past Life Recalled to Mind January 26, 1904 and November 11, 1918" reminisces about her life spent in the midwest. Not as privileged as women like Lazarus or Gratz, Goldsmith had to work her whole life, first assisting her parents, and then her husband in his business. Through it all, she remained faithful to Judaism and demonstrated this dedication in her capacity as a Mother in Israel. After proclaiming proudly that both her mother's and father's ancestors belonged "to the house of High Priests called in the Bible the Levits" she directly addressed her children saying, "I wish to state this so you may know my dear children that there is good blood in your veins" (1). The whole memoir, which is dedicated to the children, served to inform the younger Gold-smiths that their parents and ancestors were noble Jews who worked hard when necessity demanded but who never relinquished their faith. The mother explicitly reminded her children of their proud past and implicitly told them of their future duty to carry on the "good blood" of the family and of the Jews. In so doing, she assumed the responsibility for morally and religiously educating her children and thereby helped preserve not only her immediate family but the larger family of Jews. In other words, by utilizing available behavioral and linguistic codes, she lived up to the standards of the mythic Mother in Israel.

Rebekah Hyneman's mid-century narrative poem, "Zara" *(Leper)*, based on "an appeal in behalf of the Jewish nation" by E. L. Mitsford, offers us an opportunity to view the transformation of myths not so much into everyday experiences as into a literary statement. In this sixty-stanza poem, the Moslem ruler Mahmoud desires Zara, a "peerless Hebrew maid," for his harem. Both "peerless," with its connotation of sexually innocent, and "Hebrew" are significant, because Mahmoud believes that "if fraud or treachery could beguile/Her soul from its pure faith, the rest were easy spoil" (verse 4). The coupling of sexual "faith" and religious faith becomes pronounced in the climax of the poem, when Zara chooses to die rather than submit to Mahmoud or renounce her Jewish identity. Zara's expression of devotion is also one of sexual defiance:

> Fiend, thy power
> Availeth naught, for that fair, fragile flower,
> Crushed by thy hand, uprises calm and strong;
> Her pale lips move in prayer . . .
> . . . o'er the assembled throng
> Roll the clear liquid words of Israel's Shemong. (Stanza 58)

Although "Zara" takes place in an exotic setting, far removed from that of nineteenth-century America, Hyneman forcefully communicated her image of the perfect Jewish woman. Physically and spiritually inviolate, women like Zara would continue, as they always had, to protect and perpetuate Jewish ideals.

Several late-century writers projected similar images of the traditional Mother in Israel, despite the fact that they were living in what was, presumably, a progressive period. Louise Mannheimer (1845–1920), for one, in her 1892 poem, "In Memoriam," idealized the literal Jewish mother. This perfect creature's hands

> Ministered to every need;
> And with tender care took heed,
> In the nights so long and dreary
> Of the suffering, till distress
> Eased, their gentle touch did bless.

These same hands also

> Lit for us, in splendor bright,
> On each Sabbath eve the light.

This mother's voice sweetly soothed "Childish trouble, childhood's pain," and urged the children "to highest goal" with its "low but clear" "words of wisdom." Even after her death, this dear woman's "spirit hovers nigh," for "Mother's love can never die" (99–100).

The image of the mother here seems untouched by the "woman question." This Mother in Israel was remembered for her devotion to her children and to Jewish rituals, not for her college education or even her work with a Ladies' Aid Society. In valorizing her Jewish mother, or the generic Jewish mother, Mannheimer employed a familiar and acceptable code, a code which itself relied on traditional myths. The myths of the Jewish woman as mother and Sabbath-maker could not and would not change quickly because they seemed to offer protection against the terrors of new demands and changing expectations.

In her talk "What Has Judaism Done for Woman?" presented at the 1893 Jewish Denominational Congress at the World Parliament of Religions, Henrietta Szold (1860–1945) also reiterated seemingly unchanged expectations for Jewish women. Szold, one of the most "notable of Jewish spinsters," was the daughter of a Baltimore rabbi who received both Jewish and secular educations (Baum et al. 42). She was known for her twenty-three years of often unrecognized work at the Jewish Publication Society of America and for her Zionist activity, principally her founding of Hadassah, a "literary Zionist women's society" which became and still is an "organization dedicated to meeting the health needs of the people of Palestine" (Baum et al. 44).

Szold, one of the few women speaking at the congress, devoted most of her talk to a brief history of women in Judaism. During the days of the Patriarchs, she stated, women were held in high esteem. This changed in later periods, she suggested, because although "Israel's ideals of womanhood were high . . . the nations around acted according to a brutal standard, and Israel was not likely to remain untainted" (307–8). Szold concluded by answering the question, what is the Jewish woman?

> She is the inspirer of a pure, chaste family life, whose hallowing influences are incalculable; she is the center of all spiritual endeavors, the confidante and fosterer of every undertaking. To her the Talmudic sentence applies: "It is woman alone through whom God's blessings are vouchsafed to a house. She teaches the children, speeds the husband to the place of worship and instruction, welcomes him when he returns, keeps the house godly and pure, and God's blessings rest upon all these things." (309–10)

Despite the fact that Szold is remembered for her pioneering and progressive vision of Judaism's place in the world, this early example of her beliefs echoes mid-century myths of the Jewish woman's roles in the family and home. Here, as a young woman, Szold still relied on familiar codes; later, she would have to find new ones to help her negotiate the unfamiliar territory of a publicly involved, politically astute Jewish woman.

Two pieces of fiction from the final decades of the century also perpetuate the myth of the Mother in Israel, and, like Hyneman's "Zara," rely on historical settings to demonstrate the unswerving devotion of the Jewish woman. E. L. Stern's 1889 short story, "Ruth—A Story of Palestine," set in "the beautiful land of Bethlehem—Judah, during the time the people of Israel were governed by Judges" (*Menorah* 38:9, 139), glorifies the spirit and actions of Ruth. Stern follows the outline of the Old Testament story which narrates how Ruth, a Moabite (enemies of Jews) had married a Jew, Mahlon, and then dedicated her life to her mother-in-law Naomi after both were left widowed. In Stern's rendition, Ruth is the model woman: shy, retiring, hard-working, and loyal. Despite her Moabite ancestry, she unselfishly loves her Jewish husband and mother-in-law.

Although the characters are too pure and perfect to be real, they nevertheless convey Stern's belief in the goodness of Jews and of women. The idealized "Moabitess" whose life was among and dedicated to Jews, is actually the perfect, pious, and loyal Jewish woman. The sons, too, are loyal Jews, husbands, and children, and Naomi is a "Mother in Israel" to these sons and her daughters-in-law. All the characters are mythic models toward which American Jewish readers of *The Menorah* could aspire. Looking backward in its historical setting, the story paints a picture of a mythical past when Jews did not doubt their faith and when men and women acted according to strictly demarcated gender rules.

Sara Miller's novel *Under the Eagle's Wing*, published ten years later in 1899, also hearkens back to a period long past when Jews were Jews and life seemed less complicated. The novel is set in Egypt of the Middle Ages when Jews passed as Moslems in public and practiced Judaism in private. Despite the discomfort this sometimes caused, it was clear that the Jewish characters understood the masquerade as a survival tactic. They never lost or questioned their Jewish identities, as so many Jews who were trying to be Americans were doing in the 1890s.

The novel tells of the young Joseph Ibn Assan's journey to Egypt to be a goldsmith in the smithy of Moses Ibn Maimon (Maimonides). Upon his arrival he falls in love with Esther, daughter of Maimon's brother David. The young lovers meet secretly since a girl is not permitted to talk to boys. Esther also breaks conventions when she reads scholarly books. She does, however, perform one female duty: she *persuades* Joseph not to avenge his father's murder. Miller's novel, like Stern's story and Hyneman's "Zara," finds its creative space by superimposing traditional nineteenth-century myths of Jewish life and gender roles on ancient settings. Joseph proves his manhood by accomplishing a dangerous mission for Maimon. Esther proves her womanhood by believing in mercy and love. Although she reads and converses with men as an equal, she does not ride off to prove herself. Rather, she stays at home and influences those around her to be moral.

The works just discussed display no conflict between myths of traditional and modern Jewish womanhood, despite the fact that several of them were written in the last decades of the nineteenth century. Mrs. Henry Meyers, on the other hand, in her 1898 speech, "Woman's Work in the World," did recognize the changes that were taking place around her but shaped those changes into familiar molds. She told the New York section of the National Council of Jewish Women that it is

> a more responsible work to train the minds of an immortal soul, and a much higher work than to rule a state. Therefore woman's work begins in the home, although it need not end it there. She must educate herself and devote herself to high purposes before she can superintend the education of her children to any noble or beneficent purpose. (*Am Jewess* 6, 277)

Sounding like the mid-century Gratz and Hyneman, Meyers reminded her listeners that even now, in the late 1890s, when women had gained more power and were no longer relegated to second-class activities, the Jewish woman still accomplished her greatest "work" by influencing those around her, particularly in her role as mother. By converting new ideas about woman's powers and functions into traditional Jewish myths of woman's duties, Meyers attempted to invent a conciliating code through which she and her audience could continue to believe in their cultural worth as mothers and wives.

Wolf's presentation of female characters also reflects the search for a code which would reconcile traditional and new myths of Jewish womanhood. Ruth Levice in *Other Things Being Equal* (1892), for example, is a modern, middle-class American Jewish young woman who goes to the theater, helps the poor, and goes so far as to fall in love with a Christian man. Yet she is also a devoted Jewish daughter who follows her parents' advice, even when that advice includes not marrying the Christian. Wolf puts Ruth's obedience in context by offering the following explanation of Jewish "daughterhood":

> A Jewish girl's life is an open page to her family. Matters of small as well as of larger moment are freely discussed. The result is that while it robs her of much of her Christian sister's spontaneity, which often is the latter's greatest charm, it also, through the sagacity of more experienced heads, guards her against many indiscretions. This may be a relic of European training, but it enables parents to instill into the minds of their daughters principles which compare favorably with the American girl's native self-reliance. (66)

The comparison between Jewish and Christian "girls" dramatizes Wolf's perception of Jewish womanhood. Founded on close family ties, it relies for its strength on "principles." Although she leads a modern life, Ruth remains the mythic Jewish daughter, more interested in pleasing her parents than in acting "spontaneously."

Despite Wolf's explicit statement about Jewish girls in her 1892 novel, the young Jewish woman in *Heirs of Yesterday* (1900), Jean Willard, has little in the way of family connections beyond the uncle with whom she lives. She seems more independent, to possess more "American . . . self-reliance" than Ruth, yet she still has certain female duties to perform. Specifically, she must lead a man, Philip May, back to his religious base. Through his admiration and love for Jean, Philip realizes that "passing" as a non-Jew is dishonorable. Wolf makes the connection between religion and women's roles explicit when she has Philip exclaim, " 'you have become my religion—if you are Jewish, must I not too be a Jew?' " (285). Like the mid-century Anna Malchoir in Hyneman's "The Lost Diamond," Jean guides Philip back to the faith of his father. Traditional yet modern, Jean represents the turn-of-the-century Jewish woman who, despite her musical accomplishments and independence, still cares for her men. She also provides another example of the way in which American female responsibilities, in this case the duty of the woman to oversee the man's spirituality, were superimposed on a Jewish backdrop—after all, it is a Jewish woman who helps a Jewish man see the folly of "passing" in non-Jewish society.

All of the works just discussed portray Jewish women as perfect types. But America was not Paradise, and real Jewish women did not always fit the ideal. Leah (Lee) Cohen Harby (1849–1918) addressed some of the problems facing assimilated Jewish women. Herself a Daughter of the

American Republic and a Daughter of the American Confederacy, she was very self-conscious of her American identity and wanted other American Jews, particularly women, to be respectable American citizens. Harby's critique and corrective, "Our Women and Their Possibilities," was a response to a query in the *Jewish Messenger* for solutions to the problem of young Jewish men no longer calling on marriageable Jewish women. Speaking to pampered, middle-class females "as one of their faith" who in "kindness . . . point[ed] out their errors; in all earnestness . . . suggest[ed] the remedies," Harby blamed an "erroneous system of education, which fail[ed] to make [young women] reliant and independent in their opinions, or brave enough to advocate and act up to them" (Marcus, *Documentary* 344).

Harby proceeded to detail some of the "Jewess's" faults:

> She is too much given to dress and fashion—valuing her attire by its *cost* rather than by its appropriateness to her style, or the occasion. She desires thus to outshine her neighbors with this evidence of greater means. . . . A kind of self-consciousness is about her, which robs her of all repose of manner, causing her to attract attention by voice or exaggerated gesture. She is affected in her deportment at table while in company, but eats too much and too often when alone. . . . (Marcus, *Documentary* 345)

In addition, Jewish "girls seldom engage in intellectual employments. They sew, embroider, crochet—keeping time to their needles with many a tale of gossip and many an unkind scandal." According to Harby, this last vice "arises from lack of reading and unstored minds" (Marcus, *Documentary* 345–46). Harby's remedy for these ills? Cultivate a Jewish home life, not a social life, teach girls to read and appreciate good literature, and show them how to converse appropriately and intelligently. Once the girls who are thus trained grow into women, men will indeed want to call and marry.

Although Harby's stance was that of a social critic and reformer, her solution to the "problem" of Jewish courtship remained grounded in familiar myths. She asserted, for example, that in education "woman's influence reaches its highest plane, moving children through their mothers, husbands through their wives, and men generally through that beautiful power wielded over their sex by all true womanhood" (Marcus, *Documentary* 347). She concluded by expanding on the need for womanly "influence" within the family:

> A woman's idea of honor should be higher than a man's, as her purity is greater; yet her charity should be all-embracing, as she knows her own weakness and appreciates her own strength.
> Cultivate self-reliance. A woman with resources within herself

stands independent of fortune and imparts that quality to her children. Her resources are those of the minds that furnish refined pleasures, entertainment, and culture to the home whose ornament she forms. Such a home asks nothing from society, but gives much to it. A child raised in such an atmosphere will never value wealth above principle, or appearance more than worth. From such family circles will come those who will place Jewish social life upon its proper plane. Theirs will be an arduous task but a noble one, one of exaltation and redemption, to be extended to both sexes of those who share their faith. (Marcus, *Documentary* 349–50)

Harby's original audience, readers of *The Messenger*, was composed primarily of assimilated, English-speaking Jews. Through her attack on their complacency, we get a glimpse of the other side of middle-class Jewish life; we see the corruptive decadence assimilation can engender, and the disintegration of the exalted Jewish home life. No doubt Harby exaggerated to force her readers to see their faults. Even after taking this into account, however, we still have an American Jewish woman telling others like herself to educate themselves in order to guide their families correctly, to make a home a desirable place to be, and to cultivate their minds instead of their wardrobes. While Harby asked her female readers to behave according to standards of American decorum, she implicitly warned them not to forget the values of Jewish home life, or, in other words, to play the role of Mother in Israel in order to preserve Judaism.

Harby's advice resembled that given to Christian women: educate yourself to be a better wife and mother, make your home inviting, and pamper your family, not yourself. It was uniquely Jewish, however, in its admonitions not to abandon Jewish values and customs, as well as in its attempt to counteract negative stereotypes of pampered, ignorant Jewish girls. More than many of the other writers in the tradition, Harby understood the codes that guided Jews in their activities within the larger American middle-class culture, and she wanted others like herself to share her insight. Perhaps this explains her articulation of conservative rather than progressive views on women's roles, despite the 1883 date of "Our Women"; it is safer to repeat the familiar when one does not want to draw attention to one's otherness.

Role Models

The four writers I discuss in this section (Nina Morais, Mary M. Cohen, Leah Harby, and Josephine Lazarus) composed biographical-critical sketches of other women (and in three cases, Jewish) writers.[8] Through the process of measuring their own aspirations and accomplishments against those of the experienced women, the novices came to understand both the limitations and the creative potential they would encounter. Although I would not call "role models" a defining theme for American Jewish women writers, it is a significant pattern which reveals the ways in which American Jewish women were struggling to fuse both American and Jewish myths of womanhood as well as traditional and progressive gender expectations. Also significant is that in the case of Morais, Cohen, and Harby, we have rare and important evidence of "intra-textuality"—of women within the tradition reading others within the tradition.

In 1885, Morais wrote a biographical sketch of Rebekah Hyneman for the *American Jews Annual (5646)*. The younger author admitted that the older was not one of the "seers of literature" whose compass pivots "rest upon earth, but whose ends touch the stars." Rather, Hyneman's compass "was small; already the atmosphere of a new generation sifts its dust of forgetfulness upon her." Yet "her spiritual life was a beautiful one; its work bears inspiration to the Jewish heart and is of historical import in the annals of Jewish literature in America" (np). Throughout the seventeen pages that follow, Morais implied that Hyneman's work had value only for the Jewish community, not for the larger secular world of letters. The last line of the essay reads, "Yet it may be, that had Rebekah Hyneman forsaken the hermitage of her spirit, the glowing Judaic fervor of her work would be wanting, and it is because of the treasure of Jewish thought that those lines seek to revive her memory for a brief space among the people that she loved." The limited scope and influence of Hyneman's work disappointed Morais, who seems to have been searching for a guide whose compass could touch the stars, who could transcend the mediocrity of poetry "marred by a striking disregard of the ordinary regularities of metrical composition."

Morais expressed disappointment not only in Hyneman's literary production but also in the fact that "She was not a woman of advanced views. Her voice was not heard among the apostles of Abolition, nor in the incipiency of that great movement which has brought to women some legal justice and some educational opportunity," although she "state[d] repeatedly her conviction that a broader and more thorough culture for woman is expedient and necessary." Despite this last observation, Hyneman's "life of seclusion which misfortune and diffidence made for her, was not adapted to such mental experience as compels a thoughtful and earnest intellect to bear the brunt of the social battle" (np).

In an apologetic, and even gently indulgent tone, Morais explained that Hyneman did not fight social battles, nor even leave profound memories in people's minds. Yet she wanted to rescue her from oblivion—provide her with her deserved creative space—particularly as a Jewish American woman writer. Feeling a tie to her through their common status as Jewish women who wrote, she sought a literary place not only for Hyneman, but for herself as well. And in asking her fellow Jews to recognize the love and piety Hyneman felt toward Judaism, and grant her homage in return, she also asked for acceptance for herself as a Jewish woman author. Morais also wrote about Hyneman, I believe, in the hope of discovering a guide through the labyrinthine codes of gender and religious-cultural expectations. However, instead of finding liberation in Hyneman's life and writing, she found constriction. Ultimately, Morais had to forge her own trail, unassisted by Hyneman's traditional beliefs and behavior.

Eight years later, in 1893, Mary M. Cohen (1854–1911) wrote a similar essay, "Emma Lazarus: Woman; Poet; Patriot," for *Poet-Lore*. Here again, we see a younger writer turning toward an accomplished older writer for guidance as well as for affirmation of her own identity. Cohen was born, raised, and educated in Philadelphia. Her father, a businessman, and her mother were both English-born. She wrote numerous essays for both the Jewish and secular press, and she took an active role in the Jewish, literary, and philanthropic life of Philadelphia. She was also a member of the American Social Science Association. She appears never to have married.

Cohen found the "example of [Lazarus's] womanly worth, of her poetic genius, and of her patriotic fervor" a "proud joy, a constant inspiration." In addition, she proclaimed the memory of Lazarus as "undying—as everlasting as the beauty of her thought, the gentleness of her spirit, and the strength of her soul" (331). By praising Lazarus for her femaleness, artistry, and Americanness, Cohen sought to demonstrate to other Americans that a Jewish woman, herself included, could be a "woman, poet, and patriot" simultaneously.

Of the three characteristics, "woman" seems to have caused Cohen the most consternation. Even as late as 1893, she needed to justify repeatedly the "unwomanly" activity of literary production, explaining that a woman could be a poet and a patriot without sacrificing her femininity. This is where Lazarus could be so useful; with her "quiet, unpretentious manner," as well as her philanthropic activities such as assisting the Eastern European immigrants who began arriving in the 1880s (321–22), she fit a recognizable model of female decorum. Repeatedly, Cohen emphasized that these womanly traits strengthened, rather than weakened, Lazarus's other identities, particularly that of "poet." She proclaimed, for example, that "It is a noble thing to be a woman; it is a proud thing to be a poet. What is it, then, to be at once woman and poet!" (329). Clearly, Cohen was referring to herself as much as to Lazarus in this declaration of justification.

The title of Harby's essay summarizes its significance: "Penina Moise: Woman and Writer" (1905). Obvious in its simplicity, it nevertheless expresses Harby's own interest in Moise. Throughout the piece, Harby remains respectful of the older woman and writer, always tenderly describing her efforts in behalf of family and students, and always praising her poetry. About her generosity of spirit, Harby wrote,

> Penina Moise was no summer friend; she was staunch and true. . . . Her whole life proved her sincerity, and all those who were in misfortune sought her out, and were better for having been with her. Her example taught endurance and thought of others, for she had the moral courage and strength of will to "veil her suffering in mirth." (30)

About Moise's piety Harby wrote, "These hymns of hers are the voices of her life—supplication, resignation, and praise, worship, aspiration, and rejoicing, the cry of the soul, the uplifting of the mind, faith, belief in God's mercy through all events and in every phase of mortal existence" (28). And about her poetry Harby commented, "all that she wrote had distinct original value" (19) whether it were a war ditty or a hymn.

The cumulative effect of Harby's rhetoric is a portrait of a saint—a woman who courageously suffered blindness and neuralgia, who never complained but selflessly nurtured others, even when she herself was in pain. By describing her in such exalted language, Harby made Moise a type of perfect Jewish womanhood whose memory should remain unsullied. Even her poetry should remain above criticism, emanating as it did from such an exceptional woman. Unlike Morais and Cohen, Harby did not use the older poet to help guide her to her own creative space; instead, the younger woman wanted American Jewish readers of the *American Jewish Year Book* to remember and pay tribute to the "woman and writer" who so nobly embodied the attributes of American Jewish womanhood.

Josephine Lazarus (1846–1910), sister of Emma and herself an author, sought guidance from non-Jewish women writers as well as from Jewish women. It is important to note that her attraction to the non-Jewish writers Louisa May Alcott and Margaret Fuller did not translate into a denial of her Jewish heritage but into a search for answers to the puzzles of her own intellectual and nontraditional life. And her sketches of sister Emma and Madame Dreyfus, both Jewish, suggest a need to understand her Jewish identity, an identity she sought to broaden.

The essays on Alcott and Fuller both appeared in *The Century,* the former in 1891 and the latter in 1893. Although Lazarus obviously respected each author's accomplishments, she tempered her praise with "directness and sincerity." In sketching Alcott's life, Lazarus emphasized the popular author's pragmatism, which was noble yet ultimately limiting:

> So sturdy and practical a will, so firm a grasp on reality, so determined and even conscious a reaction against the exaggerations of idealism, made her the excellent, helpful woman that she was, but also, per-

haps, prevented the higher flight, the *"elan"* which might have borne her still more aloft, within sight of illumined and infinite horizons. (66)

Lazarus returned to the image of limitation a few sentences later when she remarked that Alcott's "deep spiritual life which was the source of so much energy and self-surrender" sustained her family materially rather than endowed her with "clearer insight gained, the indwelling satisfaction and repose, the vistas and heights whereto we may also aspire" (67). Looking to Alcott for help in climbing those heights, Lazarus was frustrated in finding not a scaler of transcendent mountains but a self-sacrificing guardian of duty (67). Ambivalent in her own ideas about women's responsibilities and capabilities, Lazarus found in Alcott confirmation of rather than rebellion against conventions.

In assessing Margaret Fuller, Lazarus seems to have been describing her own conflicts, particularly when she stated that "Opposing forces were constantly at war within her—the intellect and the emotions, the large, unasking sympathies, and the close, hungry human affections" (932). Intelligent and interested in great ideas, Fuller nevertheless longed for a home where she could rest, intellectually and spiritually. She found this place, metaphorically, in her marriage to Giovanni Angelo Ossoli and in motherhood, "the clue to all life's mazes," the event which refreshed her whole being (930). According to Lazarus, however, the fulfillment of domestic needs did not resolve all of Fuller's conflicts:

> For so complex a nature as hers, what was needed was some large, unifying principle that could coordinate all the facts of life, and bring them into harmony and accord; in other words, some deep spiritual conviction, that inner vision and touch of the divine which opens out horizons always luminous, and deeps where there is forever peace. Lacking this, her ideals were always human, her kingdom was of the earth, and she never gained that full mastery and knowledge of the earth which alone can make us free—free of self and the limitations of sense. (932)

Lazarus criticized Alcott and Fuller for the same inability, finally, to transcend this world and uncover ultimate ideas and truths. Disappointed when she discovered that these venerable American women were no freer than she herself, she equivocally noted their achievements, always returning to images of flightlessness and limitation.

The subjects of Lazarus's remaining two sketches are Jewish women: sister Emma and Madame Dreyfus. In both of these, she seemed to need to articulate idealized images of Judaism and womanhood in order to convince herself and her readers that her unique identity was valuable. In "Emma Lazarus" (which appeared as an essay in *The Century* as well as in

The Poems of Emma Lazarus), for example, she used such phrases as "'the miracle' of [Jewish] survival" and "the genius of Judaism,—that absolute interpenetration and transfusion of spirit with body and substance" (*Poems of EL* 23).[9] She also praised her sister's unique character and writing, both the result of being Jewish and female simultaneously (*Poems of EL* 38).

In *Madame Dreyfus: An Appreciation* (1899), Lazarus focused less on the woman as a unique individual and more on the type of perfect womanhood she represented. In the third paragraph of the pamphlet, for example, Lazarus described Dreyfus, wife of the French army Captain Alfred Dreyfus (falsely accused of treason in 1894 and finally pardoned in 1900), as an "immortal" star, an

> ideal of true womanhood which not one of us can contemplate without being lifted by it into its own radiant sphere, made better, truer-hearted, more steadfast and devoted, more brave and capable to meet whatever circumstance, whatever fortune or misfortune in life, because it reveals and illumines for us the very depths of our woman's nature, the courage that never failed . . . the well-spring of a woman's soul, the hidden source of life, of strength, of victory for herself and others, the very secret and core of her womanhood. . . . (8–9)

As Lazarus described her, Madame Dreyfus possessed "womanliness . . . something innate and inherent to the soul and spirit of woman . . . a something of which she can never, and ought never, to rid herself, and without which she can not win the unbounded sympathy and homage of mankind" (13–14). This "something innate" might very well be "the simple capacity of loving, truly and unselfishly—with that forgetfulness of self in whomsoever, in whatsoever she truly loves, whereby she truly finds herself" (49).

Despite the conservative (for 1900) bent of these observations, Lazarus did recognize that

> woman is entering to-day into a new consciousness, a new knowledge and experience of herself and of the world; restless, impatient to throw off old restraint and allegiance, in order that she may test and prove her own powers and freedom . . . that she may more fully know herself—her own, her real, her whole self, not in another, but in herself. (9–10)

Ironically, Lazarus's reiteration of traditional myths did little to help women know themselves more fully; in reality, her pamphlet projected an image of a woman, and Woman, as a domestic creature whose only "test" of her "power and freedom" came through self-abnegation. Also ironic is the fact that Lazarus, an independent and, in many ways, unusual woman, voiced traditional mandates for "womanliness." Like Catharine Beecher, Lazarus justified herself by explicitly demonstrating that she knew the rules, that she could deliver a fully coherent manifesto on the traditional roles for women. Her words, rather than her actions, would insure her own "womanliness."

The extended essay on Dreyfus is interesting not only for its statements about women but also because Dreyfus was Jewish. Although Lazarus did not dwell on this shared identity, she concluded her "appreciation" by discussing anti-Semitism as well as Alfred Dreyfus's Jewishness. But she then quickly proclaimed that Madame Dreyfus would be remembered not because she was Jewish but because she was a "starry soul, who takes her place among the Immortals, among those 'not born to die' " (54). A Jewish woman could, Lazarus seems to have been suggesting both here and in "Emma Lazarus," fulfill all of the requirements of proper womanhood, and even stand as a perfect model of that ideal. Encoding her own need for acceptance through the veil of Dreyfus's and sister Emma's images, Lazarus sought that coveted space where she could be both woman and Jew.

Like Morais and Cohen, Lazarus looked to other women who had discovered passageways through the maze of gender myths. Although the role models proved disappointing as often as they proved helpful, the process of writing about other women seems to have provided a method for these authors to explore and even solidify their own attitudes. Manifesting both an "anxiety of authorship" as well as an "anxiety of influence," these metaphoric daughters gingerly criticized their mothers even as they thanked them for having the courage to expose themselves in the public arena of American authorship.

As the above examples have demonstrated, writing by American Jewish women was neither uniform nor constant. However, what much of this writing has in common is a shared perception and acceptance of gender roles. Yet some Jewish women did voice frustration and displeasure with their assigned roles. In this way they resembled the growing number of non-Jewish women who began to argue for women's rights. Ernestine Louise Rose was the most active of these Jewish women, delivering speeches at the women's rights convention in Syracuse in 1852, as well as in smaller meetings such as The People's Sunday Meeting of Boston in 1851. Rose repeatedly argued that women were created the equals of men and therefore should not be deprived of their rights in marriage or politics.

While other Jewish women might have agreed with Rose, they rarely, if ever, articulated their feelings as vociferously or as publicly. Louisa B.

Hart, for example, expressed impatient displeasure with gender inequality, but it was her diary, rather than an assembly, which heard her opinions. In an 1842 entry she wrote,

> Woman's fate, and woman's feelings, how often descanted on, how rarely understood! Man, like the bee, wanders from flower to flower; one is beautiful to his eye, another by her mental graces awakens his intellectuality, thus gratifying, because developing his own hidden stores. . . . Credulous being! Know that the very power to choose prevents his choice; the beauty that caught his eye now fails; the mind that incited his has lost its inspiration . . . all, all have ceased to interest, because there remain yet unwon, things as beauteous and lovely. What heeds he that the sting remains behind? Thou art a woman, and 'tis thy fate to endure; wherefore this power give to man if he may not exercise it? . . . All, all are prostrate at the shrine of man's caprice, of man's vanity, but he heeds it not; 'tis woman's province to be sought, 'tis man's privilege to woo, to win, and to leave her to her fate. (8:4, 1)

Hart's bitter words convey not the exalted glory of being a True Woman or a Mother in Israel but, rather, the slave-like role of a woman whose victimization was fated and therefore immutable. As unusual as these words sound, their very existence suggests that Jewish American women of the mid-nineteenth century were neither satisfied with, nor blindly accepting of, gender myths. Even if Hart's outpouring sprang from personal disappointments, her experiences could not have been entirely unique, and her biting rhetoric should be heard as a vivid enunciation of what other women also felt but did not so dramatically articulate.

More typically, as most of this study makes clear, the American Jewish woman writer sought compromise, not controversy. Interested in reassuring herself and others that she deserved the appellation American and Jew, she attempted to find space for herself between the myth of the Mother in Israel and of the True Woman. Often she clung to old coded patterns of Jewish womanhood, while occasionally she reached for newer, American patterns, particularly when she examined her gender. Never did she forget, however, that hers was a unique identity, strengthened and enriched by its dual nature.

V.

American and
Jewish Nationalities

The great majority of nineteenth-century American Jewish women publicly and self-consciously sought a passport that carried dual citizenship. As cumbersome as it might have been, in the ideal it provided its bearers with an identity that reconciled the demands placed on them by their two nations. The nature of these demands as well as the processes by which the Jewish women inscribed their complex identities into a variety of public and private texts constitute this chapter's theme. These processes fall roughly into three groups: emphasis on one's American identity; emphasis on one's Jewish identity; giving equal weight to both. It should be noted that even with the first two, the writers were always conscious of their multiple loyalties, and of their gender. This chapter, unlike those which precede and follow it, does not attempt to provide chronological developments, except in the first section.

The women who celebrated their American identities often invoked the myths of freedom, tolerance, and opportunity—the myths which seem to distinguish America from other nations. Often they called upon these myths to reassure other Americans that they understood and appreciated their civil rights and that they were loyal citizens. Intimately connected with these feelings of loyalty were strong feelings that America, the land of liberty and choices, should not harbor anti-Semitism. Writers who emphasized the merits of Judaism warned the American Jewish community not to ignore, and subsequently lose, its Jewishness. Myths about Jewish perseverance, wisdom born of persecution, and "Diasporic" national identity formed a backdrop for many of their writings. And the Jewish women who attempted to fuse the American and Jewish components of their identities pondered intermarriage, leading a Jewish life which was American-like, and even a new religion which combined the best elements of Judaism and American Christianity.

For nineteenth-century American Jews, the issue of nationality raised complex questions about loyalty and identity: Could one be American and Jewish at the same time? Could one always show equal loyalty to both? Was Judaism a race or a religion? What did it mean to be a citizen of a nation which had no geographic boundaries, or of one which did? Did the German and Sephardic Jews really share with the Eastern European Jews a common national identity? Was America the new Israel, the promised land, an end to the Diaspora?

Hovering around many of these questions is a feeling of unease—an "anxiety of displacement"; that is, the women within the tradition experienced a sense of exile even on their American "native ground." Constantly reminded that they were not Anglo-Saxon Protestants, they experienced a feeling of displacement because they were "other" as Jews (and as women). In most cases, the anxiety compelled them to work diligently to establish for themselves and their families a secure place in America.

The 1899 *A Tent of Grace* by Adelina Cohnfeldt Lust (b. 1860) provides an excellent starting point for this chapter; with references to American freedom, Jewish pride, anti-Semitism, and intermarriage, it creatively represents the "anxiety of displacement" as well as the larger theme of American and Jewish loyalties.[1] Although set in mid-nineteenth-century Germany, the characters' problems are, not coincidentally, similar to those of late nineteenth-century American Jews. The protagonist of the novel, Henrietta (Jetta) Cagena, a young Jewish woman, experiences tremendous violence in her brief life. After the death of her mother, Jetta (age twelve) is sent out into the world by her stepfather. While selling animal pelts, she is brutally attacked by non-Jewish children. Later, an ignorant, anti-Semitic mob led by the same children now grown up makes Jetta into a scapegoat for the death of Lieschen, a little girl whom Jetta had actually loved.

In the interval between the two attacks, Jetta has lived with the kindly Christian family, the Felderns. Herr Feldern, an open-minded pastor, explains to Jetta, and to the reader, that Judaism is:

> "part and parcel of thyself, as much as the blood which goes to nourish thy heart; nay, more so, because 't is the spiritual part of thee, that which never dies,—thy passport to the Almighty One, who knows of all thy doings. 'T is a thing of ancestry, of heredity, of circumstances. . . . 'T is thy sacred, inalienable right." (159)

Herr Pastor Feldern also tells Jetta that she must always conduct herself properly so as not to bring blame upon herself or her community (160). Through this "objective" non-Jewish spiritual advisor, Lust warned American Jewish readers that Judaism is both a liability and a privilege.

Later, the novel offers another warning, this time through a bourgeois, secular Jewish character. Herr Goldman, a wealthy urban Jew who wants to marry Jetta, regarded his father's religious aspirations with tolerant contempt. He looked upon them as relics of the past and calculated to foster prejudice. . . . Creed and religion were synonymous terms with him. . . . The faith which consoles, the spirituality which ennobles and refines, makes one suffer and endure, had no place in his calculations. The forms and ceremonies which were the darlings of his father's heart he regarded as remnants of old-time superstitions. . . . He had ideals, but no spirituality. (210)

Like a number of late nineteenth-century American Jews, Goldman grows impatient with the rituals and observances of Judaism. Not understanding the sacredness of Judaism's history or the importance of its continuance, he views his creed as simply a religion, easily attended to, or even dismissed. However, Jetta's experiences brutally remind us of the "anxiety of displacement"—that the non-Jewish world always sees a Jew as a Jew, regardless of his/her level of Jewish observance. The novel's events implicitly reprimanded American Jews for their aversion to their being Jewish and warned them of the dangers of complacency and ignorance.

Intertwined with the question of Jewish identity is the issue of intermarriage. *A Tent of Grace* raises the issue through Jetta and the Feldern son, Fritz, who fall in love and want to marry. He thinks they can minimalize their religious difference, but she knows differently:

"You, the Christian, I the Jewess? . . . As long as we depend upon and mingle with our fellow creatures we, too, are penned within those narrow confines. . . . I should be a millstone around your neck. . . . Your career [as a physician] . . . would be ruined forever. . . . Strong as you may be in your love and loyal to its duties, great as may be your courage to withstand and your resolve to conquer, you would inevitably go under. And I—I should have the agony of seeing you sink, my ever-restless conscience repeating the heartbreaking refrain, ' 'Tis thy work; thou, thou hast done this.' " (277)

It is not so much the conflict between the husband and wife that militates against intermarriage, but, rather, the hostility of the outside world. And as Jetta's life demonstrates, that world can be cruel, and even savage, when it comes to Jews. The one place which seems to offer Fritz and Jetta a chance for happiness lies across the ocean, in America, " 'where liberty of thought and action prevails—where life may be begun anew and made hallowed and sweet by our own efforts' " (366). Despite the reality that many American Jews disapproved of intermarriage, the figurative "America" and its myths of liberty and new beginnings offered refuge for those seeking personal and spiritual freedom.

A Tent of Grace does not raise questions of gender; Jetta's predicament arises from her being Jewish rather than her being female. It is the commentary on the meaning of being a Jew in a potentially anti-Semitic world, the warning against complacency, the references to the choices America offers, and the investigation of intermarriage that create the novel's interest and drama. Although the cruelty of non-Jewish bigots is more graphic than in other texts, the protagonist's feelings of displacement are not unique and indeed help define the tradition of the nineteenth-century American Jewish woman writer.

American Nationality

It should not surprise us that a large number of American Jewish women writers expressed pride in their American identities and that this pride often took the form of passionate gratitude to America for welcoming Jews. However, below the surface lurked the more nervous "anxiety of displacement." Penina Moise's 1820 paean, "To Persecuted Foreigners," conveys both the pride and the nervousness:

> Fly from the soil whose desolating creed,
> Outraging faith, makes human victims bleed.
> Welcome! where every Muse has reared a shrine,
> The aspect of wild Freedom to refine.
>
> Upon OUR Chieftain's brow no crown appears;
> No gems are mingled with his silver hairs.
> Enough that Laurels bloom amid its snows,
> Enriched with these, the sage all else foregoes.
>
> If thou are one of that oppressed race,
> Whose name's a proverb, and whose lot's disgrace,
> Brave the Atlantic—Hope's broad anchor weigh,
> A Western Sun will gild your future day.
>
> Zeal is not blind in this our temp'rate soil;
> She has no scourge to make the soul recoil.
> Her darkness vanished when our stars did flash;
> Her red arm, grasped by Reason, dropt the lash.
>
> Our Union, Liberty and Peace imports,
> Stampt on our standards, graven on our hearts,
> The first, from crush'd Ambition's ruin rose,
> The last, on Victory's field spontaneous grows.
>
> Rise, then, elastic from Oppression's tread,
> Come and repose on Plenty's flowery bed.

Oh! not as Strangers shall your welcome be,
Come to the homes and bosoms of the free.

(*Secular* 177)

At first glance, the poem offers an unambivalent portrait of what America represents and offers. It can be felt as a sincere celebration of American democracy and tolerance. A poem that so passionately and publicly expresses its sentiment, however, might be carrying another encoded message, about insecurity and displacement. By reading through the code, we can see how Moise used her loud proclamation to reassure both herself and her audience that America truly insures liberty and justice for all, and that the poem provided a means for the author to inscribe herself as an American even on the grammatical level of repeating the inclusive pronoun "our." The fact that Moise wrote the poem in 1820 should remind us of the irony that even in the half century following the establishment of the "more perfect union," Jews as well as other displaced people had to work very hard to establish their right to an American identity.

The letters which Rachel Mordecai Lazarus (1788–1838) sent to Maria Edgeworth between 1815 and 1838 also reveal the "anxiety of displacement" percolating below the surface calm of pride and gratitude. The correspondence actually began when Lazarus, then a teacher in her father's "academy for young ladies," wrote to suggest that Edgeworth had depicted the character Mordecai in her novel *The Absentee* (1812) as a negatively stereotypical Jew. Although Lazarus did not know Edgeworth, she trusted that her letter would find a sympathetic listener rather than a resentful or hostile one, and she felt confident enough in her Jewish identity to challenge Edgeworth's caricature. Lazarus was born in Virginia to Jacob Mordecai and Judith Myers. In 1821 she married Aaron Marks Lazarus (a businessman and widower with seven children); they had three daughters and one son.

As part of her challenge to Edgeworth, Lazarus explained that "in this happy country [the United States], where religious distinctions are scarcely known, where character and talents are all sufficient to attain advancement, we find the Jews to form a respectable part of the community" (MacDonald 6). Having lived in Warrenton and Wilmington, North Carolina, she and her friends of "persuasions different from her own" learned to look "upon the variations of the other as things of course—differences which take place in every society" (MacDonald 6). Thirteen years later, in 1828, Lazarus again expressed satisfaction with the status of Jews in her town:

> There is such a spirit of unity and benevolence among us [townspeople of Wilmington] as ought to exist between virtuous members of the same community, and tho' many feel and even express regret at the

difference of religious sentiment which exists between us, it proves no
barrier to mutual kind offices and sincere regard. (MacDonald 163)

Perhaps in antebellum North Carolina Jews were as welcome as Lazarus
suggests. However, her religious difference *was* noted, if not condemned;
indeed, the "regret" which the other Wilmington inhabitants expressed
might have emanated from anti-Semitic feelings that Lazarus did not
want to confront. Bent on preserving an image of the unified and benevolent American town whose citizens lived together harmoniously, she
created with her words a "sentence of her own"—a world that fully
accepted her as Jew.

From Lazarus's angle of vision, America deserved accolades for its
tolerance and freedom. In 1823, she had explained to Edgeworth that she
was gratified

> to remark the spirit of liberality publicly evinced towards our Sect. An
> old Law of the State of Maryland excludes by means of a test act any
> Israelite from holding an office of trust or profit. It has been attempted
> during several sessions to abrogate this law. A candidate lately pub-
> lished a letter to his constituents stating that he should vote against
> the repeal. The illiberal spirit evinced in his mode of reasoning
> seemed to excite general indignation and elicited a number of well-
> written replies, signed by members of every Christian Sect, in which
> ample justice is done to ours. (MacDonald 46)

Like Moise, Lazarus used her words to construct an ideal America where
Jew and non-Jew accepted each other in spite of differences. Indeed, this
belief in a tolerant world had permitted Lazarus to write to Edgeworth in
the first place.

Fifty years later, Louisa Hart (who had written so bitterly of male
callousness) similarly praised America for its acceptance of Jews. On the
occasion of America's centennial celebration, Hart wrote to a friend,

> Who, more than we, the Israelites, should rejoice and be glad at the
> glory and greatness of this brave land? . . . So when Ferdinand and
> Isabella ordered the expulsion of the Jews from their realms, they also,
> in assisting through Columbus the discovery of this continent, were
> involuntarily providing them with a refuge, a home, a country. Thus
> God frustrates the evil, bestows the good. . . . Let us then rejoice, and
> be glad to commemorate the Centennial of a country for the op-
> pressed of all nations. (8:14, 2)

Hart recognized her privileged status as an *American* Jew, and like Emma
Lazarus in her poem "1492," she expressed gratitude to the nation which
had proven Ferdinand and Isabella wrong in their estimation of Jews.

Unfortunately, we do not know to whom Hart wrote the letter. If the recipient were a non-Jew, Hart's motivation might have been similar to Moise's and Lazarus's—assure Americans of your belief in the nation. On the other hand, if Hart sent this to a co-religionist, she might have been more ingenuously expressing honest gratitude for America's acceptance of persecuted people. Little seems to have changed over fifty years; in the 1870s, as in the 1820s, a woman verbally constructed an "America" which was a haven of tolerance for herself and other Jews.

A number of women created such protected space through a synthesis of their loyal American and Mother in Israel identities. That is, in order to dispel the stereotypes and racist sentiments which had the potential to destroy everything their families had achieved in America, some Jewish women wielded the pen of education, explaining to non-Jewish audiences the true nature of Jews and the reasons for anti-Semitism's malevolent existence. One such woman was Nina Morais (Cohen) whose 1881 "Jewish Ostracism in America" *(The North American Review)* poses the difficult question, "Why is the Jew still excluded from the brotherhood of humanity?" (265). More specifically, Morais investigated discrimination against Jews in America; without being hostile or antagonistic, she demonstrated that both the restrictions against transacting business on Sunday and the scheduling of school exams on Jewish holidays, for example, indirectly punished Jews for their religious beliefs (268).

These discriminatory practices seemed particularly irksome and even ironic since

> America has no extenuation for antipathy to the stranger. The American people is not a nation that traces a long line of ancestry to an aboriginal root. America is the scrap-bag of the world. . . . The American Revolution was a union of foreigners. . . . The American Constitution['s]. . . . citizen was the man, not the sectarian. Whether brought about by the course of progress, or by the exigency of the times, the American Constitution was the only resource of a nation of foreigners. American hatred of the foreigner is a paradox. (266)

Despite this paradox, the fact remained that Americans viewed the Jew as "a specimen of a whole race whose members are identically of the same kind" (269). To correct this distorted image, Morais asked that Jews be accepted as individuals with individual responsibilities (275).

Throughout her analysis, Morais remained optimistic that Jews would find their deserved place in America. The conclusion of the essay projects this optimism in a rhapsodic vision of Jewish and American interconnectedness:

> Jewish development in America is yet young—a little younger than the life of America itself. While American institutions are yet in a

molten state, the particular genius of the Hebrew has not had time to
take upon itself an American form. But there lie in the Jewish blood
the mental and moral possibilities which gave rise to prophets and
thinkers. It will infuse into the practical life of our new republic the
intellectual warmth of the sunlands. The imagination of the Orient
shall interpret the rush of Mississippi waters; the music of the Orient
shall swell with the voices of Niagara's cataract. (275)

It is difficult to read such lavish prose without hearing the crescendo of
an orchestra in the background. Despite its dramatic quality, however, the
passage drives home the argument of the essay: Americans must learn to
overcome their negative reactions to Jews and to appreciate the precious
qualities of Jews. The passage also forecasts for its Jewish readers a time
when they will be able to embrace both of their identities with pride. In
writing this essay, Morais fulfilled her role as a Mother in Israel; by both
educating non-Jews and inspiring Jews, she "fought" for the preservation
of Judaism.

Alice Hyneman Rhine (Sotheran), niece of Rebekah Hyneman, also
performed as a Mother in Israel when she wrote "Race Prejudice at
Summer Resorts" for *The Forum* (1887).[2] As the title of her article suggests, Rhine used the fact that Jews were being denied accommodations in
American hotels as a springboard for a discussion of anti-Semitism. She
accused Henry Hilton of initiating an open display of anti-Jewish sentiment when he prohibited Joseph Seligman from staying in his Grand
Union Hotel in Saratoga, New York (523). Despite the outcry from Jewish
and non-Jewish Americans alike, other hotel proprietors began to follow
Hilton's lead (524).

Rhine systematically announced, and then brought evidence against,
anti-Semitic claims "In seeking reasons for this sweeping ostracism"
(525). The complaint that Jews " 'swarm everywhere,' " for example, "is
ridiculous in the extreme" because "according to the latest statistics, the
whole number of Israelites, in a population of fifty-five million, is two
hundred and fifty thousand . . . [and they] are scattered all over the
country" (526). Charges of being irreverent as well as "ostentatious and
parsimonious" at the same time were as absurd as being too numerous.
The real problem

has its root far deeper than any dislike of [the Jew's] external or
adventitious qualities. The Christian dislike has its remoter historic
cause in the obstinacy with which Jews deny the Messiahship of
Jesus. . . . So the refusal of the Jews to accept the divinity of Christ,
with their terrible responsibility for the crucifixion, is an ever-present
ground of dislike in the Christian mind. (529)

At the risk of alienating her Christian readers, Rhine, Deborah-like in her
warrior stance, charged into the middle of the fray to confront one of the

most sensitive tension points between Jew and Christian—tension which had been mounting since news of the Russian pogroms began circulating in the early 1880s.

In the conclusion of the essay, Rhine once again put the onus of responsibility for anti-Semitism on non-Jews:

> In all civilizations, it has been said, "The Jew must be of gold to pass for silver," but when he is of thrice refined gold he is still "only a Jew." For centuries it has been impossible to say a man is a Jew without the intention to reproach him for being a Jew. For the obliteration of a prejudice so unjust the Israelite can only look forward with hope to a time when a broader culture shall prevail among his Christian fellow-men. (531)

Until that day, when Christians understand and accept Jews, "Israelites" will remain "sensible" and not "show any signs of displeasure at . . . manifestations of prejudice. Injured as they must feel themselves to be, they accept the situation and do the best they can" (530). Rhine did the best she could by exposing the part Christians (Russian as well American?) had played in promoting anti-Semitic sentiment. Not as passive as she seems to have urged other Jews to be, she openly criticized Christians for harboring anti-Semitic feelings; her outspokenness indicates real fear and anger, as well as belief in America's freedoms, particularly of religion and speech.

As one might expect, Morais's and Rhine's direct approach to prejudice and discrimination was not the only one. As Rachel Lazarus's coded words suggest, one could appear to ignore anti-Semitism. Or one could incorporate it into a religious test, as Rhine did in "Lines," a poem that predates "Race Prejudice." "Lines," published in *The Occident* in 1858, was "Written on hearing a learned Lawyer say in Court that 'the Jews were hated alike by God and man.'" The first two stanzas reaffirm the enduring faith of "Israel's race," while the last two stanzas outline the reward for that faith:

> Say not that we are cut off by Thee, Guardian of Israel's race;
> Despite of all our waywardness, in *Thy* love we hold a place;
> And in our dark and bitter hours, we still can turn to Thee;
> For guidance or for comfort, when all earthly pleasures flee.
>
> Not utterly abhorred by Thee!—man cannot trace Thy ways,
> Nor reach into Thy hidden path, Oh Thou of ancient days.
> And must we still be taunted, and told we are forgot,
> Contemned alike by Thee and man, our destiny a blot?
>
> Believe it not, believe it not! we are God's chosen still,
> To whom He hath in mercy given the records of his will!

To whom He hath in kindness said, "Fear not, for thou art mine,
I have called thee by my holy name, and glory shall be thine."

Glory, aye, Israel! as of old; Jerusalem restored,
Her temple sending forth its prayers and incense to the Lord.
Freed from the oppressor's galling yoke, poor victim of his hate,
Thy children shall rejoice, as once they mourned their bitter fate.

Clarksville, Texas.

After experiencing an "anxiety of displacement" when her fellow Americans exhibited anti-Semitism, Rhine transformed her doubt and anger into affirmation and pride. Proud of being an American, but equally proud of being a Jew, Rhine was determined to find a space in which she could honor both of her nations. Like many other American Jews, she staunchly supported the ideal of American freedom despite, and because of, her own experiences with prejudice.

Jewish Belief and Practices

Toward the end of the nineteenth century, some orthodox Jewish editors and other prominent Jews expressed concern that the American Jewish community was weakening in regard to observance of rituals and laws. It seemed that the more assimilated Jews became, the less they attended synagogue or observed religious holidays. At the same time, great numbers of Eastern European Jewish immigrants began arriving after the Russian pogroms of 1881. The Americanized Jewish women of German and Sephardic descent knew that they were linked to these "foreigners" by unbreakable bonds of religious laws and traditions, yet they shuddered at their proximity. Concerned with maintaining their middle-class status and proving their American nationality, the "uptown" ladies struggled to reconcile their racial and class loyalties.[3]

Despite this intra-Jewish tension, the theme of Jewish pride is prominent in the tradition of American Jewish women writers. Indeed, many of the writings already presented in this volume express either explicitly or implicitly the author's positive feelings about her Jewish identity. Bound up with these feelings was the woman's belief in the myth which assigned to Mothers in Israel the responsibility to keep Judaism alive, a particularly significant role in America where a secular life was possible and even advantageous in certain situations. Several Jewish women, wielding the Mother in Israel's pen of education and reform, argued that self-deceiving complacency which allowed American Jews to ignore anti-Semitic sentiments in the earlier decades of the century could no longer serve as protection against more overt manifestations of prejudice.

In order to examine the intricacies of the authors' "Jewish belief and practices," I have constructed the following section along a continuum, from those writings that express positive images of Judaism but do not ask for anything from their audiences, to those writings that beckon Jewish readers to renew their appreciation for Jewish values and rituals. I place Adah Isaacs Menken (1835–1868) at one end of the continuum not because she ignored her audiences, but because she played to those audiences as an actor, not as a Jew.[4] For Menken, the role of actress helped shape the role of Jew. Whether or not she was born Jewish, she embraced Judaism as a powerful source of emotions which she then used on the stage.[5]

A flamboyant theater figure, Menken gained notoriety for her role as "The Naked Lady"—playing Mazeppa, she appeared on stage in flesh-colored tights and strapped to the side of a horse. Menken's private life also attracted attention; she married four times, once or twice before legal divorces were completed, and presumably enjoyed a number of affairs with men such as Alexander Dumas and Algernon Swinburne. A week after Menken's death in 1868, a volume of her poems, *Infelicia*, appeared; the book was dedicated to Charles Dickens.[6] Printed by four different British and American firms in 1868 alone, America's J. B. Lippincott issued the volume ten times between 1868 and 1902. During her lifetime, Menken also contributed poems to *The Israelite* and *Jewish Messenger*.

"Judith," a poem included in *Infelicia*, reveals Menken's histrionic and emotional understanding of Judaism. After proclaiming in part 1 of the poem, "I see the dawn that heralds to my waiting soul the advent of power," Judith goes on in part 3:

Stand back!
I am no Magdalene waiting to kiss the hem of your garment.
It is mid-day.
See ye not what is written on my forehead?
I am Judith!
I wait for the head of my Holofernes!
Ere the last tremble of the conscious death-agony shall have
    shuddered, I will show it to ye with the long black hair clinging to
    the glazed eyes, and the great mouth opened in search of voice, and
    the strong throat all hot and reeking with blood, that will thrill me
    with wild unspeakable joy as it courses down my bare body and
    dabbles my cold feet!
My sensuous soul will quake with the burden of so much bliss.
Oh, what wild passionate kisses will I draw up from that bleeding
    mouth!
I will strangle this pallid throat of mine on the sweet blood!
I will revel in my passion.

At midnight I will feast on it in the darkness.
For it was that which thrilled its crimson tides of reckless passion
　　through the blue veins of my life, and made them leap up in the
　　wild sweetness of Love and agony of Revenge!
I am starving for this feast.
Oh forget not that I am Judith!
And I know where sleeps Holofernes.

Unlike the Old Testament's figure, Menken's Judith violently revels in blood and gore. And unlike Hyneman's timidly courageous "Female Scriptural Character," Menken's character derives power from sexual passion as well as from national pride. This hero plays to an audience, reciting a climactic soliloquy at the end of a moving scene. Concerned less with Judith's faith and more with her dramatic triumph, Menken, the poet and actor, saw in the hero the potential for a moving part she herself wanted to perform.

Many of the other poems in *Infelicia* exhibit the same type of emotional display. Even "Hear O Israel" and the Civil War poem, "Pro Patria," depend on emotionalism for their impact. In the former, the prophet Jeremiah exclaims in the last lines of the poem,

> Look at these pale hands and frail arms, that have rent asunder the
> 　　welded chains that an army of the Philistines bound about me!
> But the God of all Israel set His seal of fire on my breast, and
> 　　lighted up, with inspiration, the soul that pants for the Freedom
> 　　of a nation!
> With eager wings she fluttered above the blood-stained bayonet-
> 　　points of the millions, who are trampling upon the strong
> 　　throats of God's people.
> 　　　　　　　　　Rise up, brave hearts!
> The sentry cries: "All's well!" from Hope's tower!
> Fling out your banners of Right!
> The watch fire grows brighter!
> 　　　　　　　All's well! All's well!
> 　　　　　　　Courage! Courage!
> The Lord of Hosts is in the field,
> The God of Jacob is our shield!

Unconcerned with anachronistic lapses, Menken created highly dramatic renditions of religious and secular events. Utilizing the linguistic codes of drama (perhaps melodrama), she imbued her poetry and her faith with the passion of her stage life. And by identifying herself as a Jew, she found an audience for her poetry in Jewish newspapers. Her use of Judaism and of audiences emanated from a self-absorbed theatrical persona rather than from a sense of religious conviction or womanly responsibility.

Less self-interested than Menken, Octavia Harby Moses and Penina

Moise wrote poems which take Jewish events as their subjects and convey positive images of Judaism. Moses's "Lines for the Day of Atonement and Ten Penitential Days (Sept. 28, 1860)," for example, stresses the sacredness of Yom Kippur. The poem begins,

> From the trouble and the turmoil,
> From the busy walks of Life,
> From the accents soft of Pleasure,
> And the struggles fierce of Strife,
> Turn aside, oh! restless mortal,
> Calm awhile thine eager soul,
> Pause, ere yet Death's stern-browed Angel
> Thee and time, shall both control.

The last stanza reads:

> Strive with earnest, strong endeavor
> Thought as well to act, to guard.
> Aid the weak, the sorrowing comfort,
> Loving others, love thy God!
> Thus before His awful presence
> Let thy great Atonement be,
> Mercy's wings shall shield His splendor,
> While His peace descends on thee.

Although these lines articulate what sound like sentimental Christian conventions (expressing love for God through love for other human beings, attaining peace through the admission of sins committed and atoned for), they, and the other four stanzas of the poem, proclaim gratitude for the Jewish Day of Atonement—for the annual opportunity to reflect upon one's transgressions. Moses never doubted the value of this uniquely Jewish method for admitting, accepting, and atoning for sin.

Similarly, Moise did not allow doubt to intrude upon her stern portrait of Judaism in "Lines. On the Following Inscription Fronting the New Synagogue. 'Know Before Whom Thou Standest.'" However, this poem does take a more "reformist" stance than Moses's, as stanzas one, two, eight, and nine reveal:

> A voice of power from the elder time
>   A voice that homage from the Earth commandeth,
> On Israel calls with energy sublime,
>   To know in whose dread presence he here standeth.
>
> It bids him at the portal put away
>   His sandal sullied o'er with sordid dust;

In godliness his spirit to array
  Or ere he seeks the merciful and just.

. . . .

Enter not lightly then the house of prayer,
  Nor hymn with lip of guile the praise of God;
Balm will be found for meek contrition there
  For contumacy, an impeding rod.

Behold yon testimonial tablets traced
  By Judah's providence with outstretched hand
List to the voice that thunders from the waste
  "Know ye, before whose majesty ye stand!"

(Sewlar 275–76)

Further on the continuum than Moses's "Lines for the Day of Atonement," this poem reminds its readers that the Jewish God who sternly demands compliance punishes those who do not obey. It does not, however, offer guidance on how to retrace one's steps to this God, nor does it lend sympathy to those who have lost their way. It stresses the power of Judaism and its God.

Sarah Cohen's 1847 "The Last Plague," published in *The Occident and American Jewish Advocate,* also presents a powerful Jewish God who punishes non-believers.[7] Through a historical dramatization of the tenth plague (death of the firstborn Egyptian son), this sketch presents the Egyptian priests as foolish in their desire for power, and Pharaoh himself as fickle, persuaded by these priests not to heed Moses's warnings. While grief-stricken Egyptians crowd the streets and storm the palace, the Israelites "with thanksgivings and songs of praise to the God of all worlds for their deliverance . . . turn for ever their steps from the land of their hard captivity" (105). Containing only a hazy plot and characters, the incidents in the sketch serve to expose the Egyptians' perfidy and the Jews' faithfulness to their God. Through this thinly veiled code, "The Last Plague" asked Jewish readers to reconsider the historical significance of their heritage and to return, if "wandering," to their faith and their powerful God.

Hyneman's "Israel's Trust" also indirectly asks its readers to accept their Jewish identities. In stanzas three through six, the speaker proclaims,

Thine, wholly Thine, through every change,
  Through scorn, and agony, and shame!
Though aliens in every land
  Our heritage is still the same.

Borne down beneath insulting foes,

Defamed, dishonored, and oppressed,
Our country fallen and desolate,
Our name a by-word and a jest—

Still are we Thine—as wholly Thine
As when Judea's trumpets' tone
Breathed proud defiance to her foes,
And nations knelt before her throne.

We are thine own; we cling to Thee
As clings the tendril to the vine;
Oh! 'mid the world's bewildering maze,
Still keep us Thine, for ever Thine!

(*Leper* 142–43, stanzas 3–6)

Although the poem includes references to the "scorn, and agony, and shame" of being a Jew, it underlines the "proud defiance" associated with remaining faithful to God and to Judaism. Like Rhine's poem "Lines," "Israel's Trust" turns opprobrium into a test of devotion, and it assumes that all Jews will want to pass the test. This inclusive rhetoric subtly casts a net for Jewish readers even as it creates an almost inviolable image of Jewish devotion.

Another one of Hyneman's poems from *The Leper*, "The Chosen," goes a step further in commanding its Jewish readers:

Go forth erect and fearless, with God's impress on thy brow,
  The promise of His changeless love within thy trusting heart;
Proud nations shall revere thy might, and crowned heads shall bow,
  And acknowledge thy supremacy, all kingly as thou art!

(stanza 1)

A stanza later it continues:

Tho' the oppressor's hand be on thee, yet fearlessly pass on—
  Tho' temptations may surround thee, and bewildering meteors shine—
A strong right arm is guiding thee, until the goal is won;
  Oh! who would not brave perils for a heritage like thine?

And tho' thou drain'st in agony, the cup of grief and shame,
  While dark tempests low'r around thee, and poison'd shafts are hurl'd—
The time will come, forsaken one, when thy insulted name
  Will be held a badge of honor by the mightiest in the world.

The time is not far distant when thy light will shine once more,
  As in thy days of freedom, when thy proudest deeds were done;

And thy splendor shall return to thee far brighter than of yore—
Press thou but nobly to thy task, and fearlessly pass on.

                                        (110–11, stanzas 3–5)

In no uncertain terms, the poem directs its Jewish readers to bear the brunt of prejudice because the "time will come" when the title Jew will be a "badge of honor." Utilizing the code of direct and honest address, it unquestionably urges Jews to persevere and thereby find a great reward, although it does not offer tangible advice about how to remain faithful.

In "The Lost Diamond," which appeared in *The Occident* in 1862, Hyneman offered the concrete guidance she only alluded to in "The Chosen." The story's series of loosely related episodes depicts, among other things, how one daughter, Esther, is nursed after an accident by a rich Christian, Mrs. Eldridge, who wants to adopt and convert Esther and will pay the Melchoir family handsomely for the transaction, while another daughter, Anna, is loved by and loves an apparently Christian doctor, Lascelle, who turns out to be Jewish. The story ends happily with everyone well provided for.

Throughout, the virtues of Jewish family life are exaggerated. No Melchoir ever strays from Judaism or the family; it would be impossible to deny one without destroying the other. Esther feels that she cannot relinquish her faith, even for her family's economic well-being through Mrs. Eldridge's proposal, and Anna knows in her heart and mind that she cannot marry a non-Jewish man. Hyneman's story depends on familiar codes which emphasize the pride, family cohesiveness, honesty, and unswerving devotion of Jews. It informs its readers that poverty is insignificant when measured against a loving family and the stability of Judaism, as well as that family and Judaism are intricately connected. "The Lost Diamond" must have awakened pride in Jewish readers by accentuating the noble components of Judaism and celebrating Jewish family life.

In a much more subtle way, Miriam del Banco's "Friday Night" (1888) also functions to reinforce Jewish family values through sentimentality. The pleasing picture of a warm hearthside where weekly cares melt away seems to have been designed to entice Jewish readers of the Reform *Menorah* to observe Jewish customs.

Friday night! come draw the curtain;
I am weary with the week;
Sit before the grate-fire with me.
And together let us speak;
Put aside your books and papers,—
It is neither night nor day,
And the Sabbath hour approaches;
Put your endless toil away.

. . . .
Over yonder hangs a picture
Sheltered from the dancing gleam;
. . . .
See, it seems the Sabbath Spirit,
Cloth'd with pure and tender grace;

Calling to your mind the missing
Angels of our household band,
Who, on bygone Sabbath evenings,
Sat beside us, hand in hand;
Bringing back our hopes and longings,
Crowning them with light divine,
Showing us our vain endeavors
Softened by the glow of time;

Speaking of its own sweet image
As our fathers knew it best,—
Beautiful in true thanksgiving
For the day of peace and rest;
Teaching us to break the shadows,
Hovering o'er its lov'd face.
With the glowing light of fervor,
Kindled by our ancient race.

But I know I'm only dreaming,
'Tis a picture—nothing more,—
Image of some lovely maiden
Famed in song or fairy lore;
Drop the curtain, watch the fire
Till the shadows flee the light;
Rest awhile within its gleaming,
On this peaceful Sabbath night.

The poem is less concerned with describing a real situation and more with creating a familiar mood. Even its hypnotic rhythm seems aimed at soothing the world-weary Jewish readers of the *Menorah*. Although nothing explicitly tells these readers to return to Jewish customs, the poem's imagery follows Jewish codes which celebrate the Sabbath eve and its attendant family harmony and Jewish devotion.

As we move further along the continuum, we begin to see statements composed for the explicit purpose of reminding Jews how special, but also how precarious, a Jewish American identity is. In "Nationality and the Jews," for example, Nina Morais (Cohen) argued against the "conception of national character" based on racial homogeneity. In this 1892 essay, she explained to the Reform Jewish readers of *The Menorah* that the "political philosophy" which claims that "peoples of different ancestry can never form an harmonious nation; they cannot assimilate; their special characteristics are normal and ineradicable" would "be a direct impediment to all the beneficent forces which nurture a real civilization" (32).

Although the specific occasion for the essay was Russian persecution of Jews, Morais spoke also about xenophobic attitudes which persisted in America. She forcefully reminded her audience that "The idea of alienism . . . in [one's] native land . . . comes to all American Jews, when social distinctions . . . force upon the Jew the knowledge that he is among his fellow-citizens, but not of them." The American Jew, Morais continued,

> may be content to bear his yoke; he may even honor it as a badge of higher service. But his spirit cannot be submissive when he listens to the horrors of the Russian crime, and he notes the silence or the averted ear of Christianity. . . . he is made aware . . . that the Anglo-Saxon is the only native American, and that all other races are aliens. Then he reflects that perhaps the soil of his birth, the soil that holds the dust of friends of his heart, that soil so dear to him, does not claim him as her veritable child—he has no share in her motherhood. (36)

Evoking vivid images of displacement and of "native grounds," this passage exposes Morais's desire for that space between her two nations, that space which allowed for, and even supported, differentness. Not that she wanted those who were "different" to isolate themselves. Unlike Emma Lazarus, who had argued that Jews needed to become more "tribal" in order to combat anti-Semitism (*An Epistle to the Hebrews* 30), Morais claimed that "Modern existence cannot long be tribal. The destiny of mankind is cosmopolitan. . . . In spite of ourselves, we must be humanized, not tribalized. Our very word 'humanity' is all-pervasive" (34). Although they did not agree on "tribalism," both Lazarus and Morais sought the same goal: informed Jews who could assess their status in America critically, rather than naively. Non-Jewish Americans needed to overcome their prejudices, to be sure, but Jews themselves could not complacently ignore their neighbors' anti-Semitism.

Mary Cohen's "Jewish Working Girls" also addressed Jewish readers (of *The Jewish Messenger*); the directive was, maintain a united, caring Jewish community in America. Ironically, the article undermined this surface purpose by subtly reinforcing prejudices which assimilated Jews held against Eastern European Jews. For example, Cohen described the fate of many "working girls" (i.e., Eastern European young women) who left their jobs at the age of sixteen or seventeen to marry, explaining that at first, the wife's new home "is as snug and pretty as she can wish." But, she warned,

> after an interval of ten years or so, this is frequently all changed. The husband falls sick perhaps, and loses his position as clerk or salesman;

consequently, the burdens of nursing, cooking, sewing, washing, and
providing for the whole family fall entirely on the mother. . . . She,
poor woman, though she scarcely acknowledges it even to herself,
bitterly regrets her imprudence in marrying without the means necessary for support, and without the domestic knowledge which would
have enabled her to keep a clean, cheerful home for husband and
children; to make them look neat instead of slovenly; to surround
them with an atmosphere of peace and comfort instead of misery and
pauperism. (5)

Unintentionally patronizing, and naive, Cohen explained that these
"Jewish working girls" would be better off if they took positions as
domestics where they could learn how to keep house and where they
would be protected by kind employers. In addressing these potential
employers and instructors in after-work programs, Cohen pleaded, provide "these tired, discouraged workers, of your race and creed" with "love,
sympathy and counsel." "Minister to them with innocent social pleasures," she continued, and "give them knowledge instead of ignorance;
spirituality instead of indifference; faith instead of despair" (5). Such
statements reveal not only the class tension between Sephardic/German
and Eastern European Jews but also the responsibility which the Americanized Jews felt for their co-religionists. In addition, such imperatives
admonished assimilated readers to remember their own "spirituality" and
"faith."

I began this section with Adah Isaacs Menken, who seemed unconcerned with the situation or experience of other American Jews. I end it
with Emma Wolf who, in two of her novels, offered answers to difficult
questions for skeptical, assimilated American Jews. Wolf particularly
addressed the concerns of those Jews who considered Judaism a pale
religion at best and a liability to one's social and business standing at
worst. She emphasized, for one thing, that a Jew is " 'invested with certain
hereditary traits that are unconvertible. Every Jew bears in his blood the
glory, the triumph, the misery, the abjectness of Israel' " (*Other Things
Being Equal* 175). And even though that inheritance grows fainter in each
successive generation, still a Jew is a Jew, particularly to the Christian
world (175–76).

In *Heirs of Yesterday*, Wolf repeated that Jews cannot separate themselves " 'from the ancient heredity' " because " 'There is something in the
roots of every one of us, a something which has got implacably mixed
with our blood and is inseparable from it, which had made us what we are
long before oppression came near us' " (238). That "something" depends
on an intangible code of ethics that has been preserved "in ghettoes"
through the generations. It also depends on a system of belief, with God as
its keystone: " 'in the eternal flux and variety of all things, forms, and

ceremony, and dogma, God remains. . . . While God stands, the Jew stands' " (242).

Wolf's protagonist in *Heirs of Yesterday,* Jean Willard, understands the significance of such statements. This model modern American Jewish woman, who "read the daily papers and other current literature" (64), does not define her religion by a dogma, "nevertheless, she was a Jewess— having been born one," carrying in her blood the history of all Jews (64, 62). Intelligent, musical, and socially adept, the young woman never denies her Jewish identity nor tries to be anything but Jewish. She accepts her heritage as an integral part of who she is, equivalent to her sex or the color of her eyes.

In contrast, Philip May rejects Judaism as both a birthright and as religious dogma. May, the son of a German Jewish immigrant who clings to his Jewish beliefs and even to his "foreign" accent, is reluctant to acknowledge his Jewish identity both in his non-Jewish social circle as well as in his professional life as a physician. He wants to deny his background because " 'to be a Jew . . . is to be socially handicapped for life' " (35). As Wolf demonstrated through May, even the assimilated Jew did not always find easy acceptance in American society. However, although she understood May's predicament, she made clear that Jews who deny their Judaism are cowardly and/or ignorant, and Christians who are unjust to Jews are also cowardly and/or ignorant.

Eight years before *Heirs of Yesterday,* Wolf had more tentatively explored the related issues of Jewish identity and assimilation in *Other Things Being Equal* (1892). Although the characters are not so neatly identifiable as the "good Jews" and "bad Jew" of *Heirs of Yesterday,* they, too, struggle with questions of assimilation. In an early scene, for example, Jennie Lewis, cousin of the main character Ruth Levice, asks " 'What does possess your parents to mix so much with Christians?' " Ruth replies, " 'Fellow-feeling, I suppose. We all dance and talk alike; and as we do not hold services at receptions, wherein lies the difference?'." Jennie retorts that " 'There *is* a difference' " which Christians never let Jews forget (10). Later in the novel, Jennie poses another difficult question: why do you use the expression Day of Atonement rather than Yom Kippur? " 'Because 'Atonement' is English and means something to me' " (129), Ruth responds. English, and not Hebrew, or even German, was the language of assimilated Jews.

Questions such as Jennie's were not abstract meditations for many American Jews of the late nineteenth century. Indeed, a large number of these Jews resembled the Levices in socializing with non-Jews, observing few Jewish holidays, and identifying more with American society than with an ancient Hebrew race. And like the Levices, Americanized Jews were pondering the complicated question of whether a Jew should marry a non-Jew. Wolf forced the issue by having Ruth Levice fall in love with a

Christian, Dr. Herbert Kemp; she resolved the issue by maintaining that a Jew and a Christian could marry, provided each respected the other's identity. Although she did not advocate the denial of one's Judaism, even when one married a non-Jew, she refused to ignore the social problems experienced by Jews or the reality of Jews who were not comfortable with that identity.

The settings of Wolf's novels are American, and the characters are American Jews who are more the former than the latter (their names are anglicized and their habits middle-class American). Many of them struggle to resolve their feelings about being Jewish in a predominantly Christian America. Like the characters, Wolf and the other writers discussed here also sought answers to questions about the significance of a Jewish national identity. Ironically, the affirmation of that identity served to alleviate the "anxiety of displacment" by providing the much-needed sense of inclusion in a native place.

Jewish American Fusion

As Morais poetically predicted, a synthesis of the American and Jewish spirit would evolve when the "imagination of the Orient . . . interpret[ed] the rush of Mississippi waters; [and] the music of the Orient . . . swell[ed] with the voices of Niagara's cataract" ("Jewish Ostracism" 275). Jewish women proposed three methods for achieving this visionary union. The first, intermarriage, provided the Jewish partner with a convenient passport into American culture. The second, shaping one's life so that it mirrored an American's, offered a safe avenue to assimilation. And the third, a new religion that borrowed elements of both Christianity and Judaism, called traditional codes into question. With any one of these, a Jewish woman could mitigate the effects of native exile.

In nineteenth-century America, the centuries-old threat of Judaism's dissolution through intermarriage became seemingly more immediate in the face of full Jewish integration into American life. However, at the same time that many Jews opposed marriage outside the fold, others recognized and even accepted the fact that Jews who were a small minority would marry those in the majority as the natural outcome of social interaction. These intermarriages provided the Jewish partner with a neat vehicle for sustaining both her/his Jewish and American identity, assuming s/he continued to identify as a Jew.

Early in the century, Rebecca Gratz expressed strong sentiment against intermarriage.[8] In an 1819 letter addressed to her friend, Maria Fenne Hoffman, Gratz wrote, "My cherished friends and the companions of my choice have generally been worshippers of a different faith from mine—and I have not loved them less on that account. But in a family connection I have always thought conformity of religious opinions essential" (Osterweis 141). Despite this feeling, Gratz grew to love her brother's two consecutive non-Jewish wives, and she assuaged her fears when she observed that Benjamin continued to practice Jewish rituals after the marriages. In principle she opposed intermarriage, but in the personal context of family, she forsook the principle.

Almost half a century later, in the 1862 "The Lost Diamond," Hyneman permitted no leniency on the subject of intermarriage, despite the irony that her own mother, a Christian, had married a Jew. Perhaps it was *because* she was a convert that she had to be more militantly devout, particularly in a public forum. In her story, Anna Malchoir has difficulty simply admitting her amorous feelings for a non-Jewish man, trained as she has been never to marry outside Judaism. Hyneman leaves little doubt that Anna would have suffered in silence rather than act on her love and thereby unsettle the solidarity of both the Malchoir family and of the extended community of Jews.

In the final decade of the century, Wolf openly confronted intermarriage through the relationship between Ruth Levice and Herbert Kemp, a non-Jewish doctor, in *Other Things Being Equal*. More equivocal than Hyneman, Wolf (like Gratz) was willing to consider the personal ramifications of Jews and non-Jews falling in love even as she acknowledged the dangers of such unions. Through Ruth's father, Jules Levice, Wolf outlines these dangers: both the Christian and Jewish worlds would ostracize the Jewish woman (176–77) and eventually husband and wife might come to resent the other's religious difference (180, 183). Also through Jules, Wolf resolves the plot's conflict; on his deathbed, this concerned father admits that he has been narrow in his thinking and had not fully understood that we are all human in the eyes of God. The New Testament inscription for the novel, " 'And now abideth Faith, Hope, Love, these three; but the greatest of these is love,' " reinforces Jules's revelation even as it bridges the distance between Old Testament Jew and New Testament Christian.

Despite this tidy resolution, Wolf did raise some difficult questions in the novel. Herbert tells Jules, for example, " 'it was a great oversight on your part when you threw your daughter . . . into Christian society,—put her right in the way of loving or being loved by any Christian, knowing all along that such a state of affairs could lead to nothing. It was not only wrong, but, holding such views, it was cruel' " (174). Where should American Jews draw the line? Wolf implicitly asked. At socializing at all with Christians? At being escorted to the theater by them? At marrying them? Wasn't the last boundary too far if you had already crossed the others?

Unlike "The Lost Diamond," which resolved the conflict of a Jewish woman loving a non-Jewish man by simply removing the obstacle in the fairy-tale conclusion, in which Anna Malchoir's love object Dr. Lascelle reveals himself to be Jewish, *Other Things Being Equal* offered no easy solution. Wolf made it clear that her doctor is most certainly Christian and that he will not convert to Judaism; the two lovers will have to learn to live with their differences. But she also made it clear that a Jew does not lose his or her Judaism by marrying out of the faith. As Rosa Sonneschein (editor of *The American Jewess*) wrote in a review, "Orthodoxy finally yields to the power of humanity. . . . Jewish religious scruples crumble into dust when attacked by the strong impulses of the human heart. . . . 'Why should Christians and Jews not marry?' asks and answers the author, ingeniously holding out the possibility of such a union without violating religious convictions' " (1:6, 295). The fact that Sonneschein felt compelled to defend Wolf's solution to the question of intermarriage suggests that even by the end of the century American Jews could not easily accept intermarriage; while such unions did seem to provide that coveted space between American and Jewish culture, they also threatened the very existence of the Jewish nation and therefore could not function as an ideal solution to the "anxiety of displacement."

Two memoirs help illustrate the second method of fusion. One, by Emily Fechheimer Seasongood (1852–1941), exposes the ways in which assimilated Jews often mimicked American habits. Seasongood was reared within the well-established German Jewish community in Cincinnati. Tutored in German, as well as in piano, drawing, dancing, and embroidery, for a little while she also attended a school connected with the synagogue where she studied English, German, and Hebrew. When she was a child, her parents took the family to Europe to visit their ancestors' birthplaces. Her gowns were made by the most expensive dressmaker in Cincinnati after she entered society (76), and she spent summers in various watering spots. Much of her time was taken up with visiting or entertaining guests; even her honeymoon trip to Chicago, New York, and Boston consisted of visiting friends.

Seasongood's memoirs could have been written by any "lady" of the mid-nineteenth century, except for the composition of the social circle to which the writer belonged. Here was a group of German Jews leading lives that mirrored but did not seem to intersect with middle-class non-Jews. Seasongood maintained Jewish codes of behavior by studying Hebrew and following German Jewish Reform rituals. At the same time, she validated her American identity by acting according to American codes, such as calling on friends and attending balls. The next generation went even further in integrating itself into American life; Seasongood's son, Murray, born in 1878, studied law at Harvard and was elected mayor of Cincinnati in 1926.

The 1895 diary of Sarah Meyerfield Blach reveals even more than Seasongood's the mixing of American and Jewish customs. Blach spent her time traveling, making calls, receiving visitors, reading, attending the opera and theater, having dresses made, and playing cards. If she were too late for temple, she went shopping instead (np). Noting the Thanksgiving turkey and cranberry sauce on Thursday, November 28, 1895, a Chanukah party and songs on December 12, "an elegant Christmas dinner" on December 25, "Pesach cleaning" on March 25, 1896, and a " 'Seder' " on March 28, Blach indicated no discomfort with celebrating American, even Christian, and Jewish holidays. As an assimilated "modern" American Jewish woman, she participated in American middle-class activities but socialized almost entirely with other Jews and marked the Jewish holidays. Like Seasongood, she adopted certain American traditions even as she observed Jewish customs. This ability to discern and function according to the codes of both their nations permitted a large number of assimilated Jews to tolerate, and even transcend, their anxiety about displacement.

Josephine Lazarus's method for easing her anxiety—for affirming dual citizenship—was to create a new religion. In 1895 she published *The Spirit of Judaism*; consisting of six essays, some of which had been previously published or delivered as speeches, the volume raised crucial issues for Jews and about Jews. Like Morais before her, Lazarus advocated a fusion of identities, but she went further than Morais in suggesting that Judaism and Christianity could melt together into a new, universal religion.

The first essay, "The Jewish Question," which originally appeared in *The Century* (January 1892), was a call to "advanced and liberated Jews of Europe and America" although its initial audience was secular. Lazarus claimed that a "deeper current," "a more glowing impulse, and that quickening breath of the spirit" was needed to kindle the spiritual awakening and expansion of the Jewish religion into a flame (*Spirit of Judaism* 22). The way to achieve this? By blending Judaism's profound sense of "duty" with Christianity's "love"; one makes an individual moral, and the other, spiritual. When the head and heart unite, "Religion will have its full sway, and yet there will be none who persecute and none who are persecuted" (27).

In "The Outlook of Judaism," which she delivered as a lecture at the Chicago Exposition in 1893 to a Jewish audience and then included in *The Spirit of Judaism*, Lazarus explained that even in "our own free-breathing America, some 'wave' [of anti-Semitism] has come to die upon our shore" (59). Her solution for this anti-Semitism was a universal religion. Jews, she said, with their "prophetic instinct, their deep, spiritual insight," could "set the example and give the ideal" (63). "Judaism, Old and New," the fourth essay (also prepared for a Jewish audience—readers of the *Jewish Messenger*), reiterated the same arguments. Yes, Jews had been persecuted, and yes, in modern America many were losing the faith. However, the solution was not to retreat into ghettoes but to merge and add to Judaism "that which will make it no longer Judaism . . . by entering into the larger, spiritual life which makes no conditions, no restrictions necessary" (95).

In the fifth essay, "The Task of Judaism," Lazarus even more forcefully told her Jewish readers *(Jewish Messenger)* to lose their Jewish identity in their Americanness: "We cannot expect to become citizens of the world while we remain citizens of Judea, bound by local ties, local prejudice and interests" (163). Despite this and her other claims that Jews should become less Jewish, Lazarus here valorized the moral strength of Jews, as she had done in the first essay. "Rooted deep in our Judaism," she wrote, "is a great moral force to sway the world,—the power which makes for righteousness, the Law which is like a seed buried in the dark earth" (185).

Throughout the collection, Lazarus manifested her conflict between a belief in the myths of Jews' unique qualities and solidarity, and a universalist religion and community. As a secular, progressive Jew, she wanted to incorporate her idealization of nonoffensive Jewish traits into her glorified vision of a world with no racial and ethnic boundaries. And like her primarily assimilated Jewish readers, she needed to believe that it was possible to fuse the old segregated Jew, who was reappearing in the guise of the East European immigrant, with the new integrated American Jew. Because Lazarus felt loyal to other Jews as well as to her Christian America, she tried to synthesize her beliefs into a unique vision which would permit her to be Jew and secular citizen of America and the world.

In her analysis of Atlanta's turn-of-the-century Jewish women, Beth Wenger concludes, "German Jewish women were a highly acculturated group . . . but they maintained a careful public posture, remaining profoundly aware of the threat of anti-Semitism. In sum, Atlanta's Jewish clubwomen were simultaneously integrated within and marginal to their cultural surroundings" (333). Wenger's analysis, which can be applied to most regions of America, suggests that as much as American Jewish women longed to be like their non-Jewish neighbors, they recognized that being Jewish would always isolate them. Reminded constantly from the inside by Jewish myths as well as from the outside by anti-Semitism that they were people set apart from others both by imposition and by choice, they felt the discomfort of displacement. To ease their anxiety, the Jewish women in the tradition harnessed the power of the text to effect change in Americans' and Jews' attitudes or to create ideal nations which accepted and celebrated difference, and then used these texts to inscribe themselves into their nations.

VI.

American Jewish
Women Themselves

"All my life I have been inordinately proud of being a Jew. But I have felt that one should definitely not brag about it," proclaimed Edna Ferber in her 1939 autobiography *A Peculiar Treasure* (8). The ambivalence generated by the juxtaposition of these two sentences reminds us that the twentieth century had not resolved the dilemmas of the nineteenth; indeed, Hitler had made Jews more vulnerable than they had been for generations. Ferber's ironic use of "brag" dramatizes this vulnerability, this dilemma of the Jew: feel proud of your privileges, but do not call attention to yourself.

This tentative pronouncement of Jewish pride is one of the defining characteristics of the American Jewish women's tradition. As early as 1815 (Rachel Mordecai Lazarus) and as late as the 1890s (Emma Wolf), American Jewish women turned their attention to the theme of nationality through their questioning of the feasibility of living as American Jews. As the preceding discussion has revealed, often American Jewish women writers explored the meaning of their composite identities in segments. Toward the end of the nineteenth century, a growing number of American Jewish women sought ways to confirm, rather than simplify, the complexity of their amalgamated identities; this chapter will explore the ways in which these women celebrated this complexity.

This late-century celebration, which was both cause and effect of the increasing self-confidence of American Jewish women, took a variety of concrete forms: the accomplishment of a number of literary feats in the final two decades of the nineteenth century (for example, Emma Lazarus achieved a respected place in the library of American writers, and seven novels were published by American Jewish women in the 1890s alone); the convening of a Jewish Women's Congress in 1893; the publication of *The American Jewess*, a magazine for Jewish women, edited by a Jewish woman; and candid reflections in memoirs and autobiographies. Not surprisingly, the need and the ability to define a complex American Jewish female self continued on into the twentieth century; as I discuss in the final section of the chapter, the novels of Edna Ferber display this concern in ways which connect this modern author with her nineteenth-century predecessors.

Between September 4 and 7, 1893, ninety-three American Jewish women from over twenty-nine cities joined ranks to discuss the privileges as well as liabilities of being American Jewish women. Organized by Hannah Greenebaum Solomon, the Jewish Women's Congress convened under the auspices of the Chicago Columbian Exposition's Parliament of Religions. Most of the participants were upper middle-class women who had been involved in club and charitable work; they used the congress and their expertise to establish the National Council of Jewish Women, still in existence today.[1]

Not only the discussions about women, but the very fact of "the first gathering of Jewish women on a nation-wide basis" suggests that the "Congress was apparently revolutionary in its form" according to Deborah Grand Golomb. But was the congress "revolutionary in its content" (52)? I would respond, yes and no, in the same way Emma Wolf's novel *Joy of Life* was "revolutionary" and conservative at the same time. In challenging "traditional assumptions about Jewish women, but . . . not break[ing] entirely with those values of home and family" (Golomb 66), for example, the speakers at the congress celebrated the new woman even as they continued to extol the virtues of the Mother in Israel, just as Wolf's character Barbara Gerrish valued her college education as well as her "maternal instinct" *(Joy of Life)*.

More often than not the speakers at the congress expressed traditional views in regard to women's roles within the home and family. Julia Felsenthal explained that in the home woman "received the loyal love due her, as wife and mother and queen of the household" (125). She also suggested that the woman could serve her country from her home: "it is of the utmost importance that the home life, as the basis for true national prosperity, should be elevated and elevating" (128). Sadie American added that home "will and must remain first and most sacred" to woman; an "allwise Creator made male and female, and assigned them varied functions and duties" which "became a law of being, and no advance of civilization can change the functions nor abrogate these duties. The lines of their duties may, nay, do run parallel, but can never converge" (250). One of these female duties was the preservation of religion: "Religion, true religion, with which every thought and action are connected, is in woman's hand, because the inward life, the home, is what she makes it; therefore, it is eminently fit that from her should come the impulse to study more closely the underlying principles of her religion" (252–53).

Regarding mothers, Henrietta Frank stated firmly, "The mother is still the most potent factor in the world" (49). She had explained a few moments earlier that "If woman gains, the nation gains through her; as mothers, women mold the character of the nation, they influence their children in the most plastic years of their lives" (45). Helen Kahn Weil proclaimed, "Show me a great man—and I will show you a great mother! Show me a great race—and I will show you an unending line of great mothers!" (26).

The above statements (including the directive on religion) could have been spoken by any middle-class woman, Christian or assimilated Jew. The general nature of the comments suggests the extent to which American Jewish women had internalized the myths of their American culture and utilized familiar, unthreatening codes to express themselves. In some speeches, the Jewish women also spoke in safe codes of Jewish homes and of Jewish women's roles therein. Mary Cohen explained that home and Judaism were "inseparably joined"—the "Jewish religion and the family life one, a bond in sanctity" ("Influence" 116). This Jewish home preserved Judaism because through the daily repetition of home rituals, "It was not possible for the Jew to forget his allegiance to Judaism" (117). Perhaps even more importantly, the home and the synagogue "were the only places where the Jew could find relief from trouble and care," according to Felsenthal (125). The Jewish woman, the Mother in Israel, was to create the home life which in turn preserved Judaism. And when the family began to turn away from observance of Jewish ritual and law, she was "to convert [herself] and [her] famil[y] into reverent beings," Ray Frank stated ("Woman in the Synagogue" 65).

Without exception, the women who spoke at the congress expressed pride in being Jews and Jewish women. Eva L. Stern's praise for Judaism's treatment of women epitomizes the common sentiment: "Who in the whole history of the world was the first to elevate woman? to teach delicacy to woman? to command honor of woman, and to insist upon her rights . . .? Moses, who has purged and cleansed the morals of the world. . . . He purified thoughts about woman, and created her a place in life, next in dignity to man" (142). Although Stern was sincere, we, with one hundred years of hindsight to help us, can see the irony of idealizing the "delicacy," "honor," "purged and cleansed morals," and "purity" which Judaism used to "elevate" but also to contain women. We can also appreciate the concluding clause's ambiguous "next": alongside, or behind?

Woman's familial responsibilities were not the only concern of the delegates; as Jews who had achieved relative acceptance within American communities, the women attending the congress also felt loyal to their American nation and expressed their feelings in patriotic codes. In the benediction that opened the meeting, Ray Frank prayed, "Bless, O Lord, this our country and the President thereof, and all the people of the land" ("Prayer" 8).[2] Yet even as they voiced appreciation to America, many delegates recognized the precarious position they filled. In what must have been a sobering moment, Esther Witkowsky stated,

> There was no land of promise for the persecuted Jew of the 16th century; we have found one here in America; the Holy City may not lie within its boundaries, but the route thither certainly does. "Next year in Jerusalem" prays the orthodox Jew; let us hope that *here*, in the future, he may forget this prayer, believing that he has found what he has sought. (76)

To Witkowsky and other women at the congress, America was the land of opportunity and "promise"—the *future* Jerusalem of the west which had not yet fulfilled its promise to Jews or to other minorities. Although Witkowsky felt gratitude for the historical anomaly of America's relative tolerance of her people, she also recognized that being a Jew made her vulnerable.

Some of the assimilated Sephardic and German Jewish women at the congress felt even more vulnerable when they associated with the newly arriving Eastern European Jews who conspicuously displayed their foreign dress, speech, and customs. (Not surprisingly, few, if any, orthodox, and/or recently arrived Eastern European Jewish women participated in the congress.) Rebekah Kohut (1864–1951), daughter of a rabbi and wife of one of the century's leading rabbis and scholars, Alexander Kohut, expressed (in absentia) her and many others' desire that newly arrived Jews from Eastern Europe assimilate to American ways and appear less "Jewish." "Act in every sense as *American Jews*" she pleaded. She continued,

> It is a glorious privilege to be a Jew, but it is also glorious to be an American, and we must appreciate those privileges by acting up to them in the fullest sense of the word. Refined, chaste, quiet in our manners and dress, we must adopt the vernacular of this blessed free country, and perfect ourselves in it. No foreign tongue, no jargon! We are Israelites, but we are Americans as well. ("Discussion" 194)

While Kohut's words reveal the tension between assimilated and immigrant Jews, they also express the discomfort of a dual identity. In what can be read as a plaintive tone, Kohut, like so many other American Jewish women, asked for the right to be at once American and Jew, to proclaim with Henrietta Frank, "Judaism means progress, America means opportunity" (49).

Despite what seems to our modern eyes to be a general conservatism in the speeches, the assembled women felt strongly that they were participating in a great progressive movement. The delegates' decision to use full names rather than "Mrs. Henry XYZ," in addition to the very existence of the congress, indicates a movement away from traditional roles. As to why it had taken Jewish women longer to participate in "women's rights" activities, Sadie American explained that the Jewish woman

> needed to make no movement for herself . . . [or] for others, but has been content through her influence to impel [the man] to move. Because her work has been done largely in the home, because the man has been the medium of communication, the Jewish woman has been a little slower to feel the heart-beats of her time than have other women. (243–44)

The fact that the organizers of the congress "identified themselves first as Jews and only second as females" explains why "they chose to place their conference in the ranks of the religious rather than women's assemblies" (Golomb 66). Perhaps, as Golomb hypothesizes, Jews were too few in number to make a significant contribution to women's causes; or, perhaps, "anti-Semitism was a factor in the women's suffrage movement and kept Jewish involvement to a minimum" (55). Also possible is the Jewish women's choice "to maintain their exclusivity, motivated by fears of assimilation and proselytization, as well as a desire to promote Judaism and Jewish concerns" (55).

The rhetoric of the speeches delivered at the congress was occasionally sentimental, and often conventionally dramatic. One speaker's formulation of linguistic codes echoed another's, particularly in rearticulating the myths of womanhood and the Jewish woman's role in the family and Judaism. Yet even while the women believed in these myths and in their Jewish identities, they wanted to explore the new options becoming available to all American women. Underneath the pious and emotional phrasings of the women's speeches was great energy; feeling their potential as American Jewish women speaking to other American Jewish women, the delegates were ready to confront a challenging world.

As significant as the Jewish Women's Congress was the publication of *The American Jewess* (1895–99). "Devoted to Social, Religious and Literary Subjects," it was the only Jewish magazine devoted to the interests of women, the only illustrated Jewish monthly, and the only Jewish publication sold at newsstands (1:6, 314). The magazine printed fiction, poetry, and essays, as well as reports on the activities of the National Council of Jewish Women. Definitions of the new woman, discussions of intermarriage and, more subtly, of assimilation, informed many of the articles in the magazine; how to be an American woman was their underlying theme. Like many middle-class women's magazines of the period, the *American Jewess* directed women's choice of clothing, home, and activities (in and out of the home). Unlike other magazines, however, this

Jewish publication also directed its readers to cultivate a Jewish identity in themselves and their families.

Rosa Sonneschein, herself an "American Jewess" of Chicago, founded and edited the magazine. The daughter of a prominent Hungarian rabbi, Sonneschein had lived as a socialite in both Prague and St. Louis. Then, "After a discordant thirty year marriage, [she] had been divorced by her husband in 1892. As a defendant in the proceedings, she received no alimony and the *American Jewess* was intended to provide her with much needed income" (Berrol 22).[3]

Despite the promise of the publication's name, only 20 percent of the approximately 315 major articles printed in the forty-six issues of the magazine focus on women, and only about 17 percent, or fewer than fifty articles, are specifically about or for Jewish women (Beifield). The April 1896 issue, for example, contains: "Jewish Blood," by Dr. Friedrich Kolbenheyer, "Heinrich Heine and Women," by Ada Robek, "The Message of Spring," by Rabbi A. Moses, "Judaism" (a poem), by Rev. L. Stern, "The Development of Art," by Sophie Wolff, and "Passover Eve in Petticoat Lane," by Ada M. Levy. Included, too, were regular features such as "Medicine," "The Woman Who Talks," "Book Notes," "National Council of Jewish Women," "Household Hints," and an editorial. Poems about children and flowers, articles about foreign places, and "domestic" fiction also filled the magazine's pages.

Typical of a short poem which "filled" the bottom of page 77 in the November 1895 issue is the following, by John Quincy Adams:

> I want (who does not want?) a wife,
>   Affectionate and fair,
> To solace all the woes of life,
>   And all its joys to share;
> Of temper sweet, of yielding will,
>   Of firm yet placid mind,
> With all my faults to love me still
>   With sentiment refined.

The fact that Adams's poem was outdated by 1895 seems not to have mattered to Sonneschein; after all, the truth of the words was underscored by the founding father's authorship.

The articles by both men and women which did deal with Jewish womanhood often reiterated the dictates for proper female behavior. In "The Ideal Jewess" (March 1897), Rabbi David Philipson defined the ideal Jewess as "religious," as one who makes her home a "temple and considers it her first and highest duty in life to have it pervaded with an atmosphere of peace and religious calm," as one who guides her children, and gives what time she can spare from her home to the unfortunate and needy; the ideal Jewesses are "women whose lives are noiseless, who live at home, wives and mothers, without the ambition that spurs men to strive for renown, but their days are full of such richness of beautiful life" (4:6, 257–62).

In May of 1898, Sonneschein's editorial directed Jewish women to save the Sabbath and thereby "rekindle the spirit, which imbued the Home with religious devotion exercised it benevolent influence upon every member of a family [*sic*]" (7:2, 97). Always, however, Sonneschein stresssed the American half of the American Jewess. In "The American Jewess," she explained that the family has taken on an American character; children, for example, regard parents as dear, good friends, but not as authorities (6:5, 208). And while the Jewish woman is still the ruler of the household, she is by no means only a homebody (208). Most importantly, she

> loves her country intensely. Her patriotism is innate and imperishable, and for her country she would sacrifice her gold and her jewels. . . . Rachel, the mother in Israel, need not weep for her American daughters. Although a new era has dawned with changed conditions, and although she takes part in the joys and sorrows of the nation and is eager to reach the new and the beautiful, she nevertheless remains Jewish in spirit, in feeling, in faith and in conviction. (209)

Once again we see the familiar codes of the loyal American and loyal Jew. Although nothing in Sonneschein's description even hints at confusion, we can surmise that such exuberant prose functioned on some level to cover up questions and doubt.

Repeatedly, the women readers received dual messages about their roles and identities. On the one hand, Esther Rusky stated in "Progress: Its Influence upon the Home" that all of progress and all of culture is to be found in the ideal Jewish home, and that "Both of these inestimatable blessings are in the power of all Jewish women to have" (1:5, 228). On the other hand, Sara Drukker explained that "Old environments have been removed, the old needs of the home no longer exist. Why shall women still be trained in the old way?" (4:6, 273), and even Sonneschein herself pronounced that women should be equal in synagogue (2:2, 112). Selma Berrol suggests that the contradictions in *The American Jewess* as well as other magazines such as *Ladies' Home Journal* and *Good Housekeeping* "reflected the ambivalence of middle-class American women in a transitional period in their history when they had their feet firmly planted in the nineteenth century but their heads had begun to turn to the twentieth" (30–31).

The fiction in *The American Jewess* was most often unrelated to Jewish women's concerns. Written by men and women, Jews and non-Jews, Americans and foreigners, it was usually conventional and noncontroversial. Like the editors of other Jewish periodicals, Sonneschein had difficulty in procuring fiction and often resorted to writing stories herself. One of these "Between Two Worlds" (4:4 and 4:5), with its suggestive title, depicts not only a Jewish son's devotion to his mother but also the humanity of both Christians and Jews. Sonneschein brings out this latter theme through two characters, the young, American, Christian Mrs. Alwood, and the elderly, European, Jewish Mrs. Bamberg. Each woman behaves nobly and civilly, even in the face of tremendous personal tragedy. It is important to note that the foreign Jewish woman in this story is not the uncouth, ignorant Russian immigrant; she is, rather, the ideal middle-class mother. Readers of the *American Jewess* probably agreed with Sonneschein that immigrants should neither neglect their duty of trying to "amalgamate" nor stubbornly retain the customs and mannerisms distinguishing the stranger (2:9, 493). In other words, they did not want their Americanness questioned by association with obviously un-American Jews.

Despite Sonneschein's best efforts, *The American Jewess* never became a financial success. Even using the magazine as an unofficial mouthpiece of the National Council of Jewish Women proved fruitless.[4] Although Sonneschein reported on regional chapters' activities and featured photos and biographical sketches of the council leaders, not enough council members bought copies, perhaps because Sonneschein and Solomon, the council's director, disagreed vociferously on the question of Zionism (Sonneschein supported the cause) (Berrol 23). After a little over three years, Sonneschein had to sell the magazine. The new owners did not have much more success and published only four issues before they, too, had to abandon the enterprise.

Although it boldly proclaimed that the American Jewish woman had a unique identity, *The American Jewess* could not attract and hold enough readers to make it a viable publication. Perhaps Sonneschein was correct when, in her "Valedictory," she accused American Jews of being "ashamed to have their nieghbors and the letter carriers know that they are interested in Jewish matters" (8:5, 3). Or perhaps there simply were not enough middle-class Jews to read and support yet another domestically centered magazine. Despite its limited success, *The American Jewess* serves as an emblem of American Jewish woman's unique identity, and the fact that it appeared at the very end of the century reminds us that American Jewish women were facing the new century with ever-increasing confidence in themselves.

The memoirs of Mrs. Henry Gerstley (Jennie Rosenfeld, 1859–1937) also suggest just how interrelated were one's American, Jewish, and female selves. Raised in a Chicago German Reform household, Gerstley attended religious school where she learned German and Hebrew, but she went only on Saturday afternoons and Sunday mornings. Her "simple, kindly, and moral" (41) community consisted of a "desirable lot of immigrants," many of whom became successful through hard work. The men were "respectable" and "ordinary," with little education, "who were lured here by the opportunities America afforded," and the women "worked, raised their children, nursed, sewed, and went to service regularly" (40). The community's religious observances were expressions of "something fine and spiritual in the hearts of the humble, pious men who brought them to the new land of America . . . [the customs] brought something very precious and inspiring into the home" (147). Gerstley was proud of her German Jewish parents and their co-immigrants who succeeded in America.

Despite her statements of Jewish pride, however, Gerstley maintained a measured distance, and objective stance, from her German-speaking ancestors. She spoke of their customs as quaint, but somehow alien—their ideas, especially about women's roles, were old-fashioned. Although she respected her mother for her diligence and strength, for example, she marveled at her contentment with what she called "dreadful drudgery" (40). Gerstley wanted to be a Jew, but on her own terms—as a modern American woman.

She demonstrated the American part of this during the Civil War; when "the position of the Jews in Chicago was insecure, because the feeling between the North and the South was so fiercely strained," she, and other German Jews, showed "loyalty to the government" (25). Later in the century, Gerstley became the "modern" American woman by adopting new behavior and attitudes. Specifically, she transformed her girlish diversion of providing flowers for hospital patients through the Young Ladies Aid Society into a life-long career as founder and director of the Chicago Women's Aid in 1882. She assumed this public role despite the fact that in her youth "Women's clubs were disapproved most decidedly" (40) because "they did too much to draw women away from their duties" (94) in the family and the slightly larger community of friends. In "those" days (1860s and 1870s), women "accepted their lot, and that ended it" (40).

Like Gerstley, Rebekah Kohut struggled to balance the claims of traditional and progressive Jewish American womanhood. Before she married, Kohut had decided that her real mission in life was to be "a worker in the front ranks of American Jewish womanhood" (*My Portion* 74). After she married, however, she felt that her life's work was to serve her husband and his eight children (from a previous marriage). Although she was no longer working for Jewish women, she felt herself to be performing an important Jewish duty.

That is, so it stood until late in the summer of 1893. Earlier that year, Kohut had been invited to deliver a paper at the Jewish Women's Congress. Her husband, who was ill when she was supposed to depart, became quite upset at the thought of her week-long absence. She, the devoted wife, decided not to go to Chicago. But she, the woman interested in the affairs of Jewish women, went to her room and wept. As she described the event,

> The disappointment was keen. Afterward, when I heard about the gathering of Jewish women, and of the splendid material for social service brought together by Hannah Solomon and Sadie American . . . I was sorrier than ever that I had not been present. But in later years I felt it was one of the finest sacrifices I had ever made for Alexander Kohut. (182)

Despite the fulfillment of her expected role, Kohut's sacrifice rankled and even created discord in her marriage. The tone with which Kohut described the incident in her autobiography emphasizes her conflict. Speaking with almost parodic reverence for her husband, she seems to have needed to convince herself that what she had done for him was correct. However, her honesty about her reaction to his demand, and the number of years it took her to transform the disappointment into heroic sacrifice, reveals that it took strength and discipline to be the traditional Jewish helpmate, particularly when one had "modern" American ideas, such as recognizing the need to work for the rights of women, choosing to give a public lecture, and perceiving oneself as an autonomous figure with needs and goals that went beyond the family and home.

Kohut's ability to articulate a desire to work for the development of Jewish women vividly demonstrates the keen awareness with which American Jewish women were beginning to think about themselves. Here, at the end of the nineteenth century, a Jewish woman could not only identify Jewish women's particular problems but could dedicate herself to solving those problems. It is this self-conscious dedication to her own complex self which distinguishes the turn-of-the-century American Jewish woman from her predecessors.

Concluding in the Twentieth Century

Edna Ferber (1887-1968), extremely popular and financially successful, fulfilled the tradition of the previous century's American Jewish women writers. Like many of those writers, she claimed to be proud of her heritage, yet she remained ambivalent about public declarations of her Jewish identity in her life as well as in her fiction. In *A Peculiar Treasure*, her first autobiography, Ferber explained, "It has been my privilege . . . to have been a human being on the planet Earth; and to have been an

American, a writer, a Jew" (398). Although she gives equal weight to all three components of her identity, she separates American from Jewish and implies a scale of value through the order of the list. The fact that "woman" is not included raises the question of Ferber's response to her gender, although her fiction makes clear that that part of her identity was as important to her as the others; perhaps it was so obvious to her as to need no comment.

I end my discussion of nineteenth-century American Jewish women writers with Edna Ferber because by examining her life and work we can see how the themes of the nineteenth-century tradition metamorphized in the twentieth. In Ferber, we have a highly self-conscious author who brought together an American, a Jewish, a female, and a literary sensibility. Through this sensibility, we can trace the ways in which the themes developed by the nineteenth-century writers went underground, how they became encoded in Ferber's unique "regional" formula. By breaking the codes Ferber employed over and over again, we can understand how difficult it was for an American Jewish woman to expose herself, even in the "modern" world. Most often, Ferber's particular exposure was veiled in the persona of the female pioneer, the independent lover of life. And often this pioneer was in some significant way an outsider; Ferber, like Lazarus, used this character ironically to transform the "other" (the Jew and the woman) into the "one," the insider.

Ferber grew up in a midwestern, assimilated, German-Jewish family. Specifically, she was born in Kalamazoo, Michigan, and spent her childhood in Ottumwa, Iowa, and Appleton, Wisconsin. Her maternal grandfather, Louis Neumann, emigrated to the United States from Germany in the 1840s and settled in Chicago where Ferber's mother, Julia, was raised. Although her grandfather never became wealthy, the family was firmly middle-class. Ferber's father was an emigree from Hungary and also middle-class (*Peculiar Treasure* 15). Ferber herself never married or had children. Her publications include twelve novels, eleven volumes of short stories, six plays (written with either George S. Kaufman or Norman Levy), and two autobiographies.

A Peculiar Treasure provides the most explicit revelation of Ferber's Jewish self. Very early in the volume, Ferber announces, "I should like, in this book, to write about being a Jew" (8). To Ferber, this meant being "especially privileged. Two thousand years of persecution have made the Jew quick to sympathy, quick-witted (he'd better be), tolerant, humanly understanding." But being a Jew "also makes life harder," she confessed (9). Ferber further probed the "riddle of the world's attitude toward the Jew" (61) by explaining that anti-Semitism has

> through the centuries, become a behavioristic habit, like stealing or
> arson or murder. It is a way of thinking that has been handed down

from generation to generation, like tainted blood. It is a criminal weapon used against society by the unsuccessful, the bigoted, the depraved, the ignorant, the neurotic, the failures. It thrives on terror, hunger, unemployment, hate, resentment. It is mob psychology displayed at its lowest and most unreasoning. It is a thing to fill one with a profound sadness and pity for the whole struggling human race. (9–10)

In 1939, such an observation had immediate and chilling meaning. And it was necessary for the same reasons that Alice Rhine's and Nina Morais's essays at the time of the Russian pogroms were necessary: to try once again to explain to America that it had a special mission both to uphold doctrines of freedom and tolerance, and to welcome Jews when no one else would.

As a child in Ottumwa, Ferber learned what anti-Semitism felt like. Her reponse to the feeling of "ghastly inferiority" was to formulate a "resoluton, absurd and childish, such as 'You wait! I'll show you! I'll be rich and famous and you'll wish you could speak to me'" (*Peculiar Treasure* 41). Despite the pain she associated with Ottumwa, Ferber praised America for its freedom and relative acceptance of minority groups. At the conclusion of *A Peculiar Treasure* (after a diatribe against Hitler and Germany), she exclaimed, "there floods over one an overwhelming gratitude for freedom of the spirit, freedom of the mind, freedom of the soul, freedom of the body" (398). America offered these freedoms and therefore deserved constant and vociferous thanks.

Like many of the writers who preceded her, Ferber validated her Jewish self by linking it to an American identity. She described *A Peculiar Treasure*, for example, as "the story of an American Jewish family in the past half-century, and as such is really a story about America which I know and love" (6). Four pages later she added, "America—rather, the United States—seems to me to be the Jew among the nations. It is resourceful, adaptable, maligned, envied, feared, imposed upon" (10). By equating Jew with America, Ferber avoided the conflict of choosing one nation over the other.

Also like many of the nineteenth-century writers, Ferber attempted to cast her Jewish identity not only in an American, but also in a female, mold. Her unique stamp on that mold was to transform the myths of True and Jewish womanhood into the fearless, invincible pioneer woman who was appropriately female in being dedicated to her children and to beauty, but who unabashedly used her abundant power. In the majority of Ferber's novels, it is the women who direct the action of the plot as well as function as models of correct values and behavior.

In contrast to these inventive and far-sighted female characters, Ferber's males are often childishly impulsive even when they are successful and important. Ferber comments on this difference between the sexes in her second autobiography, *A Kind of Magic:* "The major women of all my novels, plays, and short stories . . . have been delineated as possessed of strength, ingenuity, perception, initiative. This is because I think that women in general—and certainly the American female of the United States—is stronger in character, more ingenious, more perceptive and more power-possessing (potentially) than the American male" (283).

She goes on to draw the startling analogy that women are smarter than men for the same reason that Jews are smarter than non-Jews: in order to survive. For centuries, women and Jews "were held in subjection. The woman for centuries was held in subjection because she was a female; the Jew because of his religious belief in one God only, rejecting the Jew Jesus as a divinity." Because of their persecution, "the rejected Female and the rejected Jew" learned "to see through the back . . . as well as through the front of their heads" (286). In an ironic transformation, Ferber turned two conventionally negative identities—Jew and woman—into superior characteristics and claimed them as her own. In the process of self-consciously equating the power of the female and of the Jew, Ferber flaunted her marginality, implicitly proving its value.

The themes of womanhood and of national loyalties appear repeatedly in Ferber's novels. The ways in which the themes took shape, however, began to change in the 1920s. That is, with her fourth novel, *So Big* (1924), Ferber began setting her own course, establishing her own "native ground" through her fiction. In order to clarify this transition, I will discuss four novels, one which I see as part of the earlier tradition *(Fanny Herself)*, and three which trace Ferber's course into a new territory, a territory which is still demarcated by concern over gender and national identity but which contains vastly different contours *(So Big, Great Son, Ice Palace)*.

Fanny Herself (1917), Ferber's second novel, openly confronts the concerns of American Jewish women. Faintly autobiographical (Ferber's sister's name was Fannie), the novel traces Fanny Brandeis's growing acceptance of her Jewish identity. Fanny, born and bred in Winnebago, Wisconsin, sets out to find success in business but feels that being a Jew is a handicap. Brandeis's friend, a Catholic priest—Father Fitzpatrick—tells the young woman that being Jewish is an " 'asset. Outwardly you're like any other girl of your age. Inwardly you've been molded by occupation, training, religion, history, temperament and race, into something—.' " When Fanny replies that no Jewish race exists, Father Fitzpatrick continues,

> "Maybe. I don't know what you'd call it, then, you can't take a people
> and persecute them for thousands of years, hounding them from place
> to place, herding them in dark and filthy streets, without leaving

some sort of brand on them—a mark that differentiates. Sometimes it doesn't show outwardly. But it's there, inside. You know, Fanny, how it's always been said that no artist can become a genius until he has suffered. You've suffered, you Jews, for centuries and centuries, until you're all artists." (121–22)

Ferber stresses the connection between suffering and art throughout the novel. At first, Fanny does not yet understand this relationship, or her special inheritance. Because she wants to succeed, she even tells her boss that she is not Jewish. It is Clarence Hoyl, the Jewish man with whom Fanny falls in love, who finally leads her to appreciate her indomitable Jewish spirit (a modern twist on an old theme). Clarence reiterates Father Fitzpatrick's observations that suffering breeds genius:

"I tell you, Fanny, we Jews have got a money-grubbing, loud-talking, diamond-studded, get-there-at-any-price reputation, and perhaps we deserve it. But every now and then, out of the mass of us, one lifts his head and stands erect, and the great white light is in his face. And that person has suffered, for suffering breeds genius. It expands the soul just as over-prosperity shrivels it." (189–90)

By emphasizing this notion of Jewish suffering, Ferber seems to have wanted to legitimize her own identity as an artist by means of her suffering as a Jew. We can hear the Ottumwa child's defiant response to the pain of anti-Semitism in these passages.

We also hear the pain of the Jewish woman through Fanny's experiences: "She must have known it was the spirit of Molly Brandeis [her mother] in her, and of Molly Brandeis's mother, and of her mother's mother's mother, down the centuries to Sarah; repressed women, suffering women, troubled, patient, nomadic women, struggling now in her for expression" (164). It is difficult not to read this as the author's own response, particularly when one knows that Mrs. Ferber had to provide for her two daughters after her husband's health failed, and that Ferber and her mother had a close though tense relationship.

By the end of the novel, Fanny learns not to resent and apologize for being a Jew but to accept her identity as something empowering. She comes to understand that she has an ancient and noble responsibility to express for herself as well as other Jews (and particularly Jewish women) the suffering but also the glory of the Jewish spirit. The novel presents a quick and neat resolution to a complex dilemma: Jewish woman feels as if she wants to hide her Jewish identity, then Jewish woman comes to understand how valuable that identity is. Like Hyneman and Wolf before her, Ferber offered herself and her Jewish readers the reassuring message that "Jew" is a title of respect, not shame.

After *Fanny Herself,* Ferber never again wrote so explicitly about a

Jewish woman. Instead, she began to concentrate on secular women (indeed, we usually do not learn about the religious heritage of her characters). I would argue, however, that these nonreligious American women often embody the traits of Fanny Brandeis, and of the nineteenth-century American Mother in Israel, particularly in their fierce devotion to ideals of freedom and inclusivity, as well as to their families and American nation. Even the unshakable sense of personal independence which many of Ferber's female characters display reveals a usually hidden dimension of the Mother in Israel's strength. Although this independent spirit seems at first glance to contradict the Mother in Israel's presumed willingness to sacrifice herself for the good of loved ones and her Jewish community, this spirit was actually indispensable in such sacrifice. Without a strong feeling of personal power, even Rebekah Hyneman's Deborah or Judith could not perform.

At the same time that Ferber was transposing the idealized nineteenth-century woman into a twentieth-century character, she was also encoding the nineteenth-century concern with validating one's American self in a popular form by turning away from explicit Jewish character development and moving toward "regional" novels. Through these novels, she asserted her claim to a "native" American place by inscribing herself into many regions of America. That is, by researching and then describing the prairie of Illinois *(So Big)*, the Mississippi River *(Show Boat)*, Oklahoma *(Cimarron)*, Connecticut *(American Beauty)*, Michigan *(Come and Get It)*, Seattle *(Great Son)*, New York *(Saratoga Trunk)*, Texas *(Giant)*, and Alaska *(Ice Palace)*, Ferber demonstrated that America belonged to her and she belonged to America; these "regional" novels affirmed the author's insider status despite her being Jewish and female.

By imaginatively inhabiting many places, Ferber eased her "anxiety of displacement," literalized the concept of "native ground," and redefined literary "regionalism" or local color writing. That is, by fictionally wandering from state to state, rather than staying within the boundaries of a single, familiar locale, she demonstrated familiarity with American diversity and forged a composite vision of America by making all of America her region.

In *A Kind of Magic*, Ferber meditated on her regional fiction, claiming that it "unconsciously began" with her third and fourth novels, *The Girls* (1921) and *So Big*. She continued, reflecting that

> The canny thing to have done . . . was to stick to one region and keep
> hammering at it for fifty years. No thank you very much. The novels
> have ranged the United States in time and period all the way from
> 1875 to today, 1963; in background, North East South West Midwest
> Southwest Northwest Northeast. . . . A writer of fiction is concerned,
> not with geography, but with people. The rich diversity and numbers

of these still make the United States a free frontier for those of the
writing craft. (281–82)

Whether or not Ferber consciously aimed this passage at a writer such as
William Faulkner is less significant than the fact that she rejected the
brand of regional fiction which demanded attention to one place. Expressing almost contempt for those writers who found a single locale rich
enough for many works, Ferber eliminated herself from the conventional
category of regionalism.

Ferber also did not undertake the kind of "regional project" described
by John L. Thomas, which sought to locate an "antimodernist alternative
to corporate capitalism and its powerful agent, the modern state" (225). In
his analysis of the work of Lewis Mumford, Vernon L. Parrington, and Van
Wyck Brooks, all of whose work flourished between the world wars,
Thomas suggests that the "regional revival of the thirties was a national
culmination of antimodernist impulses that promised recovery of a primary, fundamental, natural community" (225). Although Ferber's regional
novels also seek to establish community as primary, fundamental, and
natural, they do not pose "alternatives" to "corporate capitalism" and the
"modern state." Indeed, some of Ferber's most admirable characters become successful capitalists, and, even more importantly, the "state" does
not function in evil opposition to community; the battle between "good"
and "bad" in her novels takes place on the level of the individual, each of
whom has the potential to succeed.

Rather than sharing the "catastrophism" of the regional writers
Thomas describes, or the single-locale focus of a Faulkner, Ferber seems
to share more with the female writers in the New England local color
tradition as described by Josephine Donovan. Josephine Donovan argues
that these New England writers, including Harriet Beecher Stowe, Mary
Wilkins Freeman, and Sarah Orne Jewett, to name just three, "did not
remain negatively fixed upon the destructive practices of patriarchal
society; rather they created a positive, other world of their own that
promoted powerful and independent women" (12). Ferber, too, created
regions in which women could and did demonstrate power. However,
unlike the New England writers, she fully integrated these women into
their communities. Her emphasis on inclusion rather than exclusion
links her to the nineteenth-century American Jewish women's tradition,
in which the theme of belonging to one's American and Jewish communities was important.

Since Ferber wrote about regions she did not know well, she relied on
library research, and often, although not always, brief visits to the site of
her novel. "I can project myself into any age, environment, condition,
situation, character or emotion that interests me deeply," she explained.
In other words, she was a citizen of an America that was regionally

diverse. And she was very proud that "only once" did she receive criticism of the "veracity and soundness of background" of her novels (*Peculiar Treasure* 277). With little time or preparation, Ferber felt she could become an insider, a native of a particular state or city. This facility enabled her to procure the American identity she craved.

Despite her attention to idiosyncratic detail, all of her regional novels were, according to Ferber, "books of the American dream, of the American nightmare, of the smallness and greatness and beauty and sordidness and romance and tragedy of a people in the United States of America" (*Kind of Magic* 125–26).[5] Such a description suggests that Ferber was interested less in geographical divisions and more in proving that America, despite its vastness and multiple regions, is one nation with an identifiable national essence. This belief manifests itself in Ferber's novels which, despite their vivid settings, utilize similar characters and narrative paths. From her earliest to her last novels, Ferber deftly employed a successful formula, a formula that included the invincible woman, passionate pledges of American allegiance, vivid descriptions of place, and a conflict (which resolves itself) between an insider and an outsider sensibility.

So Big, published early in Ferber's career, helps define the components of the formula, particularly in the way it synthesizes regionalism and female strength in one extraordinary character, Selina Peake DeJong. Through Selina we gain insight into the lives of turn-of-the-century Dutch truck farmers in Illinois, and we come to appreciate the beauty of the midwestern prairie. Recently orphaned, nineteen-year-old Selina Peake takes a teaching position in High Prairie, Illinois, in 1890. On her ride from Chicago to her new home, Selina surveys the land

> stretch[ing] away and away in the last rays of the late autumn sunlight over which the lake mist was beginning to creep like chiffon covering gold. Mile after mile of cabbage fields, jade-green against the earth. Mile after mile of red cabbage, a rich plummy Burgundy veined with black. Between these, heaps of corn were piled-up sunshine.(23)

Her companion, Klaas Pool, the unimaginative farmer with whose family she will board, does not understand how it is possible that " 'cabbages is beautiful,' " let alone " 'like chrysoprase and porphyry' " (25), and he turns Selina's vision into a joke.

As Selina soon discovers, almost all of her new neighbors are as blind as Klaas. Even her husband, Pervus DeJong, and her son, Dirk, who gives up architecture after World War I to make easy money selling bonds, cannot see the beauty in the land around them. Despite the hardships she has endured, Selina herself remains strong *because* "to her, red and green cabbages were to be jade and Burgundy, chrysoprase and porphyry. Life has no weapons against a woman like that" (27, 166). Vision without an appreciation of beauty spells blindness in Ferber's fictional worlds.

It is women who passionately understand this. The ability to imagine, to see beauty, is inseparable from their ingenuity and power, two qualities which in turn endow them with shrewd business sense. It is all of these qualities which constitute Ferber's ideal: the American pioneer woman. Petite in stature but gigantic in spirit and courage, Selina epitomizes this figure; her "strength in the jaw line . . . fine, steel-strong, sharp and clear, was of the stuff of which pioneer women are made" (18). With this pioneer determination, Selina, after Pervus's death, successfully transforms the family farm into a "prosperous and blooming vegetable garden whose output was sought a year in advance" (217). Never blinded by financial gain, Selina retains a love for the beauty of the land she tills.

In describing this region, Ferber also decriptively analyzes its inhabitants. She stresses, for example, the taciturn nature of the Dutch High Prairie "folk": "a cold people, yet kindly. Suspicious, yet generous. Distrustful of all change, yet progressing by sheer force of thrift and unceasing labour. Unimaginative for generations" (222). Pervus, who scoffs at Selina's plans for the farm, epitomizes these qualities. It is only after he dies that Selina is able to execute her highly profitable plans.

Despite her business acumen, Selina never relinquishes her appreciation for beauty or her imagination. Both of these mark her as different from the other truck farmers whose resistance to change prohibits them from becoming as financially successful as Selina. Although this spirited woman becomes an insider through marriage—even borrowing Maartje Pool's Dutch wedding dress—and land ownership, she remains an outsider; the fact that Maartje's dress is altogether too large suggests that despite her honorary Dutch status, Selina will never quite fit into the circumscribed life of the truck farmers. Yet it is this female outsider who embodies the pioneer spirit and who retains an idealistic yet workable vision of life. Through her enthusiastic spirit, Selina conveys Ferber's belief that women possess "strength, ingenuity, perception, initiative" in far greater proportion than do men. And in Selina's fictional journey into an American community, we sense Ferber's own need to proclaim herself an insider and thereby demonstrate her American identity. The fact that *So Big* won the Pulitzer Prize provided Ferber external confirmation of her American identity.

In *Great Son*, published during World War II in 1944, Ferber focused her attention on Seattle and, to a lesser extent, on Alaska. She also included several explicit expressions of strong nationalistic sentiments about America. Both on the particular level of Seattle and on the general level of America, regionalism functions in this novel as an important strategy for Ferber to verify her place as an American Jew by praising the nation which "welcomes huddled masses yearning to breathe free."

The centrality of the region of Seattle emerges in the novel's opening paragraph, where character and setting melt together:

> There was too much of everything. But not for Vaughan Melendy. Himself of heroic stature, he fitted well into the gorgeous and spectacular setting that was the city of Seattle. Towering and snow-capped like the mountains that ringed the city, he seemed a part of it—as indeed he was. Born into this gargantuan northwest region of towering forests, limitless waters, vast mountains, fertile valleys, he himself blended into the lavish picture and was one with it. (11)

In the next few pages, Vaughan Melendy fades away, leaving Seattle's natural beauty the unabashed hero of the chapter.

In the rest of the novel, the city becomes less prominent although still central to the plot and characters' lives. In chapter 13, for example, Mike Melendy (grandson of Vaughan) and Regina Dresden, a German Jewish refugee, wander through Seattle's market, "a world of color and sound and motion." There they see Japanese, "Scandinavians. Slavs. Irish. Italians. Fish, flesh, fowl, cheeses. . . . Red snappers bright orange and Indian red . . . Smelts glinting silver and blue. . . . Rome Beauties that were vast globes of pink and green" (206). Amid the exciting display of people and local produce, Mike and Regina learn about each other's past and begin to fall in love. The backdrop of Seattle's market functions in this scene to capture the youthful feelings of the two lovers as it also heightens the incongruity of their histories, Mike's characterized by the bounty of the market, Reggie's by Nazi persecution.

Ferber accentuates this difference through Reggie, who exclaims to Mike, " 'I am so happy!' " She continues,

> "It's very odd. Americans apologize for their country when there's no need at all. Or they boast about it. I can't imagine why. It's the most wonderful country in the world. One needs only to be of it, and that is enough. Like a great, great lady who can be serene and confident and sure. When they let me have my papers and I am really an American citizen I never shall apologize and I never shall boast." (205)

In repeating her refrain, "America is the most wonderful country in the world," Ferber was reassuring herself that even in 1944, she, a Jew, would find haven in America. And by describing America as a woman, she reassured herself that this haven would protect its citizens with maternal devotion, as the Statue of Liberty promised.

Unlike *So Big, Great Son* does not utilize one woman to embody the spirit of America. Instead, several types of women contribute to a composite picture of American womanhood. The pioneer emerges in Exact Melendy and Pansy Deleath, Vaughan's life-long lover and biological mother of his son Dike. The "feminine" women are Emmy Melendy (Vaughan's wife and Dike's adoptive mother) and Lina Port (Dike's wife and Mike's mother). And Regina Dresden represents a new version of the pioneer.

Madam Exact Melendy "now past ninety . . . Seattle's oldest pioneer" stands as a "civic monument" to the founding of Seattle. Pansy Deleath, in contrast to Exact, more actively embodies the pioneer persona unconcerned with conventions of propriety. Like Selina Peake DeJong, Pansy remains strong both because she feels deeply the beauty around her and because she projects natural but fierce independence.

It is clear that Ferber prefers pioneer women to "feminine" women like Emma Melendy and her daughter-in-law Lina Port. In no uncertain terms, Ferber tells us that "Emmy was a good woman and a wonderful housekeeper and a crashing bore" (34). In summarizing Emmy, Ferber writes, "A neat and fussy housekeeper, completely feminine, and abysmally dull, as are all completely feminine women" (37). Lina represents another manifestation of the "feminine"—pampered, self-centered, and manipulative. Self-conscious of her midwestern, undistinguished background, she "had set to work on herself, Pygmalion and Galatea in one," sculpting body, laugh, and smile into her idea of the perfect woman (180). A New York stage actress, she is always aware of her pose and effect; in one revealing scene, Lina plays the petulant child when she and Dike discuss her desire for a new house in Seattle. Their conversation ends with her coming over to him, linking her arm through his, twisting about and "looking up at him, rapt. 'Dike dolling, no one flatters me the way you do. . . . Oh, Dike! Lamb pie! You *are* sweet!'" (191).

Despite her European upbringing, Regina Dresden bears strong resemblance to the pioneer women of the novel. Even more to the point, it is this "outsider," this refugee, who once again embodies the values Ferber most admired. The daughter of a German Jewish father and an American non-Jewish mother who refused to leave Germany without her husband, Reggie has survived her own ordeal with her enthusiasm for life still intact. After telling Mike about her days in New York among the other "refugees," she then explains that she was different, "'still alive and eager,'" anxious to see and be part of the America her mother had told her about (228–29). In Reggie, the pioneer and the refugee blend together and produce a strong American woman whose tribulations make her even more devoted to American ideals and even more sensitive to the wondrous beauty that is America. By combining an American ideal with a "foreign" type, Ferber confirmed her own status as a Jew, an outsider, who can find safety inside America. In 1944, this was crucial not only for Ferber but for all American Jews.

Ice Palace, published thirty-five years after *So Big*, in 1958, functions as a coda to Ferber's long and productive writing career. In writing about

America's last frontier, the then territory of Alaska, she found a fitting region within which to make a final proclamation about the American land and spirit. As is true in *So Big* and *Great Son*, the region itself figures prominently in the novel, providing the focal point upon which plot and characters balance. The novel creates a vivid picture of a land which embodies the best American traits, particularly in regard to inclusiveness. Alaska does not discriminate on the basis of ethnic, religious, or racial differences, but on the heartiness of the "pioneer."

Ice Palace begins with a description of the fictional town of Baranof. On the second page of the novel, we learn that "everything in Baranof seemed exaggerated. Edges sharper. Skies bluer. Mountains higher, snow deeper, temperature lower, daylight longer, sunlight briefer, depending on the season" (10). A few pages later, we learn from Bridie Ballantyne, a longtime inhabitant of Baranof, that Alaska " 'is one fifth the size of the whole United States. . . . And Matanuska Valley can grow you the biggest cabbages in the world. . . . Sun all day and all night, summertime' " (18). Bridie also tells her "tourists" and us that " 'folks Outside [those who live in the lower forty-eight states] just don't know a thing,' " and that " 'those witless ones in Washington won't let us own the land' " (18). Bridie's editorial comments influence the way we read the descriptions of Alaska; we are compelled to take a side, to ally ourselves with "Insiders" who understand the true worth of the land.

Alaska epitomizes Ferber's ideal of inclusiveness, as is apparent in the people who serve in the Alaska legislature: " 'Gunderson . . . Kasilov . . . Taylor . . . Ellis . . . Utokok . . . D'Orsay . . . Russia, Scandinavia, Germany, Ireland, France, England, Canada' "; Alaska, Ferber claims, is " 'like every other place in the United States' " (213). Even a Polish Jew, Isador Raffsky, can become a successful store owner and hotel operator in Oogruk.

All of the Alaskan and American forces coalesce once more in a female character, Christine Storm, the " 'Norwegian and the New Englander and the Westerner and the Eskimo' " (268). She has been raised by her grandfathers, Thor Storm, descended from Norwegian royalty, the appreciator of Alaska's natural forces, and Zebedee (Czar) Kennedy, the son of New England Irish fishermen, the shrewd business entrepreneur. However, it is not simply her multinational and ethnically mixed heritage that makes Chris quintessentially American. It is also her independence, her ingenuous intelligence, and her appearance (blond hair and black eyes).

Whether in Baranof as an "insider," or in Seattle as an "outsider," Chris remains fiercely independent. The novel ends affirming her autonomy; two men, one Alaskan (and part Eskimo), and the other, a native of Seattle, want to marry Chris. She does not reply to either. All of this character's strengths stem from her " '*elan vital* . . . a vital drive, a strong life force. Enthusiasm. Vigor.' " This force is something the Jews have, according to grandfather Thor; with it, " 'They've persisted these thousands of years in spite of incredible horrors.' " Thor continues, " 'The United States has had it for centuries. . . . Alaska still has the *elan vital*. . . . It may be that the pioneer stock is still running strong in [Alaskans'] veins, first and second generation still' " (144–45). Here, in a neat equation, Ferber links together Jews, Americans, Alaskans, and pioneers. Differences dissolve in the context of "elan vital."

Chris, unlike Selina Peake and Regina Dresden, is an insider; indeed, what makes her heroic is that she can utilize her insider sensibilities even when she is an outsider in Seattle. What links her to the other heroes, however, is that she is on the literal and political margin of America simply by being an Alaskan in the first half of the twentieth century. Even more to the point, Chris shares with Selina and Reggie a pioneer spirit—independence, strength, and vitality. With this spirit, women " 'will govern the world, there will be another matriarchy' " (396). Women, as well as Alaskans and Jews, because they possess the "elan vital," must take responsibility for leading the world to a better place.

By writing about Alaska this way, Ferber painted a picture of America itself: a land uniquely composed of a variety of people who work together to create their own insider sensibility. Through this organic portrait of character and region Ferber encoded both her own anxiety of displacement and her resolution of the tension. In the process, she constructed a truly native self built from American, Jewish, and female components. At the same time, she stretched the conventional boundaries of regions and regional literature, using them to stake out an American, inclusive "native ground."

In her 1934 novel, *Come and Get It*, Ferber's character Tom Melendy exclaims, America " 'is the most vital, amazing, stirring, goofy, thrilling country in the whole world, and I care about it in a Big Way' " (498). Melendy's declaration of national pride is not simply a melodramatic caricature or the exposition of an isolated theme. Rather, it expresses Ferber's own passionate pledge of American loyalty; like the declarations of other writers in the tradition, such as Penina Moise's, Louisa Hart's and Emma Lazarus's, it emanated from a spirit of allegiance to America, the country that permitted Jews to be Jews. The theme of American loyalty marks one of the boundaries of the American Jewish women's tradition. The other boundaries are drawn by the themes of Jewish loyalty and of American and Jewish womanhood. Within this verbal territory a significant number of writers explored the challenges posed by their complex national and gender identities. To honor these writers' efforts and accomplishments, we must understand them as inhabitants of their own territory, a territory made rich by its unique combination of resources.

Notes

1. Introducing the Tradition

1. I realize that the subject of the "subject" is now problematic, and that therefore I must define my use of the term. I understand the subject as culturally and linguistically constituted, not naturally determined. In addition, I am aware that my construction of a particular "subject" depends on my own cultural, educational, and political subjectivity. While this grounding of mine must necessarily influence the way I describe and investigate the nineteenth-century American Jewish woman's tradition, I hope that on some level the writers of that tradition will supply their own "subjects."

2. Brodhead's analysis of the American literary "school" which Nathaniel Hawthorne founded is only one of many works which seek to explain the tradition of American literature. An earlier example of such work is Richard Chase's 1957 *The American Novel and Its Tradition*, which states assertively, "since the earliest days the American novel, in its most original and characteristic form, has worked out its destiny and defined itself by incorporating an element of romance." This purpose led Chase "to propose a native tradition of the novel" (viii).

3. I realize that I am making judgments all the time (which writers I include and which I exclude, how many pages I devote to a particular writer, etc.). I also realize that by calling this group of writers a "tradition" I am judging them worthy of literary status. Yet I have also self-consciously tried to avoid judgments about the writers individually and collectively; my primary goal is to describe, rather than evaluate, the tradition.

4. In order to make this whole corpus of work available, I must at times provide plot summaries and lengthy excerpts from conventional poetry. I do not include these to prove either how "good" or "bad" the work is; I do it in order to describe the tradition fully.

5. I believe that I am also contributing to the larger process through which readers of American literature will come to understand that many traditions constitute American literature; this understanding is crucial for an appreciation of diversity. I hope that my study will contribute, too, to the process by which we have begun to question the canon. By learning about "other" writers, we cannot help but see American literature differently. Although I will not often be explicitly referring to the canon debate in the following pages, it clearly provides the context for my presentation and analysis.

6. This study is not intended to be proof of my particular definitions, with the American Jewish women's tradition as evidence for my hypothesis. Rather, I am attempting to use these theoretically charged terms in order to gain access to texts that might otherwise remain locked. I believe that the concepts of myth and semiotic codes can help us understand the processes by which American Jewish women articulated both their confusion and confidence.

7. Sephardic Jews, or Sephardim, are "descendants of Jews who lived in Spain or Portugal before their expulsion in 1492. Sephardim established communities of numerical, economic, and scholastic importance in North Africa, Italy, the Near East, Western Europe, America, and the Balkan states (especially Constantinople,

Salonika, Izmir). . . . Three percent of the Jewish population in the United States are tallied as Sephardic" (Beck 284). Ashkenazic Jews, or Ashkenazim, "denotes German Jewry and their descendants in other countries. From the fifteenth to sixteenth centuries, the center of Ashkenazi Jewry shifted to Bohemia, Poland, and Lithuania. In Slavonic territories, the Ashkenazis' use of Yiddish became prominent. . . . Toward the end of the nineteenth century, Ashkenazi Jewry massively emigrated from Eastern Europe. Before World War II, ninety percent of the world's Jewish population was Ashkenazi" (Beck 278).

8. I use "America" to refer to the United States of America and its territories. I realize that during the nineteenth century the notion of "America" changed dramatically—geographically, socially, politically, and even imaginatively. The Jewish women writers were concerned less with these changes and more with establishing for themselves and their families undisputably American identities.

9. I do not want to suggest that I have included every poem or letter by an American Jewish woman. At times I have been selective, rather than inclusive. Although I recognize that this presents a seeming contradiction in my enterprise of building a tradition, and that I may have committed a gross oversight because of my "subjective" choices, I feel that a group of representative works will define the tradition more effectively than an encyclopedic list could. By searching the most widely read Anglo-Jewish newspapers of the century, including *The Occident and American Jewish Advocate, The Israelite, The American Hebrew, The [Jewish] Messenger,* and *The American Jewess,* by spending time in Jewish archives, and by consulting sources such as Jacob Rader Marcus's *The American Jewish Woman: A Documentary History,* I have come to recognize names of Jewish women who were viewed as authors, and I have tried to follow up on these names whenever possible. There might be otherwise eligible authors whose names do not sound Jewish, who used pseudonyms, or who did not gain recognition within the American Jewish community because of what they wrote or how they lived (as converts to Christianity, for example). These women will not form part of this study because I am interested in writers who did identify themselves as Jews *and* as Americans. The following is a list of other women whose names I encountered but did not include in my study because I could not be sure they were American, or even Jewish: Elizabeth F. Aaron, Caroline Cohen, Constance de Rothschild, S. A. Dinkins, Frances Hellman, Isabella R. Hess, Ella Jacobs, Laura Jacobson, Ruth Ward Kahn, Rosalie Kaufman, Deborah Kleinert, Annetta Kohn, Rosa A. Levy, Minnie D. Louis, Myrtilla Mitchell, Martha Morton, Belle Moses, Miriam Myers, Jennie W. Netter, Emma Salamon, Emma Schiff, Debbie Silver, Helen K. Weil.

10. We must also relax the distinction between paid and unpaid writers. According to Margaret J. M. Ezell, this distinction has led to a devaluing of works written by " 'solitary ladies . . . for their own delight' " (585). Few nineteenth-century American Jewish women were professional writers; the tradition I am describing would be very small indeed if it included only those who were paid for their work.

11. In her *Woman's Cause,* Linda Kuzmack suggests that Reform rabbis, "Faced with the exigencies of building a new movement plus the demands of American life, which forced men to work on the Jewish Sabbath . . . acknowledged the presence of the women filling their pews" (25). She also outlines the ways in which girls and women became active in Reform Judaism: replacing the bar mitzvah ceremony with confirmation; attending religious school; and performing charitable work within the Jewish community (25–26).

12. Although Lazarus is the only writer to whom I devote an entire chapter, I am by no means suggesting that she is the "best" writer of the tradition. In other words, I do not want to imply that I am building a canon within the tradition.

2. Mythic Ideals of American and Jewish Womanhood

1. For a discussion of the Southern Woman, whose idealized behavior and responsibilities bore striking similarities to the Northern woman's, see Anne Firor Scott, *The Southern Lady.*

2. Lynn D. Gordon, in her "The Gibson Girl Goes to College: Popular Culture and Women's Higher Education in the Progressive Era, 1890–1920," and Carroll Smith-Rosenberg, in her "The New Woman as Androgyne: Social Disorder and Gender Crisis, 1870–1936," provide valuable information regarding the attitudes toward the new woman, particularly in her role as college student. Also useful for understanding the True Woman and the new woman is Susan Coultrap-McQuin's *Doing Literary Business;* in her valuable introductory chapter, Coultrap-McQuin reminds us that even in antebellum America, when the "conservative view [one which advocated True Womanhood] was widespread," the "liberal view" had its proponents (and they argued for "women's education, legal rights, suffrage, and career opportunities"). Thus, the relationship between True Womanhood and new womanhood was not exclusively chronological; it was also constructed along a continuum of values and ideals (9).

3. In analyzing the tension between Arthur Help's "social paternalism" (the theory that "society could be regenerated by duplicating the family's benevolent hierarchy" (117)) and Sara Stickney Ellis's "social regeneration" (the theory that "family and society are . . . contiguous entities, families forming a series of enclaves that are at once a part of and separate from the larger society" (118)) in industrializing England, Catherine Gallagher notes that the "ideology of domesticity was . . . somewhat paradoxical: it was a scheme of social reform, but it was also used to preach acceptance of public strife. The ideology must simply be accepted as a contradictory system, at once associating and disassociating the spheres of public and private life" (119). Although Gallagher is discussing England, I believe that her insights regarding inevitable contradictions inherent in the ideology of domesticity illuminate a similar tension in mid-nineteenth-century America.

4. See Douglas's *The Feminization of American Culture* for a full discussion of this point.

5. It is important to note that this Mother in Israel's "power-role" most often manifested itself within sharply bounded domestic realms. Mary Poovey's observations about Victorian England can help explain the complexity of this powerful/powerless position for women. Poovey hypothesizes that Victorian English culture was based on a binary opposition between male and female, with the former using rhetoric of necessary womanly roles as a way of actually maintaining the patriarchy. She states that "The model of a binary opposition between the sexes, which was socially realized in separate but supposedly equal 'spheres,' underwrote an entire system of institutional practices and conventions at mid-century, ranging from a sexual division of labor to a sexual division of economic and political rights" (8–9). While Judaism has not used the "rhetorical separation of spheres and the image of domesticated, feminized morality" to consolidate bourgeois power (10), it has constructed a system of binary oppositions ostensibly in order to preserve the Jewish nation, but also to maintain male power. The fact that the bifurcation within Judaism has had the weight of theological and centuries-old "truths" has made it difficult and heretical to question. While the analysis of how, when, and why Jewish culture became bifurcated does not lie within the scope of this study, the fact is that by the nineteenth century, women had their religious and cultural duties, and men had theirs. What is more, the mythic construct that separated men's and women's "spheres" and endowed

men's with greater power coincided conveniently with the bifurcated system of mid-century American culture.

6. Paula Hyman questions the truth of the myths which stipulate that the family has played a significant role in preserving Judaism and that the woman is central in the family; she suggests that these myths have the potential of limiting contemporary Jewish women's choices. As an alternative, she wants to find a "usable past" that will provide us with "meaningful role models for the present" ("Jewish Family" 20).

7. In his "The Female Life Cycle and the Measure of Jewish Social Change: Portland, Oregon, 1880–1930," William Toll uses demographic data to hypothesize that among German Jews there existed a "high incidence of spinster- and bachelorhood." This was not, according to Toll, because of a lack of "suitable partners," but because a "social tradition of spinsterhood . . . led many German Jews . . . to lead single lives in the company of siblings" (314). Although he does not discuss the lives of those spinsters, I would suggest that they were most likely domestically centered on siblings, nieces, and nephews. Even if German Jewish culture sanctioned spinsterhood, it did so within carefully circumscribed gender roles.

8. The Sephardic/German American Jewish women who wrote in the nineteenth century also appear conservative when they are compared to the Eastern European women who followed them. It is difficult to imagine an Anzia Yezierska, an Emma Goldman, or a labor union organizer finding a radical voice within the middle-class German Jewish families and communities of the early to mid-nineteenth century. It should be noted, too, that the Sephardic and German Jews were conservative in regard to class; desirous of maintaining their middle-class status, they adopted and developed certain values and behaviors which aligned them more with middle-class, white Christians than with poor, immigrant, Eastern European Jews.

9. Abram Isaacs was the son of Samuel Meyer Isaacs, the founding editor of the *Jewish Messenger*. It seems that the son, Abram, became editor in 1875.

3. The Words and Worlds of Emma Lazarus

1. "The New Colossus" has had a problematic history. Presumably Lazarus, along with other eminent writers, was asked to submit a poem to a fund-raising auction for the statue's pedestal. Despite initial protests, she obviously wrote a poem. The auction was part of a larger program, a Pedestal Fund Art Loan Exhibition at the National Academy of Design. The author of the catalogue for this exhibition wrote in 1883, "The literary matter of the Portfolio [of original contributions by littérateurs and of sketches by artists] contains specimen pages of the MSS. of various authors, the list including Longfellow, Bryant, Bret Harte, Aldrich, Howell, Whitman, Cable, Mark Twain, Henry James . . . poems written for the occasion by Emma Lazarus and Julia C. R. Dorr; with letters or other autographs from President Arthur . . . Ellen Terry . . . and many other writings of interest. We select from its varied contents the following beautiful poem, which it is hoped will awaken to new enthusiasm the workers in our cause" (introductory, n.p.). The poem was "The New Colossus."

James Russell Lowell wrote to Lazarus on December 17, 1883, to tell her how much he "liked the sonnet about the Statue—much better than [he] liked the Statue itself." He continued, "But your sonnet gives its subject a *raison d'être* which it wanted before quite as much as it wants a pedestal. You have set it on a noble one, saying admirably just the right word to be said, an achievement more arduous than that of the sculptor" (Rusk 74).

Despite such praise and publicity, "The New Colossus" and the other items in the literary portfolio did not raise as much money as had been hoped. Lazarus's poem quickly faded from public view and memory. Thirty years after its composition, however, in 1903, Georgina Schuyler, of the socially important New York Schuyler family, managed to have a bronze tablet inscribed with the poem placed on an internal wall of the Statue of Liberty's pedestal. According to John Higham, the poem went unnoticed for an additional thirty years because of America's fearful reaction to the great influx of immigrants at the turn of the century. Not until this attitude changed in the 1930s could the poem become a proclamation of "welcome." The change occurred when Jews'

> efforts to escape Nazi barbarism coincided with a growing revulsion of American opinion against racism and with a steady movement of the United States toward war with Germany. In contrast to the situation in the 1880s, when Americans were turning away from a cosmopolitan, humane outlook, the circumstances of the 1930s united a particular concern for the Jews with a broader movement to strengthen ethnic democracy. (Higham 84)

In 1945, the plaque with Lazarus's poem was moved to the main entrance of the statue.

2. Samuel J. Hurwitz, in *Notable American Women*, states that both of Lazarus's "parents were descended from Sephardic Jews who had come from Portugal to the New World in the seventeenth century" (377).

3. This date appears attached to the poem in a handwritten copy book at the American Jewish Historical Society, Waltham, Mass. There might be some debate about this date since Lazarus's handwriting is difficult to decipher. As a matter of fact, Eve Merriam, in *Emma Lazarus: Woman with a Torch* (12), says that Lazarus wrote this at the age of twenty-one. However, since she does not provide a source for her information, I will use the date Lazarus herself provided.

4. I will discuss Josephine's sketches of sister Emma, as well as Louisa May Alcott and Margaret Fuller, in chapter four. In all of these, Josephine reveals her own ambivalence about her roles, as proper or progressive woman.

5. Although the biographical sketch is unsigned, critics accept that it was written by Josephine. See Vogel, for example.

6. Susan Coultrap-McQuin argues that Sara Jane Lippincott, like Josephine Lazarus, justified an apparently unconventional mid-nineteenth-century woman's writing by pointing to that writer's "womanliness": " 'whatever masks of manly independence, pride, or mocking mischief Fanny Fern may put on, she is, at the core of nature, "pure womanly" ' " (18). Ironically, such praise functioned to perpetuate myths of female propriety.

7. Critics who argue for Lazarus's early Jewish consciousness include: Albert Mordell, "The One Hundredth Birthday of Emma Lazarus"; Morris Schappes, *Emma Lazarus: Selections from Her Poetry and Prose*; Dan Vogel, *Emma Lazarus*.

Critics who argue for Lazarus's "conversion" include: Charles Angoff, who claims that it was George Eliot's *Daniel Deronda* that inspired Lazarus, *Emma Lazarus: Poet, Jewish Activist, Pioneer Activist*; Rachel Cohen, "Emma Lazarus"; Murray Frank, "Emma Lazarus: Symbol of Liberty"; Hertha Pauli, "The Statue of Liberty Finds Its Poet."

8. Not all American Jews were happy with Lazarus's and other Zionists' vision. Abram S. Isaacs, for example, the influential orthodox editor of *The Jewish Messenger*, wrote a letter to the *Century* in response to "The Jewish Problem." In this letter, "Will the Jews Return to Palestine?" Isaacs explained that "It is unwise

to advocate a separate nationality for the Jews at a time when anti-Semites are creating the impression that Jews can never be patriots, but are only Palestinians, Semites, Orientals" (156). Isaacs had also written about Lazarus's Zionism before the appearance of "The Jewish Problem," in a *Jewish Messenger* editorial titled "A Problematic Champion."

9. See Aaron Kramer's "The Link between Heinrich Heine and Emma Lazarus" for additional details regarding Lazarus's affinities to Heine.

10. The play is dedicated to George Eliot "in profound veneration and respect . . . who did most among the artists of our day towards elevating and ennobling the spirit of Jewish nationality" (*Dance to Death*, dedication). Eliot's *Daniel Deronda* was extolled by the American Jewish community as evidence of sympathy and support from non-Jews.

11. For more details regarding Lazarus's and Emerson's relationship, see Max I. Baym, "Emma Lazarus and Emerson."

12. For additional information regarding this correspondence, see George Monteiro, "Heine in America: The Efforts of Emma Làzarus and John Hay."

4. American and Jewish Womanhood

1. According to David Philipson, the editor of Gratz's letters, "the year of this letter is omitted . . . but is fixed by mention of the recent marriage of Dr. Isaac Hays to Sally Minis which took place May 7, 1834" (*Letters* 205).

2. For the purposes of this study, I am not distinguishing between ideals of Southern and Northern womanhood. Both stipulated that women should be selfless guardians of the family and of Christian values. As such, they presented similar challenges to the Jewish woman who wanted to find her place in American middle-class culture.

3. In 1911, the Charleston Section of the Council of Jewish Women compiled and published *Secular and Religious Works of Penina Moise*. In this collection, the Sabbath hymn is numbered 154 (page 136).

4. Lynn D. Gordon discusses Meyer's role in "founding" Barnard in her "Annie Nathan Meyer and Barnard College: Mission and Identity in Women's Higher Education, 1889–1950."

5. Wolf's address in 1926 was 2100 Pacific Avenue, San Francisco, a respectable neighborhood, and she belonged to the Philometh Club, a Jewish women's philanthropic group.

6. Wolf's 1916 novel, *Fulfillment: A California Novel*, traces the emotional development of a young woman, Gwendolyn Heath. The plot is unremarkable, although it does raise the question of abortion. The novel's publication date places it outside the parameters of this study.

7. An excellent analysis of popular culture's depiction of college educated women is Lynn D. Gordon's "The Gibson Girl Goes to College: Popular Culture and Women's Higher Education in the Progressive Era, 1890–1920." Gordon explains that "The heated controversy over women's higher education in the nineteenth century and the high visibility and achievements of the first woman graduates raised fears that college women would not be content with traditionally domestic lives" (211–13). In addition, she argues that "The Gibson Girl/college girl . . . represented, not so much acceptance of women's higher education, as fear of its results and an attempt to deflect social change by warning educated women about their future" (213). While I do not believe that either Meyer or Wolf were warning women readers not to attend college, both *Helen Brent* and *The Joy of Life* do depict the potential loneliness, confusion, and even social stigmatization

women might experience as the result of college educations.

8. One of these biographical tributes, Harby's on Penina Moise, technically falls outside the chronological boundaries of this study. However, since it was published only five years into the twentieth century, and since it so clearly resembles the other pieces in this section, I have decided to include it.

9. For further discussion of this essay, see chapter 3.

5. American and Jewish Nationalities

1. According to Louis Harap in *The Image of the Jew in American Literature*, Lust was born in Germany and emigrated to the United States when she was sixteen (448).

2. Rhine was born in Philadelphia in 1840. According to the *Universal Jewish Encyclopedia*, the date of her death is unknown. Her first husband was Henry Rhine, and her second husband, Charles Sotheran.

3. For further discussion of the tensions between German/Sephardic and Eastern European Jews, see Ande Manners's *Poor Cousins*, and Charlotte Baum, Paula Hyman, and Sonya Michel's *The Jewish Woman in America*.

4. Like Menken, Nadage Dorée was a popular stage performer who found an additional outlet for her creative energy in writing. Her novel, *Gèlta; or The Czar and the Songstress*, emotionally depicts the heroism of a young Jewish woman.

5. The question of Menken's Jewish identity remains problematic. According to the 1888 *Appleton's Cyclopedia of American Biography*, Menken's "father was a Spanish Jew" and her "maiden name was Dolores Adios Fuertes" (vol. 4, 299). Thurman Wilkins also believes that Menken was "born of Jewish parents" (527), although he admits that she "managed to obscure most of the facts of her background in a haze of romantic and even conflicting invention" (526–27). According to Pamela Lynn Palmer, her "ethnic background was variously French, Spanish, Jewish, Creole, Scotch-Irish, and Negroid. Among the maiden names she confided were Rachel Adah Isaacs, Dolores Adios, Marie Rachel Adelaide de Vere Spenser, Adelaide McCord, and Adah Bertha Theodora" (85). The 1894 *Dictionary of National Biography* claims that Menken adopted Judaism when she married her first husband, Alexander Isaac Menken; presumably, she retained her Jewish faith even after her divorce from Menken.

6. *The Dictionary of National Biography* states that Menken "published about 1856, under the pseudonym 'Indigena,' a volume of poems entitled 'Memories.' " However, this volume "is not in the British Museum," and, according to Thurman Wilkins, "Adah's claim that she published a volume of poems, *Memories* . . . is doubtless false" (527).

7. Isaac Leeser appended a paternalistic "Note by the Editor" to Cohen's story. The note reads, "The above sketch, descriptive of the last plague, comes to us from a subscriber, as the production of a young Jewess of New York. We are aware that it has defects, inseparable from first attempts at composition; but still we insert it, to encourage our young sister to attempt again the illustration of her faith, we trust with better success, as her experience and judgment become more matured" (105).

8. She herself presumably chose not to marry because the man she loved, Samuel Ewing, was not Jewish.

6. American Jewish Women Themselves

1. In continuing the work of the congress, the National Council of Jewish Women upheld traditional female roles even as it subtly asked members to move out from the home into the world of public service. The council, which was dedicated to religion, philanthropy, and education, would organize and encourage the study of Judaism, apply such knowledge to the improvement of Sabbath schools, and secure the aid of influential people in fighting against religious persecutions (*Jewish Women's Congress* 266–67). In other words, it would continue to fulfill female responsibilities of educating the young and preserving Judaism through a strengthening of Jewish customs as well as through fighting anti-Semitism, but it would ask its constituency to fight publicly.

2. Ray Frank (1864/5–1948) was the "first Jewish woman in America to attempt spiritual leadership"; she "symbolized Jewish women's desire for increased equality in Jewish life" (Kuzmack 34). Frank, a popular lecturer who delivered synagogue sermons in Reform congregations, never claimed to be a rabbi, yet she did receive "several requests to function as a congregational rabbi" (36). Despite her unconventional vocation, "she opposed the suffrage campaign" and "promoted a traditional concept of motherhood" (36). Such seeming disjunctions should remind us, again, that myths of womanhood were dramatically metamorphizing at the turn of the century.

3. Sonneschein's grandson David Loth corroborates, explaining, "As the defendant, she got no alimony and I always understood that she launched *The American Jewess* partly because she had to earn a living" (Porter 130).

4. According to Linda Kuzmack, "The *American Jewess* supported and often vied with the fledgling National Council of Jewish Women for leadership of the campaign for Jewish religious suffrage. The journal went beyond the NCJW's official position, however, in asserting unqualified support for national suffrage and demanding that Jewish women receive the right to religious leadership, including the rabbinate" (42). Kuzmack also claims that "Sonneschein founded the *American Jewess* as a feminist platform advocating women's social, political, communal, and religious emancipation" (40) and that the magazine functioned as "a standard-bearer of the feminist movement within the Jewish community" (41). Although I note a number of essays and editorials devoted to progressive women ("Progressive Women" by Mrs. Esther Herrman, for example), the presence of essays such as "Ideal Motherhood" by Ella E. Bartlett suggests to me that Sonneschein, like many of her turn-of-the-century peers, conveyed ambivalent attitudes about women's rights; I hesitate to call either Sonneschein or *American Jewess* "feminist."

5. Ferber never wrote regional novels about Europe. Although she visited various European countries for extended periods of time, she did not make them the subjects of her novels. Ironically, she sometimes was engaged in the writing of an American regional novel while in Europe.

Bibliography

Adams, Charlotte. "A Hebrew Poet of the South." *The Critic* 12 (1889), 327–28.

Adler, Rachel. "A Mother in Israel: Aspects of the Mother Role in Jewish Myth." In *Beyond Androcentrism: New Essays on Women and Religion.* Ed. Rita M. Gross. Missoula, Mont.: Scholars Press for the American Academy of Religion, 1977. 237–55.

Admetus, by Emma Lazarus. Review of. *Lippincott's* 8 (1871), 526–27.

Alcott, Louisa May. *Little Women; or, Meg, Jo, Beth, and Amy.* Boston: Roberts Brothers, 1868.

American, Sadie. "Organization." In *Papers of the Jewish Women's Congress.* Philadelphia: Jewish Publication Society of America, 1894. 218–62.

The American Hebrew, 1879–1888.

The American Israelite, 1854–1896.

The American Jewess, 1895–1899.

Ammons, Elizabeth. *Conflicting Stories: American Women Writers at the Turn into the Twentieth Century.* New York: Oxford University Press, 1991.

Angel, Marc D. *La America: The Sephardic Experience in the U.S.* Philadelphia: Jewish Publication Society of America, 1982.

Angoff, Charles. *Emma Lazarus: Poet, Jewish Activist, Pioneer Activist.* New York: Jewish Historical Society of New York, 1979.

Antin, Mary. *The Promised Land.* New York: Houghton Mifflin, 1912.

Appleton's Cyclopedia of American Biography. Ed. James Grant Wilson and John Fiske. New York: D. Appleton, 1888.

Ardener, Edwin. "Belief and the Problem of Women" and "The Problem Revisited." In *Perceiving Women.* Ed. Shirley Ardener. New York: John Wiley, 1975. 1–27.

Auerbach, Nina. *Woman and the Demon: The Life of a Victorian Myth.* Cambridge: Harvard University Press, 1982.

Baker, Harriet Newell Woods (Aunt Hattie). *Lost but Found; or, The Jewish Home.* Boston: Graves and Young, 1867.

Barthes, Roland. *Mythologies.* New York: Hill and Wang, 1957.

Bartlett, Ella E. "Ideal Motherhood." *American Jewess* 1 (1895), 279–81.

Baum, Charlotte, Paula Hyman, and Sonya Michel. *The Jewish Woman in America.* New York: New American Library, 1975.

Baym, Max I. "Emma Lazarus and Emerson." *Publications of the American Jewish Historical Society* 38 (1948–1949), 261–87.

Baym, Nina. "Melodramas of Beset Manhood: How Theories of American Fiction Exclude Women Authors." *American Quarterly* 33 (1981), 123–39.

———. *Woman's Fiction: A Guide to Novels by and about Women in America, 1820–1870.* Ithaca: Cornell University Press, 1978.

Beck, Evelyn Torton. Ed. *Nice Jewish Girls: A Lesbian Anthology.* Trumansburg, N.Y.: Crossing Press, 1982.

Beifield, Martin B., Jr. "A Study of *The American Jewess.*" Term paper, Hebrew Union College. On file at American Jewish Archives, Cincinnati. May 1972.

Bennett, William J. *To Reclaim a Legacy: A Report on the Humanities in Higher*

Education. Washington, D.C.: National Endowment for the Humanities. November 1984.

Bercovitch, Sacvan. *The American Jeremiad.* Madison: University of Wisconsin Press, 1978.

Berkin, Carol Ruth, and Mary Beth Norton. *Women of America: A History.* Boston: Houghton Mifflin, 1979.

Berkowitz, Henry. "Dowries for Our Daughters." *The Menorah* 10 (1891), 68–76.

Berman, Jeremiah J. "The Trend in Jewish Religious Observance in Mid-Nineteenth-Century America." *Publications of the American Jewish Historical Society* 37 (1947), 31–53.

Berman, Saul. "The Status of Women in Halakhic Judaism." In *The Jewish Woman: New Perspectives.* Ed. Elizabeth Koltun. New York: Schocken, 1976. 114–28.

Berrol, Selma. "Class or Ethnicity: The Americanized German Jewish Woman and Her Middle Class Sisters in 1895." *Jewish Social Studies* 47 (1985), 21–32.

Biale, Rachel. *Women and Jewish Law: An Exploration of Women's Issues in Halakhic Sources.* New York: Schocken, 1984.

Birmingham, Stephen. *The Grandees: America's Sephardic Elite.* New York: Harper and Row, 1971.

Blach, Sarah Meyerfield. Diary, 1895–1896. Located at American Jewish Archives, Cincinnati.

Blicksilver, Edith. Ed. *The Ethnic American Woman: Problems, Protests, Lifestyle.* Dubuque, Iowa: Kendall/Hunt, 1978.

Bloom, Allan. *The Closing of the American Mind.* New York: Touchstone (Simon and Schuster), 1987.

Borden, Morton. *Jews, Turks, and Infidels.* Chapel Hill: University of North Carolina Press, 1984.

Braude, Ann. "The Jewish Woman's Encounter with American Culture." In *Women and Religion in America.* Vol. 1: *The Nineteenth Century.* San Francisco: Harper and Row, 1981. 150–92.

Brav, Stanley. "The Jewish Woman, 1861–65." *American Jewish Archives* 17 (1965), 34–75.

Brenni, Vito J., and Betty Lee Spencer. "Edna Ferber: A Selected Bibliography." *Bulletin of Bibliography* 22 (1958), 152–56.

Brodhead, Richard. *The School of Hawthorne.* New York: Oxford University Press, 1986.

Bromfield, Louis. "Edna Ferber." *Saturday Review* (15 June 1935), 10–12.

Buhle, Mary Jo. *Women and American Socialism, 1879–1920.* Urbana: University of Illinois Press, 1981.

Burton, Katherine. "A Princess in Israel: Emma Lazarus." *Catholic World* 157 (1943), 190–95.

Cancian, Francesca. *Love in America: Gender and Self-Development.* New York: Cambridge University Press, 1987.

Cantor, Aviva. *The Jewish Woman: 1900–1980: Bibliography.* Fresh Meadows, N.Y.: Biblio, 1981.

Cassirer, Ernst. *Language and Myth.* New York: Dover, 1946.

Catalogue of the Pedestal Fund Art Loan Exhibition at the National Academy of Design. December 1, 1883.

Chambers-Schiller, Lee Virginia. *Liberty, A Better Husband; Single Women in America: The Generations of 1780–1840.* New Haven: Yale University Press, 1984.

Chase, Richard. *The American Novel and Its Tradition.* Garden City, N.Y.: Doubleday, 1957.

Clebsch, William A. *From Sacred to Profane America: The Role of Religion in American History.* New York: Harper and Row, 1968.

Cogan, Frances B. *All-American Girl: The Ideal of Real Womanhood in Mid-Nineteenth-Century America.* Athens: University of Georgia Press, 1989.

Cohen, Bernard. *Sociocultural Changes in American Jewish Life as Reflected in Selected Jewish Literature.* Rutherford, N.J.: Fairleigh Dickinson Press, 1972.

Cohen, Fanny. "Fanny Cohen's Journal of Sherman's Occupation of Savannah." Ed. Spencer B. King, Jr. *Georgia Historical Quarterly* 41 (1957), 407–16.

Cohen, Mary M. "Emma Lazarus: Woman; Poet; Patriot." *Poet-Lore* 5 (1893), 320–31.

———. "The Influence of the Jewish Religion on the Home." *Papers of the Jewish Women's Congress.* Philadelphia: Jewish Publication Society of America, 1894. 115–21.

———. "Jewish Working Girls." *Jewish Messenger* 53:1 (1883), 4–5.

Cohen, Naomi. *Encounter with Emancipation: The German Jews in the United States 1830–1914.* Philadelphia: Jewish Publication Society of America, 1984.

Cohen, Rachel. "Emma Lazarus." *The Reform Advocate* (24 September 1927), 184–89.

Cohen, Sarah. "The Last Plague." *The Occident and American Jewish Advocate* 5 (1847), 97–105.

Cohen, Mrs. S. J. [Picken]. *Henry Luria; or, The Little Jewish Convert: Being contained in the memoir of Mrs. S. J. Cohen. . . .* New York: John F. Trow, 1860.

Cohn, Bertha. Obituary. *American Hebrew* 30 (1887), 85.

Conn, Peter. *The Divided Mind: Ideology and Imagination in America, 1898–1917.* New York: Cambridge University Press, 1983.

Conrad, Susan P. *Perish the Thought: Intellectual Women in Romantic America 1830–1860.* Secaucus, N.J.: Citadel, 1977.

Cott, Nancy. *The Bonds of Womanhood: "Woman's Sphere" in New England, 1780–1835.* New Haven: Yale University Press, 1977.

Coultrap-McQuin, Susan. *Doing Literary Business: American Women Writers in the Nineteenth Century.* Chapel Hill: University of North Carolina Press, 1990.

Cowan, Philip. "Emma Lazarus." In *Autobiographies of American Jews.* Ed. Harold U. Ribalow. Philadelphia: Jewish Publication Society of America, 1965. 26–37.

———. "Home Influence." *American Hebrew* 1 (1879), 1.

"The Dance to Death," Review of. *Lippincott's* 31 (1883), 216.

Daniels, Doris Groshen. "Colonial Jewry: Religion, Domestic and Social Relations." *American Jewish Historical Society Quarterly* 66 (1977), 375–400.

Dash, Joan. *Summoned to Jerusalem: The Life of Henrietta Szold.* New York: Harper and Row, 1979.

David, Sophia. Obituary. *Occident and American Jewish Advocate* 24 (1867), 480.

Dearborn, Mary. *Pocahontas's Daughters: Gender and Ethnicity in American Culture.* New York: Oxford University Press, 1986.

de Beauvoir, Simone. *The Second Sex.* New York: Bantam, 1961. Originally published by Knopf in 1953.

Degler, Carl. *At Odds: Women and the Family in America from the Revolution to the Present.* New York: Oxford University Press, 1980.

Del Banco, Miriam. "Friday Night." *Menorah* 4:1 (1888), 43–44.

De Sola Pool, D. "Some Letters of Grace Seixas Nathan, 1814–1821." *Publications of the American Jewish Historical Society* 37 (1947), 203–11.

Dickinson, Rogers. *Edna Ferber: A Biographical Sketch with a Bibliography.* New York: Doubleday, Page, 1925.

Dictionary of National Biography. Ed. Sidney Lee. London: Smith, Elder, 1894.

Diffley, Kathleen. "Reconstructing the American Canon: E Pluribus Unum?" *Journal of the Midwest Modern Language Association* 21:2 (Fall 1988), 1–15.

Donnelly, Mabel Collins. *The American Victorian Woman: The Myth and the Reality.* Westport, Conn.: Greenwood, 1986.

Donovan, Josephine. *New England Local Color Literature: A Women's Tradition.* New York: Frederick Ungar, 1983.

Dorée, Nadage. *Gèlta; or, The Czar and the Songstress.* New York: Neely, 1897.

Douglas, Ann. *The Feminization of American Culture.* New York: Avon, 1977.

DuBois, Ellen, Mari Jo Buhle, Temma Kaplan, Gerda Lerner, Carroll Smith-Rosenberg. "Politics and Culture in Women's History: A Symposium." *Feminist Studies* 6 (1980), 26–64.

Eliade, Mircea. *Myths, Rites and Symbols: A Mircea Eliade Reader.* 2 vols. Ed. Wendell C. Beene and William G. Doty. New York: Harper Colophon, 1975.

Elwell, Ellen Sue Levi. "The Founding and Early Programs of the National Council of Jewish Women: Study and Practice as Jewish Women's Religious Expression." Diss. Indiana University, 1982.

———. Ed. *The Jewish Women's Studies Guide.* 2nd ed. Lanham, Md.: University Press of America, 1987.

Ezell, Margaret J. M. "The Myth of Judith Shakespeare: Creating the Canon of Women's Literature." *New Literary History* 21 (1990), 579–92.

Faur, Jose. "Sephardim in the Nineteenth Century: New Directions and Old Values." *Proceedings of the American Academy for Jewish Research* 44 (1977), 29–52.

Feldman, David M. "Woman's Role and Jewish Law." *Conservative Judaism* 26:4 (Summer 1972), 29–39.

Feldstein, Stanley. *The Land That I Show You: Three Centuries of Jewish Life in America.* Garden City: Anchor, 1978.

Felsenthal, Julia. "Discussion of Mary Cohen's 'The Influence of the Jewish Religion on the Home.'" In *Papers of the Jewish Women's Congress.* Philadelphia: Jewish Publication Society of America, 1894. 122–28.

Ferber, Edna. *American Beauty.* Garden City: Doubleday, Doran, 1931.

———. *Buttered Side Down.* New York: Frederick A. Stokes, 1912.

———. *Cimarron.* Garden City: Doubleday, Doran, 1930.

———. *Come and Get It.* Garden City: Doubleday, Doran, 1934.

———. *Dawn O'Hara.* New York: Frederick A. Stokes, 1911.

———. *Fanny Herself.* New York: Frederick A. Stokes, 1917.

———. *Fanny Herself,* Review of. *New York Times Book Review* (7 October 1917), 380.

———. *Fanny Herself,* Review of. "Glimpses of Reality." *Nation* 105 (18 October 1917), 431–32.

———. *Giant.* Garden City: Doubleday, 1952.

———. *The Girls.* New York: Doubleday, Page, 1921.

———. *Great Son.* Garden City: Doubleday, Doran, 1944.

———. *Ice Palace.* Garden City: Doubleday, 1958.

———. *A Kind of Magic.* Garden City: Doubleday, 1963.

———. Obituary. *New York Times* (19 April 1968), 1, 32.

———. *A Peculiar Treasure.* New York: Doubleday, Doran, 1939.

————. *Roast Beef Medium*. New York: Frederick A. Stokes, 1913.

————. *Saratoga Trunk*. Garden City: Doubleday, Doran, 1941.

————. *Show Boat*. Garden City: Doubleday, Page, 1926.

————. *So Big*. Garden City: Doubleday, Page, 1924.

Fetterley, Judith. *The Resisting Reader: A Feminist Approach to American Fiction*. Bloomington: Indiana University Press, 1978.

Flexner, Eleanor. *Century of Struggle: The Woman's Rights Movement in the United States*. Cambridge: Harvard University Press, 1959.

Frank, Henrietta. "Discussion of Helen Kahn Weil's 'Jewish Women of Modern Days.'" In *Papers of the Jewish Women's Congress*. Philadelphia: Jewish Publication Society of America, 1894. 43–51.

Frank, Murray. "Emma Lazarus: Symbol of Liberty." *Chicago Jewish Forum* (1948), 251–56.

Frank, Ray. "Prayer." In *Papers of the Jewish Women's Congress*. Philadelphia: Jewish Publication Society of America, 1894. 8.

————. "Woman in the Synagogue." In *Papers of the Jewish Women's Congress*. Philadelphia: Jewish Publication Society of America, 1894. 52–65.

Fryer, Judith. *The Faces of Eve: Women in the Nineteenth-Century American Novel*. New York: Oxford University Press, 1976.

Gallagher, Catherine. *The Industrial Reformation of English Fiction: Social Discourse and Narrative Form 1832–1867*. Chicago: University of Chicago Press, 1985.

Gates, Henry Louis, Jr. "On the Rhetoric of Racism in the Profession." Unpublished paper distributed to participants in the 1988 National Council of Teachers of English Summer Institute, "Gender Studies and the Canon." June 1988.

————. "The Subject Position." Unpublished paper distributed to participants in the 1988 National Council of Teachers of English Summer Institute, "Gender Studies and the Canon." June 1988.

————. "Whose Canon Is It, Anyway?" *New York Times Book Review* (26 February 1989), 1, 44–45.

Geertz, Clifford. *The Interpretation of Cultures*. New York: Basic Books, 1973.

Geffen, David. "Emma Lazarus: Poetess of Freedom and the Nation." *Sephardi World* 1 (January 1984, Jerusalem), 3, 29.

Gelfant, Blanche. "Sister to Faust: The City's 'Hungry Woman' as Heroine." *Novel* 15 (1981), 23–38.

Gerber, Irving. *Emma Lazarus: Poet of Liberty*. Pamphlet. American Jewish Historical Society. Ethnic Reading Series, Jewish Americans. Brooklyn: Book-Lab, 1979.

Gerstley, Mrs. Henry (Jennie Rosenfeld). Reminiscences. Located at American Jewish Archives, Cincinnati.

Gilbert, Julie Goldsmith. *Ferber: A Biography*. Garden City: Doubleday, 1978.

Gilbert, Sandra, and Susan Gubar. *The Madwoman in the Attic: The Woman Writer and the Nineteenth-Century Literary Imagination*. New Haven: Yale University Press, 1979.

————. Eds. *The Norton Anthology of Literature by Women: The Tradition in English*. New York: W. W. Norton, 1985.

Girgus, Sam B. *The New Covenant: Jewish Writers and the American Idea*. Chapel Hill: University of North Carolina Press, 1984.

Gitenstein, Barbara. "Models for Jewish-American Literature: Emma Lazarus and Cynthia Ozick." Paper presented at National Women's Studies Association Conference, Minneapolis, June 1988.

Glanz, Rudolf. "The Immigration of German Jews up to 1880." In *Studies in Jewish Americana.* Ed. Rudolf Glanz. New York: Ktav, 1970. 85–103.

———. *The Jewish Woman in America: Two Female Immigrant Generations, 1820–1929.* Vol. 2, *The German Jewish Woman.* New York: Ktav and National Council of Jewish Women, 1976.

———. "Notes on Early Jewish Peddling in America." *Jewish Social Studies* 7 (1945), 119–36.

———. *Studies in Judaica Americana.* New York: Ktav, 1970.

Glazer, Nathan. *American Judaism.* Chicago: University of Chicago Press, 1957.

Goldsmith, Sophia Heller. "In Remembrance of My Past Life Recalled to Mind January 26, 1904 and November 11, 1918." Located at American Jewish Archives, Cincinnati.

Golomb, Deborah Grand. "The 1893 Congress of Jewish Women: Evolution or Revolution in American Jewish Women's History?" *American Jewish History* 70 (1980), 52–67.

Gordon, Lynn D. "Annie Nathan Meyer and Barnard College: Mission and Identity in Women's Higher Education, 1889–1950." *History of Education Quarterly* 26 (1986), 503–22.

———. "The Gibson Girl Goes to College: Popular Culture and Women's Higher Education in the Progressive Era, 1890–1920." *American Quarterly* 39 (1987), 211–30.

Greenberg, Blu. *On Women and Judaism: A View from Tradition.* Philadelphia: Jewish Publication Society of America, 1981.

Gross, Theodore L. Ed. *The Literature of American Jews.* New York: Macmillan, 1973.

Guttmann, Allen. *The Jewish Writer in America: Assimilation and the Crisis of Identity.* New York: Oxford University Press, 1971.

Hall, Sarah Ewing. "Miss Edgeworth and the Jews." In *Selections from the Writings of Mrs. Sarah Ewing Hall.* Philadelphia: Harrison Hall, 1833. 57–60.

Halttunen, Karen. *Confidence Men and Painted Women: A Study of Middle-Class Culture in America, 1830–1870.* New Haven: Yale University Press, 1982.

Handy, Robert T. *A Christian America: Protestant Hopes and Historical Realities.* New York: Oxford University Press, 1971.

Harap, Louis. *The Image of the Jew in American Literature.* Philadelphia: Jewish Publication Society of America, 1974.

Harby, Leah (Lee) Cohen. "Our Women and Their Possibilities." In *The American Jewish Woman 1654–1980: A Documentary History.* Ed. Jacob Rader Marcus. New York: Ktav, and Cincinnati: American Jewish Archives, 1981, 344–50.

———. "Penina Moise: Woman and Writer." In *American Jewish Year Book, 1905–06.* 7. Philadelphia: Jewish Publication Society of America. 17–31.

Harris, Barbara J. *Beyond Her Sphere: Women and the Professions in American History.* Westport, Conn.: Greenwood, 1978.

Harris, Susan K. *Nineteenth-Century American Women's Novels: Interpretative Strategies.* New York: Cambridge University Press, 1990.

Hart, Bella. Obituary. *Occident and American Jewish Advocate,* 10 (1852), 64.

Hart, Louisa B. "A Memoir of Louisa B. Hart, with Excerpts from her Diary and Letters." Ed. Mary M. Cohen. *Jewish Record* 8:2–8:14 (1878–1879), pp. 1–2 of each issue.

Heilbrun, Carolyn. *Reinventing Womanhood.* New York: W. W. Norton, 1979.

Helprin, Mark. "Introduction: The Canon under Siege." In *The Best American*

Short Stories 1988. Ed. Mark Helprin and Shannon Ravenel. Boston: Houghton Mifflin, 1988.

Henry, Sondra, and Emily Taitz. *Written Out of History: A Hidden Legacy of Jewish Women Revealed through Their Writings and Letters*. New York: Bloch, 1978.

Herrman, Esther. "Progressive Women." *American Jewess* 2 (1896), 404–5.

Herz, Jenny Kleeberg. "Daughters of Columbia." *Menorah* 13 (1892), 243–50.

Herzog, Kristin. *Women, Ethnics, and Exotics: Images of Power in Mid-Nineteenth-Century American Fiction*. Knoxville: University of Tennessee Press, 1983.

Heschel, Susannah. Ed. *On Being a Jewish Feminist: A Reader*. New York: Schocken, 1983.

Higham, John. *Send These to Me: Jews and Other Immigrants in Urban America*. New York: Atheneum, 1975.

———. *Strangers in the Land: Patterns of American Nativism,1860–1925*. New Brunswick: Rutgers University Press, 1955.

Hirsch, E. D., Jr. *Cultural Literacy: What Every American Needs to Know*. New York: Vintage, 1988.

Hirshler, Eric E. Ed. *Jews from Germany in the United States*. New York: Farrar, Straus and Cudahy, 1955.

Horowitz, Steven P., and Miriam J. Landsman. "The Americanization of Edna: A Study of Ms. Ferber's Jewish American Identity." *Studies in American Jewish Literature* 2 (1982), 69–80.

Howe, Irving. *World of Our Fathers*. New York: Harcourt, Brace, Jovanovich, 1976.

Huhner, Leon. "The Jewish Woman in America." Address delivered before the Council of Jewish Women at Temple Emanu-El, New York, November 21, 1905. Pamphlet located at American Jewish Historical Society.

Hurwitz, Samuel J. "Emma Lazarus." In *Notable American Women*. Vol. 2. Cambridge: Belknap Press of Harvard University Press, 1971. 377–79.

Hyman, Paula. "The Jewish Family: Looking for a Usable Past." In *On Being a Jewish Feminist: A Reader*. Ed. Susannah Heschel. New York: Schocken, 1983. 19–26.

———. "The Other Half: Women in the Jewish Tradition." In *The Jewish Woman: New Perspectives*. Ed. Elizabeth Koltun. New York: Schocken, 1976. 105–13.

Hyneman, Rebekah. *The Leper and Other Poems*. Philadelphia: A. Hart, 1853.

———. "The Lost Diamond." *Occident and American Jewish Advocate* 19 (March 1862), 551–55; 20 (April), 10–15; (May), 71–75; (June), 117–23; (July), 163–71.

Isaacs, Abram. "The Daughters of Israel." *Jewish Messenger* 39:8 (1876), 4.

———. "The Jewess in Authorship." *Ladies' Home Journal* 9 (October 1892), 17.

———. "A Lesson To Mothers." *Jewish Messenger* 38:21 (1875), 4.

———. "Our Daughters." *Jewish Messenger* 39:12 (1876), 4.

———. "A Problematic Champion." *Jewish Messenger* 53:4 (1883), 4.

———. "Will the Jews Return to Palestine?" *Century* 26 (1883), 156–57.

Jacob, H. E. *The World of Emma Lazarus*. New York: Schocken, 1943.

Jamison, A. Leland. Ed. *Tradition and Change in Jewish Experience*. Syracuse: Syracuse University Press, 1978.

Janeway, Elizabeth. *Man's World Woman's Place: A Study in Social Mythology*. New York: Delta, 1971.

Jehlen, Myra. "Archimedes and the Paradox of Feminist Criticism." *Signs* 6 (1981), 575–601.

The Jewish Messenger, 1857–1888.

Jewish Women's Congress, Papers of. Philadelphia: Jewish Publication Society of America, 1894.

Johnson, Claudia D. "Adah Isaacs Menken." In *American Actress: Perspective on the Nineteenth Century.* Chicago: Nelson Hall, 1984. 147–57, 189–90.

Kaplan, Temma. "Politics and Culture in Women's History: A Symposium." *Feminist Studies* 6 (1980), 44.

Karp, Abraham J. "Jewish Perceptions of America: From Melting Pot to Mosaic." In *Tradition and Change in Jewish Experience.* Ed. A. Leland Jamison. Syracuse: Syracuse University Press, 1978. 244–56.

Katz, Jacob. *Out of the Ghetto: The Social Background of Jewish Emancipation, 1770–1870.* Cambridge: Harvard University Press, 1973.

Kaye/Kantrowitz, Melanie, and Irena Klepfisz. Eds. *The Tribe of Dina: A Jewish Women's Anthology.* Montpellier, Vt.: Sinister Wisdom Books, 1986.

Kazin, Alfred. "The Jew as Modern Writer." *Commentary* 41 (1966), 37–41.

———. *On Native Grounds.* New York: Reynal and Hitchcock, 1942.

Kelley, Mary. *Private Woman, Public Stage: Literary Domesticity in Nineteenth-Century America.* New York: Oxford University Press, 1984.

———. "The Sentimentalists: Promise and Betrayal in the Home." *Signs* 4 (1979), 434–46.

Kerber, Linda K. "Separate Spheres, Female Worlds, Woman's Place: The Rhetoric of Women's History." *Journal of American History* 75 (1988), 9–39.

Kirk, G. S. *Myth: Its Meaning and Functions in Ancient and Other Cultures.* Berkeley: University of California Press, 1970.

Kohler, Kaufmann. "Esther or the Jewish Woman." Lecture delivered February 26, 1888, at Temple Beth-El, New York. Pamphlet no. 16, located at Hebrew Union College Library.

Kohut, Rebekah. "Discussion of Minnie D. Louis' 'Mission Work among the Unenlightened Jews.' " In *Papers of the Jewish Women's Congress.* Philadelphia: Jewish Publication Society of America, 1894. 187–95.

———. *My Portion (An Autobiography).* New York: Thomas Seltzer, 1924.

Kolodny, Annette. "Dancing through the Minefield: Some Observations on the Theory, Practice and Politics of a Feminist Literary Criticism." *Feminist Studies* 6 (1980), 1–25.

———. "The Integrity of Memory: Creating a New Literary History of the United States." *American Literature* 57 (1985), 291–307.

———. "A Map for Rereading: Or, Gender and the Interpretation of Literary Texts." *New Literary History* 11 (1980), 451–67.

Koltun, Elizabeth. Ed. *The Jewish Woman: New Perspectives.* New York: Schocken, 1976.

Korn, Bertram Wallace. "German-Jewish Intellectual Influences on American Jewish Life 1824–1972." In *Tradition and Change in Jewish Experience.* Ed. A. Leland Jamison. Syracuse: Syracuse University Press, 1978. 106–40.

———. Ed. *A Bicentennial Festschrift for Jacob Rader Marcus.* Waltham and New York: American Jewish Historical Society and Ktav, 1976.

Kramer, Aaron. "The Link between Heinrich Heine and Emma Lazarus." *Publications of the American Jewish Historical Society* 45 (1955–1956), 248–57.

Kuklick, Bruce. "Myth and Symbol in American Studies." *American Quarterly* 24 (1972), 434–50.

Kulwin, Clifford M. "The American Jewish Woman as Reflected in Leeser's *Occident,* 1843–1869." Term paper, Hebrew Union College, Spring 1980.

Kuzmack, Linda. *Woman's Cause: The Jewish Woman's Movement in England*

and the United States, 1881–1933. Columbus: Ohio State University Press, 1990.

Langer, Suzanne. *Philosophy in a New Key: A Study in the Symbolism of Reason, Rite and Art.* Cambridge: Harvard University Press, 1942.

Lauter, Paul. "Race and Gender in the Shaping of the American Literary Canon: A Case Study from the Twenties." *Feminist Studies* 9 (1983), 435–62.

Lazarus, Emma. *Admetus and Other Poems.* New York: Hurd and Houghton, 1871.

———. *Alide: An Episode of Goethe's Life.* Philadelphia: J. B. Lippincott, 1874.

———. "American Literature." *The Critic,* o.s. 1:12 (1881), 164.

———. "Cruel Bigotry." *American Hebrew* 15 (1883), 14.

———. "A Day in Surrey with William Morris." *Century* 32 (1886), 388–97.

———. "The Eleventh Hour." *Scribner's* 16 (1878), 242–56.

———. "Emerson's Personality." *Century* 24 (1882), 454–66.

———. *An Epistle to the Hebrews.* New York: Federation of American Zionists, 1900.

———. "Henry Wadsworth Longfellow." *American Hebrew* 11 (1882).

———. "The Jewish Problem." *Century* 25 (1883), 602–11.

———. "Judaism the Connecting Link between Science and Religion," *American Hebrew* 12 (1882), 28.

———. MS notebook of poems at American Jewish Historical Society, Waltham, Mass.

———. "Outside the Church." *Index* 3 (1872), 399.

———. *Poems and Ballads of Heinrich Heine.* New York: R. Worthington, 1881.

———. *Poems and Translations: Written between the Ages of Fourteen and Sixteen.* New York: H. O. Houghton, 1866.

———. *The Poems of Emma Lazarus.* 2 vols. New York: Houghton Mifflin, 1888.

———. "The Poet Heine." *Century* 29 (1884), 210–17.

———. "Progress and Poverty." *New York Times* (2 October 1881), 3.

———. "Russian Christianity vs. Modern Judaism." *Century* 24 (1882), 48–56.

———. *Songs of a Semite: The Dance to Death and Other Poems.* New York: The American Hebrew, 1882.

———. "The Taming of the Falcon." *Scribner's* 19 (1879), 196.

———. Untitled poem for the opening of the Concord School of Philosophy on July 23, 1884, included in "Emerson and the Concord School." *The Critic,* o.s. 5: 31 (1884), 55.

———. "Was the Earl of Beaconsfield a Representative Jew?" *Century* 23 (1882), 939–42.

Lazarus, Josephine. "Emma Lazarus." In *The Poems of Emma Lazarus.* 2 vols. Boston: Houghton Mifflin, 1889. Also appeared as "Emma Lazarus" in *Century* 36 (1888), 875–84.

———. "Louisa May Alcott." *Century* 42 (1891), 59–67.

———. *Madame Dreyfus: An Appreciation.* New York: Brentano's, 1899.

———. "Margaret Fuller." *Century* 45 (1893), 923–32.

———. *The Spirit of Judaism.* New York: Dodd, Mead, 1895.

Lears, Jackson. *No Place of Grace: Antimodernism and the Transformation of American Culture 1880–1920.* New York: Pantheon, 1981.

Learsi, Rufus. *The Jews in America: A History.* New York: World, 1954.

Leeser, Isaac. "How to Educate Jewish Girls." *The American Jewish Woman 1654–1980: A Documentary History.* Ed. Jacob Rader Marcus. New York: Ktav, and Cincinnati: American Jewish Archives, 1981, 129–32.

Lerner, Gerda. "The Lady and the Mill Girl: Changes in the Status of Women in the Age of Jackson, 1800–1840." In *A Heritage of Her Own: Toward a New*

Social History of American Women. Ed. Nancy Cott and Elizabeth Pleck. New York: Simon and Schuster, 1979, 182–96.

———. *The Majority Finds Its Past: Placing Women in History.* New York: Oxford University Press, 1979.

Lesser, Allen. "La Belle Menken." In *Weave a Wreath of Laurel.* New York: Coven, 1938, 21–35, 71.

Levin, Nathaniel. "An Apostrophe to Women by a Southern Gentleman." In *The American Jewish Woman 1654–1980: A Documentary History.* Ed. Jacob Rader Marcus. New York: Ktav, and Cincinnati: American Jewish Archives, 1981, 152–56.

Levinger, Rabbi Lee J. *Anti-Semitism in the U.S.* New York: Bloch, 1925.

Lévi-Strauss, Claude. *Myth and Meaning.* New York: Schocken, 1979.

———. "The Structural Study of Myth." In *Structural Anthropology.* New York: Basic Books, 1963, 206–31.

Lust, Adelina Cohnfeldt. *A Tent of Grace.* Boston: Houghton Mifflin, 1899.

MacDonald, Edgar. Ed. *The Education of the Heart: The Correspondence of Rachel Mordecai Lazarus and Maria Edgeworth.* Chapel Hill: University of North Carolina Press, 1977.

Madison, Charles A. *Jewish Publishing in America: The Impact of Jewish Writing on American Culture.* New York: Sanhedrin, 1976.

Manners, Ande. *Poor Cousins.* Greenwich, Conn.: Fawcett Crest, 1972.

Mannheimer, Louise. *Poems in German and English.* New York: Privately printed, 1921.

Marcus, Jacob. "The American Colonial Jew: A Study in Acculturation." In *Tradition and Change in Jewish Experience.* Ed. A. Leland Jamison. Syracuse: Syracuse University Press, 1978. 75–88.

———. *The American Jewish Woman 1654–1980.* New York: Ktav, and Cincinnati: American Jewish Archives, 1981.

———. *The American Jewish Woman 1654–1980: A Documentary History.* New York: Ktav, and Cincinnati: American Jewish Archives, 1981.

———. *Memoirs of American Jews.* 3 vols. Philadelphia: Jewish Publication Society of America, 1955.

Margolis, Max L., and Alexander Marx. *A History of the Jewish People.* Philadelphia: Jewish Publication Society of America, 1927.

Markley, Robert. *Two-Edg'd Weapons: Style and Ideology in the Comedies of Etherege, Wycherley, and Congreve.* New York: Oxford University Press, 1988.

Martin, Jay. *Harvests of Change: American Literature 1865–1914.* Englewood Cliffs, N.J.: Prentice-Hall, 1967.

Martin, Wendy. "Seduced and Abandoned in the New World: The Image of Woman in American Fiction." In *Woman in Sexist Society.* Ed. Vivian Gornick and Barbara Moran. New York: New American Library, 1971. 329–46.

Mayo, Louise A. *The Ambivalent Image: Nineteenth-Century America's Perception of the Jew.* Rutherford, N.J.: Fairleigh Dickinson University Press, 1988.

McDonnell, Colleen. *The Christian Home in Victorian America.* Bloomington: Indiana University Press, 1986.

McWilliams, Carey. *A Mask for Privilege: Anti-Semitism in America.* Boston: Little Brown, 1948.

Mead, Sidney E. *The Lively Experiment: The Shaping of Christianity in America.* New York: Harper and Row, 1963.

Menken, Adah Isaacs. *Infelicia.* Philadelphia: J. B. Lippincott, 1868.

The Menorah, 1886–1899.

Merriam, Eve. *Emma Lazarus: Woman with a Torch*. New York: Citadel Press, 1956.

Mersand, Joseph. *Traditions in American Literature: A Study of Jewish Characters and Authors*. New York: Mordern Chapbooks, 1939.

Meyer, Annie Nathan. *Barnard Beginnings*. New York: Houghton Mifflin, 1935.

———. *Helen Brent, M.D.: A Social Study*. New York: Cassell, 1892.

———. "The Higher Education for Women in New York City." *The Nation* 46:1178 (1888), 68–69.

———. *It's Been Fun*. New York: Henry Schuman, 1951.

———. Ed. *Woman's Work in America*. New York: Henry Holt, 1891.

Meyer, Michael A. *The Origin of the Modern Jew: Jewish Identity and European Culture in Germany 1749–1824*. Detroit: Wayne State University Press, 1967.

Meyers, Mrs. Henry. "Woman's Work in the World." *American Jewess* 6 (1898), 274–79.

Miller, Sara. *Under the Eagle's Wing*. Philadelphia: Jewish Publication Society of America, 1899.

Moers, Ellen. *Literary Women: The Great Tradition*. Garden City, N.Y.: Doubleday/Anchor, 1977.

Moise, Penina. *Fancy's Sketchbook*. Charleston, S.C.: J. S. Burges, 1833.

———. *Secular and Religious Works of Penina Moise, with a Brief Sketch of Her Life*. Charleston: Charleston Section, National Council of Jewish Women, 1911.

Monteiro, George. "Heine in America: The Efforts of Emma Lazarus and John Hay." *Turn-of-the-Century Women* 2 (1985), 51–55.

Morais, Nina. "Jewish Ostracism In America." *North American Review* 133 (1881), 265–75.

———. "The Limitations of Sex." *North American Review* 132 (1881), 79–95.

——— (Cohen). "Nationality and the Jews." *Menorah* 12:1 (1892), 30–37.

———. "Rebekah Hyneman." *American Jews' Annual*, 5646 (1885), np.

Mordell, Albert. "The One Hundredth Birthday of Emma Lazarus." *Jewish Book Annual* 7 (1948–1949), 79–88.

———. "Some Final Words on Emma Lazarus." *Publications of the American Jewish Historical Society* 39 (1949–1950), 321–27.

Morton, Leah (Elizabeth Stern). *I Am a Woman—and a Jew*. New York: J. H. Sears, 1926.

Moses, Anna J. *Esther: A Play in Five Acts*. Cincinnati: Bloch, 1887.

Moses, Octavia Harby. *A Mother's Poems: A Collection of Verses*. Published by her children and grandchildren, 1915.

Murray, Henry. Ed. *Myth and Mythmaking*. Boston: Beacon, 1960.

Nathan, Maud. *Once upon a Time and Today*. New York, 1933. Rpt. New York: Arno Press, 1974.

———. "A Woman's View of Christianity's Millstone." *North American Review* 162 (1896): 252–55.

Neidle, Cecyle S. *America's Immigrant Women*. Boston: Twayne, 1975.

The New English Bible with the Apocrypha. Samuel Sandmel, General Editor. New York: Oxford University Press, 1976.

The Occident and American Jewish Advocate, 1843–1869.

Ogden, Mrs. C. A. *Into the Light; or, The Jewess*. Boston: Loring, 1868.

Osterweis, Rollin G. *Rebecca Gratz: A Study in Charm*. New York: G. P. Putnam, 1935.

Overton, Grant M. "Edna Ferber." In *The Women Who Make Our Novels*. New York: Moffat, Yard, 1922.

Palmer, Pamela Lynn. "Adah Isaacs Menken: From Texas to Paris." In *Legendary Ladies of Texas*. Ed. Francis Edward Abernethy. Dallas: E-Heart Press, 1981. 85–93.

Papishvily, Helen Waite. *All the Happy Endings: A Study of the Domestic Novel in America: The Women Who Wrote It, The Women Who Read It, in the Nineteenth Century.* New York: Harper, 1956.

Pauli, Hertha. "The Statue of Liberty Finds Its Poet." *Commentary* 1 (1945), 56–64.

Philipson, David. Ed. *The Letters of Rebecca Gratz.* Philadelphia: Jewish Publication Society of America, 1929.

"Poems by American Women." *Scribner's* 19 (1879), 194–98.

Poovey, Mary. *Uneven Developments: The Ideological Work of Gender in Mid-Victorian England.* Chicago: University of Chicago Press, 1988.

Porter, Jack Nusan. "Rosa Sonneschein and *The American Jewess:* The First Independent English Language Jewish Women's Journal in the United States." *American Jewish Historical Quarterly* 68 (1978), 57–63.

———. "Rosa Sonneschein and *The American Jewess* Revisited: New Historical Information on an Early American Zionist and Jewish Feminist." *American Jewish Archives* 32 (1980), 125–31.

Porterfield, Amanda. *Feminine Spirituality in America: From Sarah Edwards to Martha Graham.* Philadelphia: Temple University Press, 1980.

Pratt, Norma Fain. "Culture and Radical Politics: Yiddish Women Writers, 1890–1940." *American Jewish History* 70 (1980), 68–90.

———. "Transitions in Judaism: The Jewish American Woman through the 1930s." *American Quarterly* 30 (1978), 681–702.

Price, Warwick James. "Three Forgotten Poetesses." *The Forum* 47 (1912), 361–76.

Radway, Janice. *Reading the Romance: Women, Patriarchy, and Popular Literature.* Chapel Hill: University of North Carolina Press, 1984.

Raphael, Marc Lee. "The Early Jews of Columbus, Ohio: A Study in Economic Mobility." In *A Bicentennial Festschrift for Jacob Rader Marcus.* Ed. Bertram Wallace Korn. Waltham and New York: American Jewish Historical Society and Ktav. 1976, 435–52.

Reznikoff, Charles. *The Jews of Charleston: A History of an American Jewish Community.* Philadelphia: The Jewish Publication Society of America, 1950.

Rhine, Alice Hyneman. "Lines." *The Occident and American Jewish Advocate* 15 (1858), 489.

———. "Race Prejudice at Summer Resorts." *The Forum* 3 (1887), 523–31.

———. "Woman in Industry." In *Woman's Work in America.* Ed. Annie Nathan Meyer. New York: Henry Holt, 1891. 276–322.

Righter, William. *Myth and Literature.* Boston: Routledge and Kegan Paul, 1975.

Robinson, Lillian S. "Treason Our Text: Feminist Challenges to the Literary Canon." *Tulsa Studies in Women's Literature* 2 (1983), 83–98.

Rodenas, Adriana Mendez. "Tradition and Women's Writing: Toward a Poetics of Difference." In *Engendering the Word: Feminist Essays in Psychosexual Poetics.* Ed. Temma F. Berg. Urbana: University of Illinois Press, 1989. 29–50.

Rosaldo, Michelle Zimbalist, and Louise Lamphere. Eds. *Woman, Culture, and Society.* Stanford: Stanford University Press, 1974.

Rose, Ernestine L. *An Address on Woman's Rights: Delivered before the People's Sunday Meeting in Cochituate Hall on October 19, 1851.* Boston: J. P. Mendum, 1851.

Rosenberg, Rosalind. "In Search of Woman's Nature, 1850–1920." *Feminist Studies* 3 (1975), 141–54.

Rosenberg, Stuart. *America Is Different.* New York: Thomas Nelson, 1964.

Rosenblatt, W. M. "The Jews: What They Are Coming To." *The Galaxy* 13 (1872), 47–60.

Rosenbloom, Joseph R. "Some Conclusions about Rebecca Gratz." In *Essays in American Jewish History.* Cincinnati: American Jewish Archives, 1958. 171–86.

Rosenwaike, Ira. *On the Edge of Greatness: A Portrait of American Jewry in the Early National Period.* Cincinnati: American Jewish Archives, 1985.

Rothman, Sheila M. *Woman's Proper Place: A History of Changing Ideals and Practices, 1870 to the Present.* New York: Basic Books, 1978.

Ruchames, Louis. "New Light on the Religious Development of Emma Lazarus." *Publications of the American Jewish Historical Society* 42 (1952–1953), 83–88.

Rusk, Ralph L. *Letters to Emma Lazarus in the Columbia University Library.* New York: Columbia University Press, 1939.

Ryan, Mary P. *Womanhood in America.* New York: Franklin Watts, 1983.

Sachar, Howard M. *The Course of Modern Jewish History.* New York: World, 1958.

Sarna, Jonathan. "Appendix." *The American Jewish Experience.* Ed. Jonathan Sarna. New York: Holmes and Meier, 1986. 296–97.

———. "The Impact of the American Revolution on American Jews." *The American Jewish Experience.* Ed. Jonathan Sarna. New York: Holmes and Meier, 1986. 20–28.

———. "Introduction." *The American Jewish Experience.* Ed. Jonathan Sarna. New York: Holmes and Meier, 1986. xiii–xix.

———. *Jacksonian Jew: The Two Worlds of Mordecai Noah.* New York: Holmes and Meier, 1981.

———. "Jewish-Christian Hostility in the US: A Jewish Perspective." In *Uncivil Religion: Interreligious Hostility in America.* Ed. Robert Bellah and Frederick Greenspahn. New York: Crossroad, 1987. 5–22.

———. "The Jewish Publication Society 1888–1988." *Jewish Book Annual* 45 (1987–1988), 42–53.

———. Ed. *The American Jewish Experience.* New York: Holmes and Meier, 1986.

Saum, Lewis O. *The Popular Mood of Pre–Civil War America.* Westport, Conn.: Greenwood, 1980.

Schappes, Morris U. *A Documentary History of Jews in the United States, 1654–1875.* New York: Citadel, 1950.

———. *Emma Lazarus: Selections from Her Poetry and Prose.* New York: Cooperative Book League, Jewish-American Section, International Workers Order, 1944.

———. Ed. *Letters of Emma Lazarus.* New York: New York Public Library, 1949.

Schneidau, Herbert. *Sacred Discontent.* Berkeley: University of California Press, 1976.

Scott, Anne Firor. *The Southern Lady: From Pedestal to Politics, 1830–1930.* Chicago: University of Chicago Press, 1970.

Scott, Joan W. "Gender: A Useful Category of Historical Analysis." *American Historical Review* 91 (1986), 1053–75.

———. "Women's History: The Modern Period." *Past and Present,* 101 (1983), 141–57.

Seasongood, Emily. *My Memoirs.* Located at American Jewish Archives, Cincinnati.

Sebeok, Thomas A. Ed. *Myth: A Symposium*. Bloomington: Indiana University Press, 1955.

Seelav, Robert. *Emma Lazarus: Poet of the Homeless*. Pamphlet. American Jewish Historical Society, 1949.

Shapiro, Ann R. *Unlikely Heroines: Nineteenth-Century American Women Writers and the Woman Question*. Westport, Conn: Greenwood, 1987.

Shaughnessey, Mary Rose. *Woman and Success in American Society in the Works of Edna Ferber*. New York: Gordon, 1977.

Showalter, Elaine. "Feminist Criticism in the Wilderness." *Critical Inquiry* 8 (1981), 179–205.

———. *A Literature of Their Own: British Women Novelists from Bronte to Lessing*. Princeton: Princeton University Press, 1977.

Silverman, Joseph. "Place of Woman in Modern Civilization." *Menorah* 21 (1896), 399–406.

Singerman, Robert. "The American Jewish Press, 1823–1983; A Bibliographic Survey of Research and Studies." *American Jewish History* 73 (1984), 422–45.

Sklar, Kathryn Kish. *Catharine Beecher: A Study in American Domesticity*. New Haven: Yale University Press, 1973.

Sklare, Marshall. *America's Jews*. New York: Random House, 1971.

———. Ed. *The Jew in American Society*. New York: Behrman House, 1974.

Smith, Barbara. "Toward a Black Feminist Criticism." In *All the Women Are White, All the Blacks Are Men, but Some of Us Are Brave: Black Women's Studies*. Ed. Gloria T. Hull, Patricia Bell Scott, and Barbara Smith. Old Westbury, N.Y.: Feminist Press, 1982. 157–75.

Smith, Barbara Herrnstein. "Contingencies of Value." In *Canons*. Ed. Robert von Hallberg. Chicago: University of Chicago Press, 1983. 5–39.

Smith, Daniel Scott. "Family Limitation, Sexual Control, and Domestic Feminism in Victorian America." *Feminist Studies* 1 (1973), 40–57.

Smith-Rosenberg, Carroll. "Beauty, the Beast and the Militant Feminist: A Case Study in Sex Roles and Social Stress in Jacksonian America." *American Quarterly* 23 (1971), 562–84.

———. *Disorderly Conduct: Visions of Gender in Victorian America*. New York: Oxford University Press, 1985.

———. "The Female World of Love and Ritual: Relationships between Women in Nineteenth-Century America." *Signs* 1 (1975), 1–29.

———. "The Hysterical Woman: Sex Roles and Role Conflict in Nineteenth-Century America." *Social Research* 39 (1972), 652–78.

———. "The New Woman as Androgyne: Social Disorder and Gender Crisis, 1870–1936." In *Disorderly Conduct: Visions of Gender in Victorian America*. New York: Oxford University Press, 1985, 245–96.

———. "Puberty to Menopause: The Cycle of Feminity in Nineteenth-Century America." *Feminist Studies* 1 (1973), 58–72.

Sochen, June. *Consecrate Every Day: The Public Lives of Jewish American Women, 1880–1980*. Albany: SUNY, 1981.

———. *Herstory: A Woman's View of American History*. New York: Alfred, 1974.

———. "Identities within Identity: Thoughts on Jewish American Women Writers." *Studies in American Jewish Literature* 3 (1983), 6–10.

———. *The New Woman: Feminism in Greenwich Village, 1910–1920*. New York: Quadrangle, 1972.

Sollors, Werner. *Beyond Ethnicity: Consent and Descent in American Culture*. New York: Oxford University Press, 1986.

———. "Literature and Ethnicity." In *Harvard Encyclopedia of American Ethnic Groups.* Ed. Stephan Thernstrom. Cambridge: Harvard University Press, 1980. 647–65.

Sonneschein, Rosa. Untitled review. *The American Jewess* 1 (1895), 294–95.

Spacks, Patricia Meyer. *The Female Imagination.* New York: Alfred A. Knopf, 1975.

Spitz, M. "The Model Wife." *American Israelite* 28:38 (1882), 1.

Stern, E. L. "Ruth—A Story of Palestine." *Menorah* 38:9 (1889), 139–40.

Stern, Eva L. "Charity as Taught by the Mosaic Law." *Papers of the Jewish Women's Congress.* Philadelphia: Jewish Publication Society of America, 1894. 133–44.

Stern-Taeubler, Selma. "The Motivation of the German Jewish Emigration to America in the Post-Mendelssohnian Era." In *Essays in American Jewish History.* Cincinnati: American Jewish Archives, 1958. 247–61.

Stewart, Grace. *A New Mythos: The Novel of the Artist as Heroine 1887–1987.* Montreal: Eden Press Women's Publications, 1981.

Stowe, Harriet Beecher. *The Pearl of Orr's Island: A Story of the Coast of Maine.* Boston: Ticknor and Fields, 1862.

Sulzberger, Cyrus L. "Emma Lazarus as a Jew." *American Hebrew* 33 (1887), 79.

Szold, Henrietta. "What Has Judaism Done for Woman?" *Judaism at the World's Parliament of Religions.* Cincinnati: Union of American Hebrew Congregations and Robert Clarke, 1894. 305–10.

Tarshish, Allan. "The Economic Life of the American Jew in the Middle Nineteenth Century." In *Essays in American Jewish History.* Cincinnati: American Jewish Archives, 1958. 263–93.

Thernstrom, Stephan. *Poverty and Progress: Social Mobility in a Nineteenth-Century City.* New York: Atheneum, 1977.

Thomas, John L. "The Uses of Catastrophism: Lewis Mumford, Vernon L. Parrington, Van Wyck Brooks, and the End of American Regionalism." *American Quarterly* 42 (1990), 223–51.

Toll, William. "The Female Life Cycle and the Measure of Jewish Social Change: Portland, Oregon, 1880–1930." *American Jewish History* 72 (1983), 309–32.

Tompkins, Jane. *Sensational Designs: The Cultural Work of American Fiction 1790–1860.* New York: Oxford University Press, 1985.

Trachtenberg, Alan. *The Incorporation of America: Culture and Society in the Gilded Age.* New York: Hill and Wang, 1982.

Universal Jewish Encyclopedia. New York: Universal Jewish Encyclopedia Company, 1948.

Vickery, John B. Ed. *Myth and Literature.* Lincoln: University of Nebraska Press, 1966.

Vogel, Dan. *Emma Lazarus.* Boston: Twayne, 1980.

Wagenknecht, Edward. *Daughters of the Covenant: Portraits of Six Jewish Women.* Amherst: University of Massachusetts Press, 1983.

Wald, Lillian. *The House on Henry Street.* New York: Henry Holt, 1915.

Walden, Daniel. "Jewish Women Writers and Woman in Jewish Literature: An Introduction." *Studies in American Jewish Literature* 3 (1983), 1–5.

Walker, Cheryl. *The Nightingale's Burden: Women Poets and American Culture before 1900.* Bloomington: Indiana University Press, 1982.

Watts, Emily Stipes. *The Poetry of American Women from 1632 to 1945.* Austin: University of Texas Press, 1977.

Weigle, Marta. *Spiders and Spinsters: Women and Mythology.* Albuquerque: University of New Mexico Press, 1982.

Weil, Helen Kahn. "Jewish Women of Modern Days." In *Papers of the Jewish Women's Congress.* Philadelphia: Jewish Publication Society of America, 1894. 26–42.

Weissler, Chava. "Women in Paradise." *Tikkun* 2 (1987), 43–46, 117–20.

Welter, Barbara. *Dimity Convictions: The American Woman in the Nineteenth Century.* Athens: Ohio University Press, 1976.

Wenger, Beth S. "Jewish Women of the Club: The Changing Public Role of Atlanta's Jewish Women (1870–1930)." *American Jewish History* 76 (1987), 311–33.

White, Ken. "Publication Policy toward Women in *The Occident and American Jewish Advocate.*" Term Paper, Hebrew Union College, 9 January 1980.

White, William Allen. "Edna Ferber." *World's Work* 59, part 1 (June 1930), 36–38, 90.

Who's Who in American Jewry, 1926. New York: The Jewish Biographical Bureau, 1927.

Wiebe, Robert. *The Search for Order 1877–1921.* New York: Hill and Wang, 1967.

Wilkins, Thurman. "Adah Isaacs Menken." Entry in *Notable American Women 1607–1950: A Biographical Dictionary.* Vol. 2. Ed. Edward T. James. Cambridge: Belknap Press of Harvard University Press, 1971.

Williams, Blanche Colton. "Edna Ferber." In *Our Short Story Writers.* New York: Moffatt, Yard, 1920.

Witkowsky, Esther. "Discussion of Pauline H. Rosenberg's 'Influence of the Discovery of America on the Jews.'" *Papers of the Jewish Women's Congress.* Philadelphia: Jewish Publication Society of America, 1894. 74–76.

Wiznitzer, Arnold. "The Exodus from Brazil and Arrival in New Amsterdam of the Jewish Pilgrim Fathers, 1654." *Publications of the American Jewish Historical Society* 44 (1954): 80–97.

Wolf, Alice. *House of Cards.* Chicago: Stone and Kimball, 1896.

Wolf, Emma. *Fulfillment: A California Novel.* New York: Henry Holt, 1916.

———. *Heirs of Yesterday.* Chicago: A. C. McClurg, 1901 (copyright 1900).

———. *The Joy of Life.* Chicago: A. C. McClurg, 1896.

———. *Other Things Being Equal.* Chicago: A. C. McClurg, 1892.

———. *A Prodigal in Love.* New York: Harper, 1894.

Wolff, Cynthia Griffin. "A Mirror for Men: Stereotypes of Women in Literature." *Massachusetts Review* 13 (1972), 205–18.

Woodward, Helen Beal. "The Body: Adah Isaacs Menken." In *The Bold Women.* New York: Farrar, Straus, and Young, 1953. 269–80, 369.

Wyszkowski, Yehezkel. "The American Hebrew: An Experience in Ambivalence." *American Jewish History* 76 (1987), 340–53.

Yarborough, Richard. "'In the Realm of the Imagination': Afro-American Literature and the American Canon." *Association of Departments of English Bulletin* 78 (Summer 1984), 35–39.

Yezierska, Anzia. *The Bread Givers.* Garden City, 1925; New York: Persea, 1975.

———. *The Open Cage: An Anzia Yezierska Collection.* Ed. Alice Kessler-Harris. New York: Persea, 1979.

———. *Red Ribbon on a White Horse.* New York, 1950; New York: Persea, 1981.

Zaretsky, Eli. *Capitalism, the Family, and Personal Life.* New York: Harper and Row, 1976.

Zatlin, Linda Gertner. *The Nineteenth-Century Anglo-Jewish Novel.* Boston: Twayne, 1981.

Zeiger, Arthur. "Emma Lazarus: A Critical Study." Diss. New York University, 1951.

Ziff, Larzer. *The American 1890s: Life and Times of a Lost Generation.* New York: Viking, 1966.
———. *Literary Democracy.* New York: 1981; New York: Penguin, 1982.
Zimmerman, Bonnie. "What Has Never Been: An Overview of Lesbian Feminist Criticism." *Feminist Studies* 7 (1981), 451–75.

Index

Absentee, The (Edgeworth), 99
Actress, role of, for Menken, 105–6
"Admetus" (Lazarus), 52
Admetus and Other Poems (Lazarus), 52, 55–56
Alcott, Louisa May, 7, 90–91, 147 n.4
Alide: An Episode of Goethe's Life (Lazarus), 40–41
Alienation, 41, 52, 112
America as nation, 1, 17–18, 95, 96–97, 134, 136–41; Jew equated with, 131, 141; loyalty to of American Jewish women, 23, 24, 95–104, 122–23, 141. See also National loyalties
American, Sadie, 121, 124
American Hebrew, The, 41–42, 47–51, 58
American identity, 1, 8, 13, 86, 127–28, 144 n.8; for Emma Lazarus, 43, 51–58; emphasis on in women's writings, 95, 98–104; expressed by Ferber, 130, 131–32, 134, 136; fusion with Jewish identity attempted, 95, 101, 115–19; stressed in The American Jewess, 126; and the True Woman's duty, 18–20. See also American Jewish identity
American Jewess, The, 60, 120, 124–27, 150 nn.3, 4
"American Jewess, The" (Sonneschein), 126
American Jewish identity, 60, 61, 68, 111–13, 120–29; dual nature, 94, 95–98; Emma Lazarus's development of, 38, 57–59; through synthesis of American and Jewish identities, 95, 101, 115–19. See also American identity; Jewish identity
American Jewish women writers, 60–63; at end of the 19th century, 80–87, 120, 124–29; Ferber as early 20th-century example, 129–41; in the South, 69–74, 148 n.2; varied conformity to myths of American womanhood, 64–80. See also Literary tradition(s): 19th-century American Jewish women; individual authors by name
American Jews, 2, 10–14, 45, 63, 144 n.7; addressed by writers, 47–49, 72–73, 85–87, 112–15; complacency of attacked, 38, 50–51, 87, 97, 104; in the late 19th century, 120–27; women's position in Reform Judaism, 14, 144 n.11. See also Assimilated Jews; German Jews: in America; Sephardic Jews: in America
American literature, 41–42, 53, 62, 88–89;

canonical and non-canonical texts, 4, 143 n.5; place in as identity for Emma Lazarus, 38, 51–56, 120; plural traditions, 2–3, 55–56, 143 n.2, 143 n.5
"American Literature" (Lazarus), 55
Americanness, 23, 52, 53, 62; for Emma Lazarus, 37, 43, 89. See also American identity
American Novel and Its Tradition, The (Chase), 143 n.2
"Annie Nathan Meyer and Barnard College" (Gordon), 148 n.4
Anti-Semitism, 24–25, 64, 93, 147–48 n.8, 150 n.1; in America, 12, 75, 95, 100, 101–4, 112, 119, 124; Emma Lazarus's approach to, 38, 45–46, 48–51; Ferber's autobiographies on, 130–31, 132; in Germany, 13, 96–98; Josephine Lazarus's universal religion as solution to, 118–19
Anxiety of authorship, 2, 23, 93
Anxiety of displacement. See Displacement, anxiety of
Anxiety of influence, 23, 93
Ashkenazic Jews (Ashkenazim), 10–11, 144 n.7
Asmonean (periodical), 61
Assimilated Jews, 1, 29, 32, 60, 113–15, 117–18; Emma Lazarus's "An Epistle to the Hebrews" directed to, 47–49; Ferber's family as, 130; Judaism as cultural identity for, 47; and newly arrived Eastern European Jews, 123, 127; observance of Jewish rituals and laws, 104; women's conflicts, 32–35, 85–87
Assimilation, 48–49, 51, 115, 117–18, 124
Audience, as issue in establishment of a literary tradition, 9–10
Author, identity as, 38, 43, 68, 130
Authorship, anxiety of, 2, 23, 93
Autobiographies, 128–29, 129–32. See also Memoirs

"Banner of the Jew, The" (Lazarus), 50–51
Barnard College, 76, 148 n.4
Barthes, Roland, 5, 6
Beecher, Catharine, 19, 93
Berkowitz, Henry, 33–34
Beth Elohim, 72
"Between Two Worlds" (Sonneschein), 127
Biblical characters, portrayals, 66–68, 83, 105–6; of Deborah, 23, 37, 38, 47, 66–68

169

172

Index

Harby, Leah (Lee) Cohen, 47, 85–87; on
Moise, 87–88, 89–90, 149 n.8
Hart, Bella, obituary, 30–31
Hart, Louisa B., 93–94, 100–101, 141
Hawthorne, Nathaniel, 4, 143 n.2
Hay, John, 56, 58
"Hear O Israel" (Menken), 106
Heine, Heinrich, 46–47, 49, 56
Heirs of Yesterday (Wolf), 85, 113–14
Helen Brent, M.D.: A Social Study (Meyer),
76, 77–78
Herz, Jenny Kleeberg, 74–75, 80
Higham, John, 147 n.1
History: importance for Jews emphasized by
Emma Lazarus, 47–48; as setting for fic-
tion, 81, 83–84, 108
Hoffman, Maria Fenne, 115–16
Holidays, 7, 104, 107, 118
Holy texts, Jewish, women excluded from
study of, 23, 63
Home. *See* Domesticity, ideology of; Do-
mestic sphere
Hotels, American, denial of accommoda-
tions to Jews, 102–3
"How Long!" (Lazarus), 55–56
Hurwitz, Samuel J., 147 n.2
Hyman, Paula, 26, 146 n.6
Hymns, 44, 72, 90, 148 n.3
Hyneman, Rebekah Gumpert, 4, 10, 74, 85,
108–10, 133–34; Emma Lazarus con-
trasted with, 38; fiction, 66, 83; Morais's
essay, 88–89; poetry, 66–69, 81, 108–10

Ice Palace (Ferber), 132, 134, 139–41
"Ideal Jewess, The" (Philipson), 125–26
Identities
—of American Jewish women writers, 5,
22–23, 27, 37, 63, 80; attitudes toward in
Moise's poetry, 72–74; as authors, 38, 43,
68, 130; components of for Ferber, 130; for
Emma Lazarus, 38, 39, 51–56, 89; repre-
sentations of, 35
—dual, 46–47, 94, 95–98, 123
—*See also* American identity; American
Jewish identity; Jewish identity; Woman-
hood myths
Ideology, relationship to myth, 6
Immigrants, 10–14, 17, 36–37, 128, 144 n.7,
147 n.1. *See also* Eastern European Jews;
German Jews; Sephardic Jews
Independence, female, 62, 77–80, 85, 86–87,
135; of Ferber's pioneer women and the
American Mother in Israel, 134, 139, 140;
of the new woman, 17, 145 n.2; passed
from mothers to daughters, 74–75
Infelicia (Menken), 105–6
Influence, anxiety of, 23, 93
"In Memoriam" (Mannheimer), 82

"In Remembrance of My Past Life . . ."
(Goldsmith), 80–81
Insider(s), 10, 140–41
—outsiders transformed into, 36, 130, 137
—status as: for Emma Lazarus, 57; for Fer-
ber, 134, 136–37
Intermarriage, 27, 65, 95–97, 114–17, 124,
149 n.8
"In the Jewish Synagogue at Newport"
(Lazarus), 43–44
Intratextuality, 88–90
Isaacs, Abram S., 29, 61–62, 146 n.9, 147–48
n.8
"Israel's Trust" (Hyneman), 108–9

"Jewess in Authorship, The" (Isaacs), 62
Jewish American identity. *See* American
Jewish identity
"Jewish Cemetery at Newport, The" (Longfellow), 43–44
Jewish Denominational Congress (1893),
82–83
Jewish identity, 1, 8, 65, 95, 104–15; addressed in Lust's *A Tent of Grace*, 96–97;
claimed by Menken, 104–5, 149 n.5; development in Emma Lazarus, 37, 42–51,
52, 55, 57–59, 147 n.7; Ferber's concern
with, 120–21, 129–33, 141; Herz's
awareness of, 75; of historical characters
in Miller's *Under the Eagle's Wing*, 84; for
Josephine Lazarus, 90, 91–93; readers of
The American Jewess directed to cultivate, 125; rejection of addressed in Wolf's
novels, 114; retained by Zara in Hyneman's poem, 81; seen in Heine by Emma
Lazarus, 46–47; writers' attempt to fuse
with American identity, 95, 101, 115–19,
127–28. *See also* American Jewish identity
Jewish Messenger, The, 29, 61–62, 86–87,
112–13, 146 n.9, 147–48 n.8
Jewish nation, 6, 64, 81, 95–98, 145–46 n.5;
Emma Lazarus's citizenship in, 47, 50; intermarriage as threat to, 117; loyalty to
among writers, 44, 104–15. *See also* Judaism; National loyalties
"Jewish Ostracism in America" (Morais),
101–2, 103, 115
"Jewish Problem, The" (Lazarus), 45–46, 48,
147–48 n.8
"Jewish Question, The" (Josephine Lazarus),
118
Jewish Women's Congress (1893), 120, 121–
24, 128–29
"Jewish Working Girls" (Cohen), 112–13
Jews, 10–11, 63, 88–89, 147 n.7; Emma
Lazarus as public spokesperson for, 42–
51, 57–58; linked by Ferber with Amer-

n.6; by Moise, 71–74, 90, 98–99, 106–8; by Moses, 69–71, 106–7, 108; by Rhine, 103–4; translated by Emma Lazarus, 44, 46, 49

Pogroms, in Russia, 42, 45, 46, 50

Poovey, Mary, 145–46 n.5

Porterfield, Amanda, 20

Power, 19, 67, 107–8, 145–46 n.5; for Ferber, 131, 132, 133, 134, 137; of men, 31, 35, 94, 145–46 n.5; in the Mother in Israel role, 24, 145–46 n.5; of the text, 79–80; of women, 18, 60, 65, 84, 92, 135

Pride: in American identity, 98, 99; in Jewish identity, 96, 104–12, 120, 122, 128

Private sphere, 18–20, 22, 145 n.3. *See also* Domestic sphere

Private Woman, Public Stage (Kelley), 22

"Problematic Champion, A" (Isaacs), 147–48 n.8

Prodigal in Love, A (Wolf), 79–80

Professions, women in, 17, 27, 74, 76–78, 145 n.2

Public sphere, 18–20, 26, 77, 145 n.3; women's place in, 34, 60, 80, 150 n.1; writers in, 22, 38, 63–64

Rabbis, views on women, 27, 28, 32–35

"Race Prejudice at Summer Resorts" (Rhine), 102–3

Ragozin, Z., 45, 47

Reform Judaism, 14, 32–33, 110–12, 127–28, 144 n.11, 150 n.2; Beth Elohim, 72; Society of Reformed Israelites, 69

Regional fiction, 134–35; of Edna Ferber, 130, 134–41, 150 n.8

Reinhard, Richard, 49

Religion, 34, 85, 122; Josephine Lazarus's attempt to create a new, 95, 115, 118–19; the True Woman as guardian of, 7, 18–19, 20–21. *See also* Christianity; Judaism

Religious holidays. *See* Holidays

Religious persecution. *See* Anti-Semitism; Pogroms

Rewriting, as woman's power, 79–80

Rhine (Sotheran), Alice Hyneman, 24, 102–4, 109, 131, 149 n.2

Rights, 12, 28, 31, 145–46 n.5; women's, 67–68, 93–94, 124, 145 n.2, 150 n.4

Rituals, Jewish, 11, 97, 122; Yom Kippur, 107–8, 114

Rose, Ernestine Louise, 93

Russia, persecution of Jews, 42, 45, 46, 50, 112

"Russian Christianity vs. Modern Judaism" (Lazarus), 45, 57

"Russian Jews and Gentiles" (Ragozin), 45, 47

"Ruth—A Story of Palestine" (Stern), 83

Sabbath Hymn (number 154) (Moise), 72, 148 n.3

Schuyler, Georgina, 147 n.1

Screens: domestic duties as, 39; in women's writings, 39, 42

Scribner's (magazine), 58

Seasongood, Emily Fechheimer, 117

Secular and Religious Works of Penina Moise, 148 n.3

Secularism, 1, 27, 44

Selflessness of women, 7, 18, 39

Self-reliance, 74–75, 85, 86–87

Seligman, Joseph, 12, 102

"Separate Spheres, Female Worlds, Woman's Place" (Kerber), 19

Sephardic Jews (Sephardim), 8, 10–11, 37, 143–44 n.7, 147 n.2

—in America, 12–13, 31–35, 48, 146 n.8; attitudes toward Eastern European Jews, 12, 96, 104, 113

Short stories. *See* Fiction

Showalter, Elaine, 3

Silverman, Joseph, 34

Single Blessedness, Cult of, 20–21

Single men, 65, 146 n.7

Single women, 20–21, 25, 34, 146 n.7

—writers as, 64, 71, 78, 82, 89; Emma Lazarus, 39; Ferber, 130

Sklar, Kathryn Kish, 19

Smith, Barbara, 3

Smith-Rosenberg, Carroll, 18, 145 n.2

So Big (Ferber), 132, 134, 136–37, 140

Sollors, Werner, 7, 10

Solomon, Hannah Greenebaum, 121, 127

Songs of a Semite (Lazarus), 49–51

Sonneschein, Rosa, 45, 117, 125–27, 150 n.3

South, the: myth of womanhood, 145 n.1, 148 n.2; writers, 69–74, 99–100, 148 n.2

Spheres of influence, 70. *See also* Domestic sphere; Private sphere; Public sphere

Spirit of Judaism, The (Josephine Lazarus), 118–19

Spirituality, 85, 88–89, 91. *See also* Religion

Spitz, M., 32

Stedman, Edmund C., 41–42

Stern, E. L., 83

Stern, Eva L., 122

Stowe, Harriet Beecher, 3, 7, 22, 135

Stuyvesant, Peter, 10–11

Suffrage: for Jewish men, 12; religious, 126, 150 n.4; women's fight for, 124, 145 n.2

Sulzberger, Cyrus L., 51, 58

Sunday Schools, Jewish, 64, 72

"Sympathy" (Lazarus), 39–40

Szold, Henrietta, 82–83

"Taming of the Falcon, The" (Lazarus), 58–59

Tanz zum Tode, Der (Reinhard), 49

DIANE LICHTENSTEIN is Associate Professor of English and Co-Chair of Women's Studies at Beloit College. Her work on American Jewish women writers has appeared in *Tulsa Studies in Women and Literature* and *Studies in American Jewish Literature*.